RAKING THE ASHES
Genealogical Strategies for
Pre-1906 San Francisco Research

Second Edition

RAKING THE ASHES
Genealogical Strategies for
Pre-1906 San Francisco Research

Nancy Simons Peterson, CG

Second Edition

California Genealogical Society
Oakland, California

Library of Congress Control Number: 2011923179
ISBN: 978-0-9785694-5-7

© 2011, Second Edition, Nancy S. Peterson
Printed in the United States of America

Published by the California Genealogical Society
2201 Broadway, Suite LL2
Oakland, California 94612-3013

Telephone: 510-663-1358 — Fax: 510-663-1596
Website: *CaliforniaAncestors.org*

Cover design and graphics by Judy Bodycote-Thomas
Cover photograph from San Francisco History Center, San Francisco Public Library
Text design by Shirley Pugh Thomson

CONTENTS

MAPS AND ILLUSTRATIONS vii

INTRODUCTION xi

PART I

   ORIGINAL RECORDS: WHAT DID AND DID NOT SURVIVE,
   WITH WORK-AROUNDS FOR LOST RECORDS

     Vital (Civil) Records: Birth, Marriage and Death 3

     Mortuary, Crematory and Coroners' Records 11

     Cemetery and Columbarium Records 19

     Religious Records 29

     Newspapers: Films, Indexes, Abstracts and Online Digitizations.......... 43

     Census Enumerations and Indexes 51

     San Francisco City Directories 55

     Municipal Records: Annual Reports, Tax Records 59

     Land Records 63

     Original and Appellate Court Records: Naturalization, Probate, Land,
       Divorce and Adoption 71

     Voting Records 85

     Immigration: Overland Arrivals, Passenger Lists and Passports 89

     Military Records 97

     Records of Fraternal Organizations and Benevolent Societies 113

     Institutional, Business and Occupational Records 117

     Pre-Statehood Spanish and Mexican Records 123

     Diaries and First-Hand Accounts 125

     Ethnic Records and Resources 127

PART II

CONTINUING THE SEARCH: ADDITIONAL RESOURCES

Biographical and Historical Publications 139
The *California Information File* 143
Records of Pioneer and Other Lineage Societies 145
Help from Internet Resources 151
Family History Library Resources 155
Local Repositories 159
Professional Research Assistance 163

PART III

RESEARCH TECHNIQUES FOR SOLVING GENEALOGICAL PROBLEMS

Assembling and Assessing Evidence 167
The Basics: the Census and City Directories 169
A Quick Survey of the Most-Used Sources 173
A Less-Used Source: Religious Records 175
Location, Location, Location.. 179
Expanding Your Search: Wider and Later 187
Naming Complications 193
Thinking Beyond San Francisco... 197
Source Summaries: Where to Find What... 199
Putting It All Together 207

APPENDIX

PRE-EARTHQUAKE NEWSPAPER COLLECTIONS: TITLES, LOCAL SOURCES AND

DATES OF COVERAGE 209

INDEX 215

ABOUT THE CALIFORNIA GENEALOGICAL SOCIETY AND LIBRARY 221

ABOUT THE AUTHOR 223

MAPS AND ILLUSTRATIONS

1) City Hall and adjacent Hall of Records following the fire ix

2) Ruins of the Hall of Justice following the fire.. x

3) General view of San Francisco following the fire xii

4) Page from earliest surviving death register (1865) 2

5) Evidence of marriage from early land index 6

6) Samples from the only civil death records available from May 1873 to
   August 1894: one Coroner's ledger and the Chinese decedents lists 9

7) Page from surviving ledger of N. Gray & Co. mortuary 10

8) IOOF Crematory ledger record 17

9) Pioneer gravestone uncovered during 1933 excavation for the
   Federal Building 18

10) Entries in 1903 Laurel Hill Cemetery burial register 23

11) IOOF Cemetery record 25

12) Typical entry from ledger of IOOF columbarium 28

13) Baptism from films at Swenson Swedish Immigration Center 31

14) *Emanu-El* newspaper article... 41

15) 1850 funeral notice from *Daily Alta* 42

16) Searching the California Digital Newspaper Collection 49

17) Page from 1852 state census 50

18) Easily mis-indexed census entry 54

19) "Chronological History of Principal Events" from
    1868-69 city directory 57

20) Typical entries from "Coroner's Report" in 1898 *Annual
    Municipal Report* 58

21) Folsom Prison convict list...61

22) San Francisco in 1848 62

23) Early San Francisco preemption claim from alcalde's records 65

24) Post-fire restoration of property title...70

25) Typical restoration of naturalization record 75

26) Page from *Register of Actions* 77

27) "Court Notes" from 1875 issue of the *San Francisco Chronicle* 80

28) Divorces from newspaper records 81

29) Appellate case summary dating to 1872 in *California Reports* 83

30) Page from San Francisco, California, 1890 *Great Register of Voters* 88

31) Passenger arrival list appearing in 1850 issue of *Alta California* 92

32) 1903 passport application 95

33) Civil War widow's pension claim... 96

34) Pages from state–held compilation of Civil War volunteers ... 104, 105

35) Page from *Record of Orphans, Half–Orphans, Etc., on State Aid 1907–1910: City and County of San Francisco* 118

36) Northern portion of San Francisco peninsula showing the location of early ranchos 122

37) Manumission record found in the alcalde's miscellaneous records... 128

38) Page from 1918 alien registration document 135

39) Witnessed departure statement and return certificate application from Chinese Exclusion Act documents at National Archives 136

40) Entry in Bancroft's *Pioneer Register & Index* 138

41) Card from *California Information File* and referenced article 142

42) Translations of alcalde land grant appeals 144

43) Capsule ancestral line in *Register of the Society of Mayflower Descendants in the State of California* 146

44) Pages from original enrollment register of Association of Territorial Pioneers of California 148, 149

45) National Archives regional facility in San Bruno 158

46) Doe Memorial Library and adjacent Bancroft Library 161

47) Biography from *History of San Mateo County, California* 166

48) Baptismal record from original ledger at Mission Dolores 176

49) Record of marriage without a license 178

50) 1853 map of San Francisco 180

51) 1906 fire destruction map 182

52) Casting a wider net: using cemetery lot maps................................ 186

53) Early San Francisco marriage certificate found in Massachusetts 189

54) Entry in 1909 Suhr Funeral Home ledger....................................... 191

55) Thinking beyond San Francisco: Marin County marriage license 196

56) Published record: First Congregational Church baptisms 198

57) Birthdates of children from widow's sheet in military pension file 201

58) Attestation of witness to marriage in widow's pension file 203

59) Early mortuary record with corresponding newspaper entry 205

60) Interior of California Genealogical Society library............................. 220

*City Hall and adjacent Hall of Records following the earthquake and fire
(from California Genealogical Society archives).*

*Ruins of the Hall of Justice following the fire
(San Francisco History Center, San Francisco Public Library).*

DISASTER!

*A*t 5:12 a.m., April 18, 1906, the ground beneath San Francisco began to tremble. Less than a half minute later the first of several episodes of violent shaking began, which within forty–five to sixty seconds left large parts of San Francisco in ruins. Gas mains, both large and small, ruptured. Both the primary water main to the city from two large reservoirs to the south and distribution mains from secondary city storage facilities were severed. Throughout the downtown section of the city multiple fires erupted, soon outrunning what little water could be found to fight them. Before the morning was over, several of the largest fires had merged into a roaring inferno that destroyed what little was left of the area immediately south of Market Street. The firestorm swept through the shambles of City Hall, the adjoining Hall of Records, and most of the business district. It destroyed a large number of churches and moved on to claim the Hall of Justice and ultimately a major portion of the records documenting the lives of most residents of the largest, most beautiful city on the West Coast. What transpired that morning and in the several fire–plagued days that followed continues to make research into the lives of nineteenth century San Franciscans a challenge for even the most experienced of genealogists.

This was not the simple courthouse fire with which many of us with southern ancestry are familiar. Over one–fifth of the population of California lived at this time in San Francisco. Within three days 4.7 square miles of the city had burned, and about half the city's population was left homeless. Although the "official" death toll was set at 478, it has since been shown that at least 3,400 lives and likely more were lost in a city that then was home to over 400,000. Losses in lives and property far exceeded those lost in the Great Chicago Fire of 1871. Not only were the documents genealogists are accustomed to accessing destroyed,

General view of San Francisco following the fire
(San Francisco History Center, San Francisco Public Library).

but also the personal effects of a large part of its citizenry were lost. Marriage
records, birth and baptismal certificates, deeds and naturalization documents
were abandoned and later destroyed as residents fled in terror to the outer reaches of
the city or to its suburbs. Hundreds of thousands of San Franciscans crossed the bay
to Oakland and Berkeley. Almost as many never returned.

EXTENT OF THE RECORD LOSS

All the records that genealogists treasure, however, were not destroyed. A
very small number of civil death records and many deeds did not burn. Some
cemetery, mortuary, and coroners' records survived. Extractions of Chinese
names from the civil death registers had already been sent to federal immigration
authorities. Occasionally a minister managed to save some of the church registers
in his custody. Federal court records escaped destruction; other federal records,
such as military and census records, were not archived in San Francisco in the
first place. Numerous publications had previously been distributed beyond
the reaches of the fire: newspapers, compilations, abstracts and reports. And,
of course, the recollections and accounts of family members, not only of San
Franciscans but also relatives in other areas, survived.

Researching the trail of pre–earthquake residents requires persistence and frequently the pursuit of more obscure records, less reliable sources and often a much broader array of evidence. On the other hand, the time and effort required frequently results in a fuller, more robust family history. A large body of indirect evidence based upon independent sources may in the end provide a clearer and more convincing argument with respect to dates and relationships than can be obtained from several pieces of direct evidence that may or may not be accurate and may or may not apply to the party in question.

The amazing growth of information technology over the past several years is in part responsible for this revision. It has resulted in availability on the Internet of transcriptions, abstracts and digitizations of many of the surviving records, which makes our search far easier. Nonetheless, those researching nineteenth century San Francisco ancestry still frequently encounter what seem to be insurmountable "brick walls."

HOW TO USE THIS GUIDE

This publication is directed towards frustrated and bewildered hobbyists, as well as towards experienced genealogists and historians, all of whom want a summary and evaluation of what is available to help and a "battle plan." I hope it will be valued by those who treasure the permanence and portability of paper, and the convenience that comes from being able to mark pages with personal notations. Those who have spent years researching San Francisco problems have developed a number of strategies that often lead to success. I have tried to include their suggestions not only in the specific sections where they apply, but also in Part III of this guide. *If this is your first experience with early San Francisco research, I strongly recommend starting with Part III.* In fact, most readers may wish to start there. This is a guide, not a novel, and need not be read from front to back. Part III presents an overview of the most commonly used sources, contains research strategies appropriate for common objectives and summarizes some of the pitfalls and self–created obstacles that often inadvertently block success. Part III now also contains summaries of post-earthquake resources, where clues to pre-earthquake events may be found, and three convenient tables summarizing parts of the book that may yield birth, marriage and death information.

Rather than include a bibliography at the end of the publication, I have chosen to insert most published references in the chapter or chapters where they are relevant. A number of sources dealing directly with the earthquake and fire, however, have been used to provide a sprinkling of color throughout the text and are not referenced at each use. These publications include *Denial of Disaster* by Gladys Hansen (San Francisco: Cameron and Co., 1989) and William

Bronson's *The Earth Shook, The Sky Burned* by (Garden City, New York: Doubleday, 1959). Both are available at the San Francisco Public Library, at the California Genealogical Society and at Sutro Branch of the California State Library. In addition to including details of the calamity itself, they also provide insight into the widespread corruption and scandals of the time. A third publication, written immediately after the disaster by Richard Linthicum, *Complete Story of the San Francisco Horror, 1906* (Chicago?: Hubert D. Russell, 1906), with an introduction by the Rt. Rev. Samuel Fallows, contains many trivial details that other accounts do not. Roger W. Lotchkin's book, *San Francisco, 1846-1856: from Hamlet to City* (Chicago: University of Illinois Press, 1997) provides outstanding historical coverage of topics ranging from land litigation to schooling and health problems and facilities. The Internet site prepared for the centennial by the Bancroft Library, University of California, Berkeley, currently found at *http://bancroft.berkeley.edu/collections/earthquakeandfire/*, contains photographs, historical background, letters written by survivors and links to other informative websites. Useful population statistics can be found posted in the Historical Census Browser, a part of the website of the University of Virginia Geospatial and Data Center (*http://mapserver.lib.virginia.edu/*).

This guide by no means represents the complete word on San Francisco sources. Since the first edition, some records have been moved; addresses and contents of electronically accessible compilations have changed; and new sources have been located or created. The transfer of private records to the city archives, which are part of the San Francisco History Room at the San Francisco Public Library, is ongoing. Many of these and other library records have been and are being digitized by Internet Archive (website: *www.Archive.org*).

There has been no attempt to list all places where specific sources may be found. Those who live far from the Bay Area may be able to find many of the publications mentioned here in large genealogical libraries or perhaps as electronic digitizations. Those that have been filmed by the Family History Library in Salt Lake City can be obtained on loan through Family History Centers and ultimately will be available as digitizations at the Family History Library website, *www.familysearch.org*. I have tried to include both current Internet addresses and the names of compiling organizations or persons so sites can be located should the address (URL) change. For want of a better name, however, I have referred to the enormous website of San Francisco data and gleanings created by Pam and Ron Filion by its present URL, *www.sfgenealogy.com*.

This guide was first published as part of the one–hundredth anniversary of the earthquake and fire, celebrated April 18, 2006 by those who love the city and by those whose ancestors perished or survived only to witness one of the greatest tragedies in the short history of our country. You may not have San

Francisco lineage in your ancestry, but instead may have lost a descendant line of a family member who went west. This guide is for you as well, and also for those countless researchers who have run up against courthouse fires and record loss at other times and other places. The strategies presented here apply everywhere.

Abbreviations

Abbreviations used for convenience throughout the text include:

CG   Certified Genealogist; service mark of the Board for Certification of Genealogists

CGS   California Genealogical Society, located in Oakland, California

CHS   California Historical Society, located in San Francisco

DAR   (California Society of the) Daughters of the American Revolution

FHL   Family History Library, Salt Lake City

IOOF   International Order of Odd Fellows

NARA   National Archives and Records Administration. The two main research centers are in Washington, D.C., and Suitland, Maryland; regional branches exist across the country, one of which is located just outside of San Francisco in San Bruno.

NPRC   National Personnel Records Center in St. Louis, Missouri

SFPL   San Francisco Public Library, main branch

Sutro   Sutro Library in San Francisco, the genealogical branch of the California State Library in Sacramento

WPA   Works Progress Administration, governmental agency of New Deal era, active in inventorying countless public documents

BACKGROUND AND ACKNOWLEDGMENTS

This project originally was conceived as an update of a publication by Kathleen C. Beals, *A Useful Guide to Researching San Francisco Ancestry* (California Genealogical Society, 1994; revised 2001). CGS members Ann Duncan and Jane Steiner surveyed library and archive holdings and initiated the table of newspaper holdings that appears in the appendix. The project was tabled when it became evident that a guide to both pre– and post–earthquake material was too large an undertaking to be completed in the time remaining before the 2006 earthquake centennial. The assignment was handed to me by then CGS president, Jane Lindsey, with a narrowed focus on pre-earthquake records. To this I added the section on research techniques. Since the first printing in the spring of 2006, new records have surfaced, record locations have changed and exciting new tools have become available. Because many post-earthquake records may need to be accessed in order to solve pre-earthquake problems, the scope of the guide has now been enlarged to include a brief coverage of later records.

The appearance of the first edition was the work of Shirley Thomson, whose many years in the publishing arena and experience with graphics imparted a professional appearance to what otherwise would have been an amateurish production. Without her help and guidance and the constant encouragement of Jane Lindsey, the first edition of this book would not have been possible. The cover and graphics in this edition have been entirely the work of Judy Bodycote, whose skill in using Adobe Illustrator and Adobe Photoshop has been invaluable.

I am equally indebted to those experienced researchers whose comments shaped the content of this and the previous publication: the late Rick Sherman, who for many years handled CGS research requests; Marie Melchiori, CG, whose knowledge of federal military records is unequaled; Verne Deubler, former president of CGS, who shares a great interest in San Francisco ancestry; Jeremy Frankel of the San Francisco Bay Area Jewish Genealogical Society; and Susan Goldstein, Manager of the San Francisco Public Library History Center and of the associated Archives of the City and County of San Francisco.

Marilyn Willats, retired law librarian for Pillsbury, Madison and Sutro, provided information for the subsection on trial case records and answered countless questions on legal research. Her advice regarding how best to present information on local libraries and archives trimmed a long list to a concise description of the most useful repositories.

A guide of this magnitude also requires volunteers willing to confirm the present location and extent of published records and resources. My gratitude especially goes out to Anne Robinson, who spent every Monday over a period of several years checking film holdings at the Catholic Regional Archives at St. Patrick's Seminary in Menlo Park.

Verne Deubler proofread this version for content; Shirley Thomson established the style sheet and guided our adherance to publishing standards. My greatest thanks go to Laura Spurrier, who kept countless typographical, grammatical and syntactical errors from ever reaching your eyes and guided me to resources at the University of California at Berkeley I otherwise would have missed. I take total responsibility for any errors that remain and ask that they be brought to my attention so that they are not repeated in future revisions.

Together we all hope this revised guide helps you to muddle through surviving records or to circumvent the profound loss of records in ways you might not otherwise have thought of.

Nancy Simons Peterson, CG
May 2011

PART I

ORIGINAL RECORDS
WHAT DID AND DID NOT SURVIVE, WITH
WORK-AROUNDS FOR LOST RECORDS

"I tell you the past is a bucket of ashes."

—Carl Sandburg

Mortuary Record of the

No.	1865 DATE	NAME	SEX	AGE Years	M'ts	Days	OCCUPATION	PLACE of BIRTH	
185	Dec 3	Ah Soy	Female	46				China	4
186	" 3	Unknown Body	Male						
187	" 3	Ung Wing Sing	do	57			Cigar Maker	do	4
188	" 3	Edward Hull	do	24			Drayman	Vermont	9
189	" 4	Frank Market	do					San Francisco	
190	" 4	Annie Dalton	Female	7	7			do	4
191	" 3	Daniel Harrington	Male					do	
192	" 4	George W Purdy	do	18			Ship Carpenter	Nova Scotia	9
193	" 4	Edward Kurtz	do			28		San Francisco	10
194	" 4	William H Davenport	do	58	1	7		Connecticut	8
195	" 4	Leopold Ojeda	do		1	2		San Francisco	2
196	" 4	Robert P Lee	do	42			Clerk	Rhode Island	5
197	" 4	Julia Young	Female			2		San Francisco	10
198	" 4	Mary Magan	do	71				Ireland	10
199	" 4	Mary C Gleason	do	2	1	24		San Francisco	
200	" 4	H Boscher	Male					do	
201	" 4	Amelant Hubert	do	50			Barber	France	
202	" 4	Gustave Mentel	do					San Francisco	

December 1865 entries (above and below) from earliest surviving death register
(available on FHL film #975,830).

City and County of San Francisco.

Previous Residence	PARTICULAR PLACE of DEATH	Date of Death	CAUSE of DEATH	PLACE of BURIAL	REMARKS
4	No 46 Globe Hotel	Dec 3	Phthisis	Lone Mt	Copper
4	Jackson St	" 2	Gen. Debility	do	Copper
9	Harrison "	" 2	Typhoid Fever	do	
4	Dupont "	" 7	Still Born	Calvary	
4	Washington "	" 3	Scarlatina	Mission	
8	5 Minna	" 3	Still Born	Calvary	
9	334 Rich	"	Inf of Brain	Lone Mt	
10	Mission "	" 4	Gen debility	Calvary	
8	719 Cal. "	" 4	Typhoid Fever	Lone Mt	
2	10 Union Place	" 3	Cholera Infant	Calvary	
5	Cosmopn Hotel	" 2	Disease of Heart	Lone Mt	
10	254 Fourth St	" 4	Convulsions	do	
10	153 Second do	" 4	Gen debility	Calvary	
8	Sutter "	" 4	Croup	do	
10	Fourth "	" 4	Still Born	Lone Mt	
	603 Montgy "	" 4	(Poison)	Masonic	
8	118 St Marks Pl	" 4	Still Born	Calvary	
	Clark St	" 2	Pneumonia	Lone Mt	Colored
10	551 Sixth "	" 3	Phthisis	Calvary	
8	Dupont "	" 4	do	do	
2	520 Vallejo "	" 3	Gen. Debility	Lone Mt	
11	Co 6th	" 5	Typhoid Fever	Calvary	

Vital (Civil) Records

While most of the vital records that were created by the City and County of San Francisco were destroyed in the earthquake and fire of 1906, a few volumes of death records and indexes, six months of death certificates, a coroner's register and an index to a little under two years of marriage records somehow survived. Those records are listed on the following page, along with the Family History Library (FHL) film numbers that can be used to access them. The FHL filmed most of the surviving records, with the exception of two *indexes* to corresponding death *registers* that did not survive. Names and approximate dates in the first of these two unfilmed indexes can at least help narrow newspaper searches. Except for two months, the second unfilmed *register* index is covered by surviving death *certificates*.

An index to all surviving civil death records was published by CGS in 2010: Barbara Ross Close and Vernon A. Deubler, *San Francisco Deaths, 1865-1905: Abstracts from Surviving Civil Records*. Entries are also part of the California Names Index, a database at the society website *www.CaliforniaAncestors.org*. Copies of original ledger entries and certificates are available from CGS for a nominal fee. The four-volume index is available from *Lulu.com* or via a link at the CGS website. Those wishing to perform searches themselves should use the films listed on the following page. The original records are stored at the San Francisco Department of Public Health, where special arrangements must be made to view them. All films are available at CGS and SFPL.

Entries in surviving indexes to death registers are grouped alphabetically by the first letter of the surname and then chronologically within an alphabetical group. Information in the registers themselves normally includes number and posting date of entry, name, sex, age (years–months–days), occupation, place of birth (state or country), social condition (married, single, widow or widower), date and cause of death, residence at time of death (usually), place of burial, physician, undertaker and additional remarks. Interestingly, the information for Chinese decedents from 1870 to February 1905, including the lost periods, was extracted prior to the earthquake and sent to Immigration. (See p. 133).

Surviving Pre-Earthquake City and County Records

			FHL Film #
Vol. 1	(Nov 8, 1865 – Sep 30, 1869)	unindexed death register	975,830
Vol. 2	(Oct 1869 – Apr 30, 1873)	unindexed death register	975,830
Vol. 3	(Apr 1, 1882 – Jun 30, 1889)	coroner's cases and index	975,831
Book M	(Aug 1, 1894 – Jun 30, 1896)	death register and index	975,832
Book O	(Jul 1, 1898 – Mar 16, 1900)	index to death register	unfilmed
Book P	(Mar 17, 1900 – Oct 22, 1901)	death register and index	975,833
Book Q	(Oct 23, 1901 – Jun 30, 1903)	death register and index	975,834
Book R	(Jul 1, 1903 – Jun 30, 1904)	death register and index	975,835
"Index"	(Jul 1, 1904 – Jan 31, 1905)	index to death register	unfilmed
	(Jul 1, 1904 – Dec 1, 1904)	death certificates	975,839-47

Index to Marriage Licenses (Jul 1, 1904 – Apr 17, 1906)   974,858

Vital record-keeping commenced with statehood as evidenced by over two thousand references to non-surviving marriage records scattered in deed indexes over the years 1850–1858. These were extracted by Kathleen C. Beals in *Index to San Francisco Marriage Returns 1850–1858* (Oakland: California Genealogical Society, 1992). Extracts were amplified with information from newspaper indexes and abstracts, found for about forty percent of the records referenced. The legal requirement for record-keeping was not established and standardized by the state until 1858, at which point references to marriages in deed indexes cease.

Following the earthquake, when proof of marriage was required, many couples provided the necessary evidence to have their marriages re–recorded. The index to re–recorded marriages is available on FHL film #974,858, which, along with all FHL films listed above, is available at SFPL and CGS. The index to marriage certificates (July 1, 1904–April 17, 1906) represents original county ledgers 24 (through August 1905) and 25 and follows (as item 2) the re–recorded marriages on film #974,858. Entries are grouped alphabetically by first letter of surname, first by groom, then by bride; within an alphabetical group, entries are chronological. Some of the names (and dates) are out of order. There are "P's," for example, among the "W's." Information includes not only certificate number, but also the name of the person performing the ceremony, which can point the way to surviving church records.[1] The curious instance of legal marriage without a license or civil recording is discussed on pp. 177-178.

---

[1] Surviving returns for marriages taking place just before the earthquake and not yet received by the recorder's office were entered in the newly created post-earthquake certificate "Book 1," but were nonetheless indexed in (surviving) Volume 25. Those returns received between April 7 and April 16, but not yet posted, were lost.

STATE–HELD BIRTH AND DEATH RECORD AND INDEXES

Beginning July 1, 1905, all vital records were required to be submitted to the state. Compliance was neither immediate nor complete. Unfortunately, copies of the pre-earthquake information sent by San Francisco were never sent to the county after the earthquake. Thus, birth and death *records* starting with July 1905 through those that were last sent before the earthquake can only be obtained from the Office of Vital Records in Sacramento.[2] For genealogical purposes, "informational" (non–certified) birth and death certificate are available. These do not require that the person submitting the request be the person named, or a parent, guardian, empowered attorney, governmental representative, or legal heir of that person.

More often, one's search begins with indexes, because the date of birth or death is not known or because there are multiple entries of the same name to examine. *Indexes* to state–held *death* records beginning July 1, 1905 are available at SFPL and CGS and on FHL films. The 1905-29 index may be searched at no charge at *http://www.vitalsearch-ca.com*. To access the FHL death index collection, enter the film #1,686,044, in the online FHL catalog. Information in the 1905-29 index includes name, initials of spouse, age, date of death, code number of the city or county where the person died, registrar number and state file number.

Online birth indexes have come and gone as privacy legislation has evolved. However, copies of the state–created electronic index purchased before restrictive legislation was enacted have been allowed to remain. CGS has a copy. It may be searched by fields such as mother's maiden name, which is useful in the case of common surnames or when the married surname is not known. A field–searchable index that permits wildcard spelling options is available at *www.sfgenealogy.com*. Information in the state birth index includes full name, date and county of birth, father's name and mother's maiden name.

STATE–HELD MARRIAGE RECORDS AND INDEXES

In California the responsibility for recording marriages lies with the County Recorder. Marriage returns were to have been reported to the state beginning July 1, 1905, but the state no longer has pre-1949 indexes to them. Thus, before 1949, unless the county in which a license was taken out is known, one must search county by county. San Francisco indexes for most of the last two years before the earthquake survived the fire and are available on FHL film #974,858. Information found here can possibly be amplified in the society section and vital record section of newspapers.

[2] Write: Office of Vital Records; 304 S Street, PO Box 730241; Sacramento, CA 94244-0241.

WORK–AROUNDS

Many work–arounds exist where records are missing. That, for the most part, is the focus of this guide. Church records of baptisms, marriages and funeral services often contain dates of birth and death. Additional work–arounds for missing civil death records are described in sections covering mortuary, crematory, cemetery, columbarium and coroners' records. Summaries of sources for missing vital records are tabulated on pp. 200-204. Newspaper films, digitizations and indexes are among the most heavily used substitutes. Issues of the *Overland Monthly* magazine for 1872 were extracted for marriages and deaths as part of "The Making of America" series, placed online by the University of Michigan and at the Rootsweb site of npmelton (Nancy Melton). Land records occasionally made reference to recent deaths, and early land record indexes from 1850 through 1858 also indexed marriage returns, an example of which is shown below. Over two thousand entries were compiled by Kathleen C. Beals (see p. 4), where entries represented the posting date, not the date of marriage.

Entries in pre-1860 land indexes may constitute the only record of some marriages.

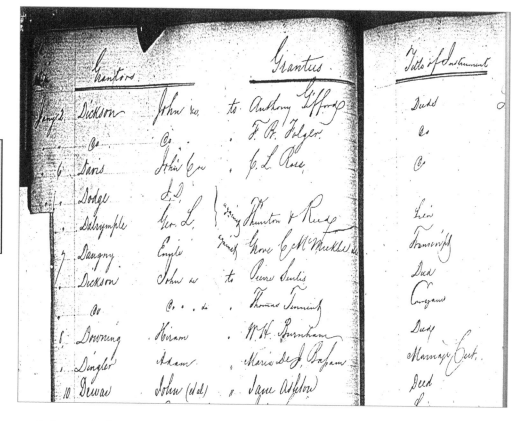

Reference to the marriage of Adam Dingler and Maria De J. Basham from the 1851 grantor index. "Marriage cert." is noted on the right-hand ledger page. The ledgers recording the marriages referenced in these indexes did not survive the 1906 fire (FHL film # 966,131).

Federal records often provide missing data. Pension applications of widows yield marriage information that may appear nowhere else. Death ledgers from Letterman Hospital at the Presidio (1898-1910) are discussed on p. 111. Newspaper accounts of divorce proceedings or court records of divorces that occurred after the earthquake and fire contain marriage information that may have been lost. Several parts of the annual *San Francisco Municipal Report* (p. 59) carry references to deaths, as do a number of San Francisco city directories in the year–end "Chronological History of Principal Events." Don't overlook census mortality schedules. Reports to the California State Board of Examiners provide dates of death for those who died in old age homes and county hospitals during the years 1883–1889; similar reports for orphanages over the same years record birth dates for orphans on state aid and often include death dates for the parents.

Databases available on the Internet are always worth checking, even though they may be incomplete and contain transcription errors. The most reliable of these is the index offered by Jim Faulkinbury. His fee–based extractions of births, marriages and deaths that appeared in the *San Francisco Call* newspaper, encompassing (at present) the years 1869–1899, is discussed on p. 46. Extractions of many of the surviving death registers were made by Rootsweb volunteers and posted online with no attribution as to sources. This database can be accessed through a link at *www.sfgenealogy.com*. The transcriptions, however, were checked against the original ledger entries and found to be grossly error–laden. Handwriting was misinterpreted, and blocks of information in the original registers were not included. The CGS publication described on p. 3 is preferred.

The clues that enable the researcher to search these substitutes with success often come from federal census enumerations, which provide the age, birth year and the birth month of those enumerated (1900), the number of years a couple has been married (1900 and 1910) and the ages and birthplaces of their children. Voter registers provide ages of registered males. Land records occasionally give clues to death dates as well as to family relationships. Other clues that may help to focus the search in substitute records come from compilations of a more general nature, such as family histories, pioneer records, ethnic records, biographies, lineage society records and such. These, along with the *California Information File,* are covered in Section II. Some compilations, particularly pioneer accounts and diary transcriptions, are reliable substitutes in those instances where they represent firsthand accounts created by the person being researched.

MISCELLANEOUS OTHER SOURCES

Some work–arounds do not cleanly fall into any of the record and source categories mentioned above. One of these is the 1906 earthquake and fire "death toll," which can be accessed in a card file in the History Center at SFPL.

Created many years ago by SFPL librarians from newspaper accounts and other documented sources, it consists of those persons known to have died as a result of the disaster, a number totaling a little under five hundred. In 1980 Gladys Hansen, then head of the San Francisco History Center at the library and its associated Archives for the City and County of San Francisco, published *Who Perished: A List of Persons Who Died as a Result of the Great Earthquake and Fire in San Francisco on April 18, 1906* (San Francisco: San Francisco Archives, 1980). This book is available at SFPL, at Sutro, on FHL film and fiche (film #1,421,964, item 8, and fiche #6048077) and as a transcription at *www.sfgenealogy.com*. Ms. Hansen continued her research over many years; the list grew, but never approached, even closely, the true number of fatalities, which is now estimated by most to be nearer to five thousand. Large numbers of the unidentified dead were residents of the Chinese community; others were transients or residents who were never reported as missing and their deaths, therefore, not investigated or recorded. It was not in the interests of the city fathers to admit to such a large number of fatalities. They most certainly desired to cover up indefensible deeds such as the shooting of looters. The city's image needed to be restored in order to encourage future settlement and re–settlement to replace the large numbers of San Franciscans who fled the city and never returned.

A second source, not discussed elsewhere in this guide, is a card file created by and kept at the California State Library in Sacramento in which reference librarians over the years recorded answers they have provided to inquiries they received. Called by the Special Collections Department the "Vital Statistics Index," it is rather haphazard, but interesting in that the name of the person making the inquiry is recorded. Thus, in some instances an entry could lead researchers to previously unidentified family members. The file was filmed by the FHL. Film numbers and the first name on each film (information not provided in the FHL catalog) are as follows:

Vital Statistics Index — First Names on Films

1,711,369	Aa . . .	1,711,484	Landrum, Richard
1,711,370	Brutt, John	1,711,485	Meune, Albert
1,711,371	DeMont, Arne	1,711,486	Peterson, Albert
1,711,372	Gold, Frank	1,711,487	Scott, Charles
1,711,373	Holman, Nadin	1,711,488	Vail, Fred

Coroner's cases (top) and transcriptions of Chinese decedents prepared from the original death register (bottom). These are the only civil death collections available between May 1, 1873 and August 1, 1894. The coroner's register, which covers April 1, 1882 through 30 June 1889, is on FHL film #975,831, available at SFPL and CGS. The transcriptions of Chinese decedents are on two rolls of microfilm classified as NARA Publication A4040 (RG85), "Mortuary Records of Chinese Decedents in California, July 1870 - April 1933."

Films of surviving vital records are available at San Francisco Public Library and the California Genealogical Society. Films of the Chinese transcription ledgers are available at NARA San Francisco in San Bruno.

Records of disinterments and shipments or reburials from early San Francisco and Gold Country graves are often recorded in these ledgers.

Example of record in surviving 1851 ledger of N. Gray & Co.
(Archives of San Francisco History Center, San Francisco Public Library;
digitizations are also available online at FamilySearch.org).

MORTUARY, CREMATORY AND CORONERS' RECORDS

When civil death records are not available, as is the case for many pre-earthquake years, mortuary, crematory and coroner's records constitute perfectly acceptable substitutes. These records were normally created shortly after the date of death and often provide names and relationships of those close to the deceased.

MORTUARY RECORDS

In April 1906, a large number of mortuaries were in business in San Francisco. Most lay within the fire zone and were destroyed, but fortunately the employees of several firms managed to rescue some or all of their records before the fire reached them. The records of N. Gray & Co., in particular, which go back to 1850, provide the basis for much of what we know about deaths in the Gold Rush era. These and others were digitized by the FHL and are being indexed.

Records of N. Gray & Co.

Nathaniel Gray, intending to open an undertaking business in San Francisco, arrived with supplies in the spring of 1850. The previous undertaker by the name of Wingate had recently been killed in an accident. After losing his supplies in a fire, Gray purchased Wingate's coffins and equipment and as N. Gray & Co., opened for business July 1, 1850. Following Nathaniel Gray's death in 1889, his son–in–law continued the business as Clark & Booth, then under the more familiar name, N. Gray. All of the records beginning in July 1850, along with many records of firms that later merged with Gray, survived. The merged firms exist today as Halsted N. Gray–Carew & English. In 2006, records predating 1920 were transferred to SFPL, where they were digitized. Researchers may examinine original ledgers in the History Room at SFPL and search both indexed and unindexed digitizations at *www.FamilySearch.org*. (To view unindexed digitizations, one must currently register at the FamilySearch website.)

The original ledgers of N. Gray & Co. mortuary and the establishments with which it merged from 1850 to 1922, were transferred to SFPL. They are also available on FHL film and as searchable digitizations at the FHL website.

Book of the Dead

In 1916, Gray's mortuary records over the years 1850–1863 were abstracted by longtime CGS president Henry Byron Phillips and CGS treasurer Bethuel Merritt Newcomb. These men gathered supplementary material from a surviving, rather poor copy of Yerba Buena Cemetery interment records (which appears to have been lost), from coroners' records and from early newspapers at the University of California. They included in their abstracts most death and burial detail, but an examination of the original mortuary ledgers at SFPL reveals that some details were not abstracted. Occasionally Gray's records mention wooden head markers at City Cemetery, the only definitive record we have for disinterments from Yerba Buena and reburials that took place about 1870.

Phillips and Newcomb prepared a number of carbon copies of their manuscript, one of which remains unfilmed in eleven bound manuscripts at the FHL and one of which is at the New England Historic Genealogical Society. NEHGS recently prepared a searchable electronic database from their copy, available online to members as part of the cemetery collection at the NEHGS website. Entries in the NEHGS database can be viewed both alphabetically and in the order in which they appeared in the manuscript. The California State Library was willed Phillips's personal copy but could not locate it when contacted.

At some unknown time before 1938, the Phillips–Newcomb manuscript was copied in duplicate onto 3 x 5 file cards so that the names could be alphabetically arranged, but not until September 1969 were the cards assembled. One set of cards is held in twelve card file drawers at Sutro Library, along with, but not interfiled with, records from a number of other early California cemeteries, including headstone transcriptions from Masonic Cemetery gathered by the DAR. The cards bearing Masonic Cemetery data are at the end of the collection, but those for names beginning with letters U–Z have been lost.

The card collection at Sutro has come to be known locally as the "Book of the Dead." It was filmed by the FHL on films #1,711,667 (item 2) and #1,711,668 (item 1). The typescript that was the source for the DAR–collected Masonic Cemetery portion (surnames A–Z) was separately filmed as FHL film #844,432. The duplicate set of cards retained by the California State Library in Sacramento was filmed on #1,711,602–604 and #1,711,667 (item 1). Following this filming, or perhaps on a third set of cards, the state library appears to have interfiled all Northern California cemetery record holdings and had the result filmed as FHL films #1,683,914–921 and #1,684,053–057. This last set of films contains much data gathered from Sacramento County also and covers to the year 1900.

In 1938 the DAR abstracted the card file data as part of a much larger project covering cemeteries throughout California. Their abstracts, however, include less information than is contained in the card file. Entries for Chinese and Native

Americans were not included. A copy of the DAR publication can be found at Sutro Library, at SFPL and on FHL film #844,431. The DAR copy has also been posted online at *www.sfgenealogy.com*.

An examination of the multiple publications and a comparison to the original ledgers reveals transcription errors and inconsistencies; the DAR version in particular leaves out many important details. Entries made from supplementary materials are easily identified in the carbon copies at the FHL as they are generally entered out of chronological order and were made using a different color carbon. The original Gray ledgers now provide an accuracy check for the card file and the various manuscripts.

Mortuaries and cemeteries usually post records of deaths in multiple ledgers, including indexes, day books, burial registers and financial ledgers. Records of the shipment of bodies to other locations, the preparation of bodies to be returned for burial by other establishments and the reinterment of exhumed remains from other cemeteries may appear only in financial accounts. Making one's way through the digitizations of these multiple ledgers, which are often chronologically overlapping, can be tedious. Nonetheless, they should all be examined or an important entry may be missed.

J. C. O'Connor Mortuary Records

J. C. O'Connor & Co. was also located within the burned area, yet its records survived, if not all, then in part. Mortuary records from 1882 to about 1920 are available on film at CGS and SFPL (FHL films #1,405,713–717). Be very careful in viewing the records. An attempt was made to arrange them chronologically and then alphabetically within time frames, but many pages are out of order and some may be missing. This mortuary appears to have had a clientele that was largely Irish Catholic. Typical entries include name, age, date and place of death, date and place of burial, place of birth, survivors' names (often just those financially responsible) and details regarding funeral and burial expenses.

Bunker & Lunt

Bunker & Lunt at 2666 Mission Street was located outside the fire zone. One ledger was found, scanned, indexed and published in 2000 by the Los Banos Genealogical Society: *Funeral Register, Bunker & Lunt, 1903–1906*. The records cover over five hundred deaths or re-interments that occurred from November 25, 1903 through March 10, 1906. Because other family information was recorded, over thirteen hundred names were indexed. Information is quite detailed, including besides name and date of death, place and date of birth, names of parents, cause of death, and burial or cremation details. This publication is shelved at Sutro Library and CGS and is available from the Los Banos Genealogical Society.

"Chinese Mortuary Records"

The National Archives San Francisco holds Microfilm publication A4040, "Mortuary Records of Chinese Decedents in California, July 1870 - April 1933." These records are not funeral home records, but were extracted from San Francisco death ledgers before and after the 1906 earthquake in order to identify ship passenger arrivals using false "paper" names. (See p. 133.)

Other Surviving Records

Some records from four other mortuaries in business prior to the earthquake and fire were saved and later merged into the present firm of Halsted N. Gray - Carew & English. Along with the ledgers of N. Gray, records of the following mortuaries were transferred to SFPL: Halsted & Co., J. S. Godeau & Co., Clark & Booth, and Carew & English. Valente, Marini, Perata & Co., still in business, has retained all its records dating back to the firm's formation in 1888.

Locating records of defunct firms or those that merged with another business can be problematic. The researcher may wish to use city directories and other sources to determine what became of mortuaries for which no information has been found and then attempt to locate descendants of the owners.

Mortuaries in Business in 1905 (information from city directories)

- Anderson, Charles A., 429 Golden Gate Ave. (reopened at 1169 Valencia)
- Bunker & Lunt, 2666 Mission St. (survived—opened at same location)
- California Burial Co., 215 Sansome St. (burned area—did not reopen)
- California Undertaking Co., 713 Post St. (reopened at 2210 Steiner)
- Carew & English, 29 Van Ness Ave. (burned area—reopened at 1618 Geary; records start in 1890)
- Clark & Booth, 612-614 Van Ness Ave. (burned area, reopened at 2198 Geary; records start January 1896)
- Craig, Cochran & Co., 429 Golden Gate Ave. (burned area—reopened at 1169 Valencia)
- Dierks, Theodor & Co., 432 Golden Gate Ave. (burned area—reopened at 900 Divisadero)
- Galagher, Henry J. Undertaking Co., 20 – 5th St. (burned area—reopened at 1314 Webster St.)
- Gantner Bros., 1209 Mission St. (burned area—reopened at 3460 – 16th St., records not saved)
- Godeau, Julius S., 305 Montgomery St. (burned area—reopened at 2123 Bush St.; records start in 1894)
- Golden Gate Undertaking Co., 2475 Mission St. (outside of burned area—open at same address in 1907)
- Gray, N. & Co., 612-614 Van Ness Ave. (records cover 1850-1896; reopened at 2198 Geary, St. allied with Clark & Booth)
- Hagen, James & Co., 49 Duboce Ave. (possibly survived—open at same address in 1907)

- Hagen, Joseph, 1705 Sacramento St. (burned area—reopened at 2540 California St.)
- Halsted & Co., 946 Mission St., (burned and reopened at 924 Fillmore St.; all records saved—start 1883)
- Iaccheri, Duclos & Co., 629 Broadway (burned area—J. Iaccheri & Co. reopened, 3032 Mission St.)
- Jacob, Charles H. & Co., 1909 Mission St. (burned area—but reopened at same address)
- Maass, H. F. Co., 917 Mission St. (burned area—reopened at 1335 Golden Gate Ave.)
- Martin, A. W. & Co., 319 O'Farrell St. (burned area—reopened at 1868 Geary St.; records not saved)
- McAvoy, O'Hara & Co., 261 Hayes St. (burned area—reopened at 2649 Market St.)
- McFadden, McBrearty & Green, 1171 Mission St. (burned area—reopened as McFadden, 1070 Haight St.)
- McGinn Bros., 222 McAllister St. (burned area—reopened at 1826 Eddy St.)
- McGinn, James Co., 214 Eddy (burned area—reopened at 832 Fulton St.)
- McMenomey, James & Son, 1057 Mission St. (burned area—did not reopen)
- Metzler, Charles J. B., 636 Washington St. (burned area—reopened as Metzler Undertaking, 1892 Folsom St.)
- Mission Undertaking Co., 601 Valencia St. (burned area—did not reopen)
- Monahan & Co., 2339 Mission St. (burned area—reopened at 1304 Guerrero St.)
- O'Connor, J. C. & Co., 769 Mission St. (burned area—some records survived and are filmed; reopened at 770 Turk St.)
- Pacific Undertakers, 777 Mission St. (burned area—may not have reopened)
- Peterson, H. P. & Co., 228 McAllister St. (burned area—reopened at 1940-42 Post St.)
- Porter & White, 423 Golden Gate Ave. (burned area—reopened at 1531 Golden Gate Ave.)
- Suhr, H. F. & Co., 1137 Mission St. (burned area—reopened at 2919 Mission St.; records date to 1901)
- Truman, Charles H. J. and Co. Funeral Home, 1919 Mission St. (burned area—reopened, 1909 Mission St.)
- United Undertakers Association, 866 Mission St. (burned area—reopened at 2608 Howard St.)
- Valenti, Marini & Co., 1524 Stockton St. (burned area—reopened at 3448 Mission St.)
- Western Addition Funeral Directors, 1724 Divisadero St. (not in burned area—open at same address in 1907)

CREMATORY RECORDS

IOOF Crematory Records

A crematory was once located on the grounds of the Independent Order of Odd Fellows (IOOF) Cemetery. Originally exempt from the ordinance that disallowed burials within the San Francisco city boundary, it was demolished following the passage in 1910 of a similar ordinance applying also to crematories.

Approximately ten thousand cremation records dating primarily from 1895 to 1911 were abstracted from the original ledgers by volunteers at CGS, where the ledgers are archived. Some cremations were of remains from disinterments of earlier burials, the earliest original burial having occurred in 1857.

Abstracts prepared from the ledgers were published by CGS in 2001 under the title *San Francisco, California, I.O.O.F. Crematory Records*. Names of the deceased are included in the California Names Index at the society website, *http://www.CaliforniaAncestors.org*, and copies of the digitized originals may be purchased from the Society. The publication can also be found at SFPL and Sutro Library. Abstracts include name, age, birthplace, date of death, and place and cause of death. The original record also includes the name and address of the person receiving the ashes (or their disposition), funeral director, name of the attesting doctor, names of next of kin and often the obituary as it appeared in the newspaper.

CORONERS' RECORDS

Except for one ledger, original coroners' records were lost in the earthquake and fire. That one ledger, "Book 3," covers only those deaths referred to the Coroner's Office from April 1, 1882 through June 30, 1889. It is archived at the San Francisco Department of Public Health and is treated as one of the few surviving vital records ledgers (which are covered in this guide on pp. 3-4). A film of this ledger, FHL film #975,831, is available at SFPL and CGS. Information provided includes date, name, color/race, age, sex, marital status, nativity (state/ country), cause of death, inquest number, crime (if any), last place of residence, autopsy (if any, by whom), and remarks (which may include occupation and condition, how long in county, reference to death certificate, etc.).

Later the Coroner's Office became known as the Medical Examiner's Office. Some records beginning in 1902 were recently discovered at SFPL in ledgers that were thought to have covered the years 1906-1956. The surviving pre-earthquake records include only descriptive death reports of unknown or unidentified individuals. Information consists of where and when the deceased was found;

who found the body; physical characteristics of the deceased; and clothing and property found on the body. Only occasionally was an identification made and a name provided. A finding aid to this holding can be found under "Archives and Manuscript Collections" at *www.sfpl.org/sfhistory*.

As a work-around, the researcher may find useful the "Coroner's Report," which was included in the annual *San Francisco Municipal Report*. It abstracted name (if known), date of death, description and disposition of property of deceased persons, but, as is the usual practice, only in the instance of those deaths that occurred under sudden, violent, unattended, unexpected or unexplained circumstances. Most municipal reports that cover the years 1861/2 through the earthquake and fire are at SFPL. CGS also holds some volumes, and many have been transcribed at *sfgenealogy.com*.

Typical record from original IOOF Crematory ledger
(from California Genealogical Society archives).

*Pioneer gravestone uncovered during 1933 excavation for the Federal Building
(San Francisco History Center, San Francisco Public Library).*

CEMETERY AND COLUMBARIUM RECORDS

Cemetery and columbarium records provide another work-around to missing death records. The search for these records, however, is not always easy. The only columbarium in San Francisco changed hands many times and fell into ruin. Almost all the old cemeteries were relocated. Most headstones were destroyed, and complete paper records did not necessarily follow removals. Together, these problems frequently make the search difficult.

CEMETERY RECORDS

The extensive record loss that the genealogical community must circumvent as a result of the 1906 earthquake and fire is exacerbated by the loss of records resulting from the forced removal of San Francisco cemeteries over the years spanning 1900 to 1942. The story of San Francisco's cemeteries and this loss is interesting and worth recounting.

A Little Bit of History

Until 1838, Mission Dolores and the Presidio military establishment were the only settlements in what would become San Francisco. Each had an adjoining cemetery closed to outside burials, and neither was located near the cove from which San Francisco grew. Until the first authorized public cemetery, Yerba Buena, was laid out in February 1850, the dead were buried in private cemeteries or in unauthorized locations wherever open land could be found. Remains from many of these early burial sites were most likely moved to Yerba Buena until it was closed to further burials in 1854, at which time Lone Mountain Cemetery opened. In 1870 the land occupied by Yerba Buena was needed for a new city hall and other commercial development. About three thousand dead were reportedly removed to Golden Gate ("City") Cemetery, a small cemetery at Land's End that had been established partly as a potter's field. The removal process was careless, however, perhaps foretelling what would occur after the turn of the century.

In 1900 the Board of Supervisors passed an ordinance effective the following year halting burials within the city limits. Only cremation and the storage of cremated remains were exempt. Pressure to close cemeteries had begun in the 1880s, and some removals from cemeteries that were short of space had already begun to take place to new locations in Lawndale, just over the San Mateo County line. Following implementation of the 1900 ordinance, interments were almost entirely redirected to the Lawndale (since renamed Colma) cemeteries.

In 1914 the Board of Health, bowing to pressure by land developers, ruled that the four largest of the existing (inactive) cemeteries, grouped about Lone Mountain in the Richmond District, were a public health hazard, and removal orders were issued. This action was followed by minimal compliance and prolonged litigation. Some removals started to take place from Odd Fellows (IOOF) and Masonic cemeteries, but there nonetheless remained considerable resistance; Laurel Hill and Calvary cemeteries successfully fought removal until the mid- to late 1930s. Initially the removal process required financial participation by surviving family members. When they could not be found or would not participate, remains were eventually gathered and reinterred in mass, unmarked mounds in Colma cemeteries. Walls, crypts and unclaimed markers were used in breakwaters in the bay and as erosion control at Ocean Beach.

Most remains in Golden Gate ("City") Cemetery were never removed at all. In addition to being the destination for indigent burials and the location of small benevolent-society enclosures, Golden Gate had received early pioneer removals from Yerba Buena. In 1908 a removal order was issued to Golden Gate, and the cemetery land was turned over to the federal government and to the San Francisco Park Commission. Some voluntary removals took place very early from small ethnic enclosures, but no funds were made available and most graves remained undisturbed. One parcel became part of the Fort Miley Military Reservation, while the other was grassed over and largely converted into Lincoln Park Golf Course. Surface markers and structures were hauled away to be used in construction or simply pushed over the cliff into the ocean. In 1921 a portion of the park parcel was dedicated to the construction of the Palace of the Legion of Honor, a memorial to WWI casualties. During excavation, close to fifteen hundred coffins and bodies were inadvertently disinterred and hastily reburied, causing widespread publicity and public agitation. In 1993 during expansion of the Palace, some three hundred corpses that appeared to date to Yerba Buena Cemetery re-interments and therefore to earliest pioneer times were unearthed and removed to Skylawn Cemetery in San Mateo.

Where They Went

San Francisco cemeteries for which some pre-earthquake records survived are described on the following pages, along with a brief outline of the history

> *Most remains in Golden Gate Cemetery, including indigent burials, early pioneer removals, Chinese burials and burials in small, benevolent society and ethnic plots were never removed at all. The cemetery was grassed over and converted in part to Lincoln Park Golf Course.*

of each and a description of what records are available. Old newspaper articles, however, suggest the existence of a number of unrecorded, private and/or unauthorized cemeteries that served during pre-1850 years. Except for occasional notations of removals to Yerba Buena Cemetery in N. Gray & Co. ledgers and in early newspapers, we have no record of these countless early burials.

The Cemetery at Mission Dolores

One of San Francisco's two earliest cemeteries, that adjoining Mission Dolores, was established in 1776. Available only to Catholics, the last burial there appears to have been in 1898. Some remains were removed to Calvary and Holy Cross cemeteries in Colma in 1889 in order to make room for a street extension. Records are available at the Mission and on film at the Catholic Archives located in Menlo Park (see p. 33). A collection of epitaphs compiled by Charles Francis Griffin and published by the DAR comprises part of the seventeen-volume DAR cemetery collection, which is available on various FHL films, including #844,413, and at SFPL and Sutro.[3] The mission epitaphs were separately bound as *Epitaphs, Mission San Francisco de Asis Cemetery (Mission Dolores), San Francisco, California* (Charles Francis Griffin, comp., San Francisco Chapter, Daughters of the American Revolution, 1950), a copy of which is at CGS. A mission history containing various vital and burial records was related by Don Inocente Garcia, then administrator of Mission San Miguel, and was translated by Thomas Workman Temple in 1974. It can be found in the Bancroft Library at the University of California (Berkeley), at SFPL and on FHL film #908,786 (item 2) under the title, *Huechos historicos de California, as told to Thomas Savage, 1878: incidents in the life of a soldier of Spain and Mexico in Alta California, 1807 to 1878.* Temple's original vital record extractions from this book are available on FHL film #944,282.

Old Hebrew Cemetery

Other than Mission Dolores records, Old Hebrew is the only pre-1850 cemetery for which some records survive. It opened in 1847 on land bounded by Broadway, Vallejo, Gough and Franklin streets. Remains were removed to two new cemeteries established in 1860-61 near Mission Dolores, Hills of Eternity (Giboth Olom) and Home of Peace (Navai Shalome). Remarkably, some records documenting this removal and referring to events in 1847 survived and are now part of the Western Jewish History Collection now archived at the Bancroft Library in Berkeley.

---

[3] The DAR cemetery books were filmed in two FHL film series which can be accessed by entering in the online catalog film numbers 844,410 and 558,289. Vol. 5 in the FHL series covers Laurel Hill; vol. 13 covers most other cemeteries except for a very few burials in vol. 16. Book versions at SFPL, Sutro and the state library may have volume numbers that do not necessarily correspond to the volume numbers in film descriptions.

Yerba Buena Cemetery

Yerba Buena, San Francisco's first public, authorized cemetery, opened in February 1850. Its location on shifting sand dunes made it unsuitable as a burial ground, forcing its closure in 1854. Burials are recorded in the records of N. Gray & Co. (p. 11). In 1870 to make way for the new city hall, remains were removed to Golden Gate ("City") Cemetery. The occasional notation "wooden marker, City Cemetery" provides the only evidence of this. Later excavations at the city hall site, however, uncovered remains that could be traced through clothing to Gold Rush years, indicating that removals were not complete (illustration p. 18).

The Old Cemetery on Goat Island (Yerba Buena Island)

Close to one hundred burials took place beginning in 1842 on Yerba Buena ("Goat") Island. Owned by the federal government, the island now anchors the San Francisco Bay Bridge. Six headstones that could still be read some ninety years later were transcribed by the DAR (see f.n., previous page).

Hills of Eternity and Home of Peace

Remains in "Old Hebrew Cemetery" (Emanu-El Hart), established at Gough and Vallejo streets in 1847, were relocated in 1860-61 to two new cemeteries, Hills of Eternity (Congregation Sherith Israel) and Home of Peace (Congregation Emanu-El), bounded by Dolores and Church, 18th and 20th streets. In 1889, thirteen thousand remains and headstones were moved from there to cemeteries of the same name in Colma. A few records from Old Hebrew are part of the Western Jewish History Collection at the Bancroft Library. Records from Home of Peace were lost in 1906, except for one ledger archived at Congregation Emanu-El. Transfer records from both cemeteries, along with old Hills of Eternity records are available at the joint cemetery office in Colma. Transcriptions of Hills of Eternity burials were provided by the San Francisco Bay Area Jewish Genealogical Society to the JewishGen online Worldwide Burial Registry.

Lone Mountain/Laurel Hill

Lone Mountain Cemetery opened in May 1854. Tolls were charged on the road leading to the cemetery, which at that time was some distance removed from the settled part of the city. Portions of Lone Mountain acreage were leased as sub-cemeteries and were later sold by the association to became separate entities: Calvary (1862), Masonic (1864) and Odd Fellows (1865). What remained of Lone Mountain took the name of another subdivision, Laurel Hill (1867).

Removals from Laurel Hill, primarily to Cypress Lawn Memorial Park in Colma, began in 1892 and continued until 1940, ultimately totaling about 35,000. Removals from the Serbian sub-section in Laurel Hill dating to 1877, had already taken place about 1901 to the new Serbian Cemetery in Colma. The final removal list compiled in 1940 by the Laurel Hill Cemetery Association is housed at the San Francisco Department of Public Health and is available on FHL film #975,838. It contains three indexes each alphabetically arranged by surname. Information usually includes full name, dates of death and burial and age at death in days, months and years. A card file at Cypress Lawn references volume and page of the original Lone Mountain and Laurel Hill ledgers, which are archived at the California Society of Pioneers. Records also include names of earthquake victims and cremations of disinterments, 1903-1936.

Many Lone Mountain burials occurring before it was renamed Laurel Hill are recorded in the ledgers of N. Gray & Co. and are part of the Book of the Dead. Laurel Hill and Lone Mountain tombstone records appear in the DAR cemetery series (see f.n. p. 21) and in two publications: *Records from Tombstones in Laurel Hill Cemetery 1853-1937* (a DAR publication shelved at SFPL and Sutro) and in Ann Clark Hart's *Lone Mountain, the Most Revered of San Francisco's Hills* (available at Sutro, CGS, SFPL and on FHL film #844,644, item 6).

The Society of California Pioneers holds all surviving Laurel Hill Cemetery ledgers, as well as many Lone Mountain Cemetery ledgers that are not at San Francisco Public Library. Evidently burials continued into 1903 before the cemetery finally complied with the city ordinance banning them.

Facing pages (top and bottom) in 1903 Laurel Hill Cemetery burial register. Note removal notations. Ledgers archived at the society begin with Lone Mountain Cemetery ledgers from 1854 and continue through cremations of remains during final disinterments in 1936.

Calvary Cemetery

This Catholic cemetery was established in 1860 and opened in 1862 on land purchased from Lone Mountain. Bordered by Geary, Turk, Parker and St. Joseph's streets, some of its earliest interments are recorded in the Book of the Dead (p. 12). The cemetery began to run out of available space in 1887, and burials started to take place instead at Holy Cross Cemetery in Colma. Descendants and the Archdiocese successfully fought relocation for many years but eventually lost; removals were finally completed in the early 1940s. While many went to Holy Cross, some also went to Cypress Lawn. Holy Cross Cemetery holds the original Calvary ledgers and a detailed card file that was prepared from them.

Masonic Cemetery

Having established their cemetery in 1864 on land purchased from Lone Mountain, the Masonic Cemetery Association resisted unpaid removals until 1923. About fifteen thousand remains were then moved over a period extending into the 1930s to Woodlawn Memorial Park in Colma, where brief records can be found. Original cemetery ledgers were lost in 1906. A 1934 compilation of the names, original cemetery locations and new locations (if at Woodlawn) is available on FHL film #975,836. Dates of death are not included. Names are arranged by first letter of the surname only and are presented in either of two parts with no indication in which section a name might be found. Masonic epitaphs recorded in 1934 by the DAR from remaining stones are part of the card file version of Book of the Dead and are available on FHL films #1,711,667-8. The FHL films are available at CGS. The Sutro Library card version extends only through surnames beginning with "T."

IOOF (Odd Fellows) Cemetery

Established in 1865 on land purchased from Lone Mountain, this very large, irregularly shaped cemetery, owned by the IOOF, was bounded in part by Turk, Geary, Parker and Arguello streets. In addition to burial sites, the grounds held a crematorium and columbarium. In 1903 directors of the new Odd Fellows Cemetery to be developed in Colma appropriated $50,000 from the IOOF endowment care fund in order to purchase the necessary land. They did so without permission, and endorsement by IOOF was withdrawn. Instead, the new cemetery was named Greenlawn Memorial Park.

When the IOOF cemetery in San Francisco was finally made to comply with removal orders, many families arranged for cremations or burials elsewhere rather than allow removal to Greenlawn, which nonetheless in the 1930s received about twenty-six thousand unclaimed remains. These were buried in a mass grave slightly removed from the regular grounds, not open to visitors but marked by a single monument. Due to lack of perpetual funding, it is not maintained. Remaining headstones and monuments from the old cemetery were used in a seawall at Aquatic Park.

Original IOOF ledgers, useful for locating records of immigrant Germans, are divided between Greenlawn Cemetery and CGS. A 1933 report made to the San Francisco Department of Public Health by the Odd Fellows Cemetery Association is available on FHL film #975,836. It consists of names of those still interred in 1931, date of death (ranges from 1865 to 1906), original location of interment and, penciled in lightly, planned location of reinterment. Greenlawn holds indexes and burial ledgers providing date and cause of death, while the indexed registers at CGS provide date of burial and funeral home. Both sets

Page from one of original IOOF Cemetery registers
(from California Genealogical Society archives).

The California Genealogical Society holds half the surviving original ledgers of this cemetery; the rest are at Greenwood Cemetery in Colma.

include removal information. CGS also holds section maps, lot and deed books, all crematory ledgers and all surviving columbarium ledgers except for one, which remains at the restored San Francisco Columbarium. Compilations of cremation ledger abstracts and some columbarium records have been published as *San Francisco, California, I.O.O.F. Crematory Records* (Barbara Close, comp., CGS, 2001) and *San Francisco, California, Columbarium Records 1847 - 1980* (Vernon A. Deubler, comp., CGS, 2003).

Golden Gate Cemetery

This smaller, outlying cemetery, also known as City Cemetery, was established in 1870, at which time it received removals from the pioneer cemetery, Yerba Buena. The books of N. Gray & Co. mortuary reference some paid removals to Golden Gate by entries that read, "Yerba Buena Cem. – Removed to City Cemetery [1870 or later] – Inscription on wood." Most burials, however, were of Chinese and indigent dead.

A number of small sub-cemeteries with ethnic or fraternal order connections were formed within Golden Gate or were moved there from previous locations, including the Greek ("Greco-Russian") Cemetery, formerly at Stanyan Street and Golden Gate Avenue, and the Chinese Cemetery, formerly just west of Laurel Hill Cemetery. Records have not been found for these and most of the following small enclosures located nearby: Caledonian (a Scots club), Chinese, French, German, Colored Masons, Greco-Russian, Japanese, Russian, Scandinavian, Slavonic-Illyric, GAR, Knights of Pythias, Master Mariners (a club), Old Friends (Quaker), Independent (or Improved) Order of Red Men, and Seamen's.

Pressures aimed toward condemnation began in the late 1880s. Some removals followed in instances when the expense was borne by family members. Most burials, however, remained undisturbed and were eventually grassed over and the surface markers destroyed. The only removal program from Golden Gate appears to have taken place in 1891, some twenty years before the city ordered removals. At that time 696 removals from "Old" Salem Cemetery, founded in 1877 by Beth Israel Congregation, went to the new cemetery in Colma. The new cemetery was purchased in 2004 by Home of Peace/Hills of Eternity.

In 1919 about eight thousand removals from Italian Cemetery (in Golden Gate) to Italian Cemetery in Colma were planned, but never took place. Some sixty headstones in Golden Gate were published by Evelyn Briggs Baldwin in 1912: *Inscriptions from City Cemetery, Thirty-fourth Avenue and Clement Street (now Lincoln Park), San Francisco, California* (FHL film 1,419,455, item 7). The same records appear in greater detail in the Phillips-Newcomb manuscript (p. 12).

San Francisco National Cemetery

Begun in 1884 as an expansion of Post Cemetery, this cemetery was closed to most burials in 1990. Located on grounds of the Presidio that now belong to the National Park Service, its records are posted online, can be accessed at *http://www.interment.net* and are also available at the cemetery. Tombstone inscriptions from here and the Veterans' Home in Napa County, over the years 1902-1944, are available on FHL film #874,359 (item 11). Included are name, birth state, death date, age at death and a brief service description if applicable.

The Presidio grounds held several older cemeteries that dated to long before 1884. The first *recorded* interment, however, took place in 1852. The U.S. Marine

Hospital Cemetery, where both American and international seamen were interred up to at least 1912, was built in 1874. This burial ground was covered with fifteen feet of landfill in the 1970s when the area was converted to other use. In 2006 as a project of the National Park Service, Jennifer McCann reconstructed 838 burials from multiple sources and published them as "The Marine Hospital Cemetery, Presidio of San Francisco, California," available as a free download from the Service through a convenient link at *http://www.sfgenealogy.com/sf/sfmarine.htm*. Records include age, date, birth country and cause of death.

Post-1900 Burials

After burials within the city limits of San Francisco ceased at the turn of the century and in many instances in the decade before that, interments of San Franciscans took place just over the county border in what is now Colma, where far more people lie beneath the ground than above. The remains of over one million people lie buried there, beneath a town that numbers slightly over one thousand residents. Records of San Franciscans buried during the years immediately before the earthquake, particularly those of Jewish residents buried in or after 1889, likely will be found in Colma at the following cemeteries:

- Cypress Lawn Memorial Park, 1370 El Camino Real, 94014; (650) 755-0580
- Holy Cross Cemetery (Catholic), 1500 Old Mission Rd., 94014; (650) 756-2060
- Home of Peace Cemetery & Emanu-El (Jewish), 1299 El Camino Real, 94014; (650) 755-4700
- Woodlawn Memorial Park, 1000 El Camino Real, 94014; (650) 755-1727
- GreenLawn Memorial Park, 1100 El Camino Real, 94014; (650) 755-7622
- Eternal Home Cemetery (Jewish), 1051 El Camino Real, 94014; (650) 755-5235
- Hills of Eternity Memorial Park (Jewish), 1301 El Camino Real, 94014; (650) 756-3333
- Olivet Memorial Park (formerly Mount Olivet), 1601 Hillside Blvd., 94014; (650) 755-0322
- Salem Memorial Park (Jewish), 1711 El Camino Real, 94014; (650) 755-5296
- Serbian Cemetery, 1801 Hillside Blvd., 94014; (650) 755-2453
- Japanese Benevolent Society (Cem.), 1300 Hillside Blvd., 94014; (650) 755-3747
- Italian Cemetery, 540 F Street, 94014; (650) 755-1511

Addresses for the two cemeteries and one columbarium in San Francisco are:

- Mission Dolores, 3321 – 16th St., San Francisco 94114; (415) 621-8203
- San Francisco Columbarium, 1 Lorraine Ct., San Francisco 94118; (415) 752-7891
- San Francisco National Cemetery, Golden Gate National Recreation Area, Lincoln Blvd. and Funston Ave., San Francisco 91208; (415) 561-2008

Columbarium Records

Ashes from the IOOF crematory not interred at other locations were placed in locations within an adjacent columbarium. Completed in 1898, the columbarium was exempted from the 1900 removal order and after the 1911 closure of the crematory continued to receive cremains from other counties. It was purchased by Bay Cities Cemetery Association about 1930, sold several years later to Cypress Abbey and soon after that, abandoned. When the property was purchased by the Neptune Society in 1980, the building was in ruins and the old ledgers water-damaged. CGS now holds the ledgers that could be saved, but they do not cover all years. Over 5,000 records have been published as *San Francisco, California, Columbarium Records 1847 - 1980* (Oakland: California Genealogical Society, Vernon A. Deubler, comp., 2003). Abstracts include name, niche location, year of birth and year of death. Occasionally year of death has been found to mark the transfer of ashes dating to a much earlier death. The columbarium has recorded names and niche locations for most inurnments, including some dating to before 1980 not found in the publication. Additional IOOF information is available as part of the research services of CGS; the society holds not only the original crematory and surviving columbarium ledgers, but also a large number of the cemetery ledgers (p. 25).

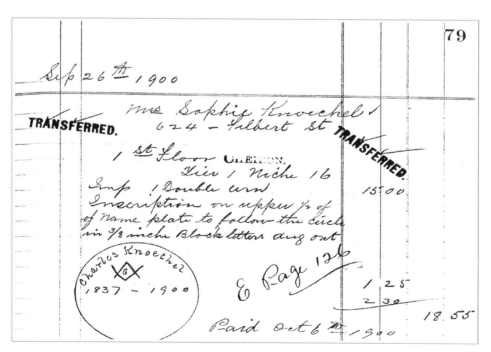

Typical entry in original ledger of old IOOF columbarium
(from California Genealogical Society archives).

*B*efore the beginning of civil registration, church records were the most used source for vital information. Even today they frequently provide detail that civil records lack. All vital records kept by the city and county of San Francisco, with the exception of a few death record ledgers and two marriage indexes, were lost. Not all churches burned, however, and more than one clergyman saved some or all of his records before the encroaching fire destroyed them.

Church records vary in content and scope according to the record-keeping practices of the various denominations. One cannot expect to find, for example, infant baptismal records in denominations that did not practice infant baptism. The genealogical information available in marriage records varies from a recording of date and two names to the inclusion also of age, residence, birthplace and parental names. Similarly, the content of death records ranges from only name and date of burial to date of death, birthplace and occasionally parental names. Confirmation records in those denominations in which confirmation was practiced vary from long lists of only names to unexpectedly more detailed information, such as parental names and place of baptism. In general, more detailed records were (and are) kept by Catholic, Lutheran, Congregational, Episcopal, Presbyterian, Methodist, Quaker and Eastern Orthodox churches, by the Church of Jesus Christ of Latter-day Saints and by Jewish synagogues.

The search for surviving records can be time-consuming. The researcher first must locate the church or synagogue a family likely attended and then determine where the records might be today. This often entails following a congregation through mergers and name changes. If you are persistent and fortunate enough to locate surviving records, you may be well-rewarded for your efforts.

LOCATING THE CORRECT CONGREGATION

Except in the instance of foreign language-speaking churches, which may have drawn their membership from wider areas, most families attended churches or synagogues fairly close to where they lived. If family records or newspaper notices of marriages and burials are of no help in determining the church a family attended, or at least in identifying a preferred denomination, then city directories used in conjunction with street maps may help to narrow the range of possibilities.

LOCATING THE RECORDS

The following pages may be of some help in locating records, but be aware that the search is often difficult. In instances where congregations ceased to exist, records may have been retained by the last clergyman or turned over to a church archive or library. Missing records may be hiding in churches that have undergone name changes or in churches that acquired them through mergers not described here. Only those denominations that traditionally offer the best chance for obtaining genealogical information are covered here. Included are: lists of confirmed holdings and some that were found in 1942 but could not be located today; records claimed to be missing or known to have been lost in 1906; and descriptions of mergers found in church literature.

Several resources at SFPL may help clarify the path that wandering congregations took. See Frank Mead and Samuel S. Hill, *Handbook of American Denominations* (Nashville: Abingdon Press, 1985) and *Yearbook of American and Canadian Churches* (many editions, 1933-1986). The book *Sacred Places of San Francisco*, compiled by San Francisco Alumnae Panhellenic (San Francisco: Presidio Press, 1985) contains brief church histories for those churches of architectural interest that still exist. Short histories of most Lutheran, Episcopal, Congregational, Methodist, Presbyterian Baptist, and Unitarian churches that were founded before the earthquake and were still in existence in 1978 can be found in *Heritage and Hope: A History of the Protestant, Anglican & Orthodox Church Movement in San Francisco on the Occasion of the 75th Anniversary Year (1978-1979) of the San Francisco Council of Churches* (Helen E. Helton and Norman E. Leach, eds.; San Francisco: San Francisco Council of Churches, 1979). Checking the section on churches and synagogues in city directories over successive years also may afford clues.

In the several years preceding 1942, the Works Progress Administration (WPA) conducted a survey of extant church records for six denominations. The findings of this survey were published in *A Guide to Church Vital Statistics Records in California, San Francisco and Alameda Counties: Six Denominations*, available at SFPL, on FHL film #897,458 (item 7) and online at *www.sfgenealogy.com*. The location of records presented in the WPA guide does not necessarily hold for today. Also, many descriptions were found to differ from what was found at archives, churches and synagogues checked in preparation for this guide. The WPA publication included only six denominations: Roman Catholic, Protestant Episcopal, Presbyterian, Methodist, Baptist and Jewish. Some holdings identified in 1942 cannot be found in extant churches or regional archives. This is not to say that they do not exist. Researchers in need of missing records should inquire at churches of the same denomination and check the sources mentioned above for clues to past mergers or name changes.

This 1897 baptism of Frank Gustaf Solvin from the filmed records of the old Swedish Evangelical Lutheran Ebenezer Church of San Francisco was provided by the Swenson Swedish Immigration Center at Augustana College in Rock Island, Illinois (courtesy of Joann MacDonald).

Pre-earthquake Roman Catholic Church Records
Available on Film at the Archdiocese of San Francisco Chancery Archives

	Baptisms	Marriages	Deaths
All Hallow's	Bp. 1871+	M. 1895+	
Cathedral of St. Mary	Bp. 1891+	M. 1891+	D. 1891+
Convent of the Good Shepherd (home)	Bp. 1885+		
Corpus Christi	Bp. 1898+	M. 1898+	
Holy Cross (Korean)	Bp. 1887+	M. 1887+	
Holy Family (Chinese Mission)	Bp. 1902+		
Mission Dolores	Bp. 1862+	M. 1776-1859	D. 1776-1822
Mission Dolores Basilica (see also pp. 21-2)	Bp. 1776+	M. 1776+	D. 1776-1876
Most Holy Redeemer	Bp. 1905+	M. 1900+	
Nativity Church (Slavonian)	Bp. 1902+		
Notre Dame des Victoires (French)	Bp. 1856+	M. 1855+	
Old St. John's	Bp. 1869+	(closed in 1891)	
Old St. Mary's	Bp. 1855+	M. 1855+	
Our Lady of Guadalupe	Bp. 1875+		
Sacred Heart	Bp. 1885+	M. 1885+	
St. Agnes'	Bp. 1895+	M. 1895+	
St. Anne's	Bp. 1904+	M. 1905+	
St. Anthony de Padua (German)	Bp. 1894+	M. 1894+	D. 1894+
St. Boniface Church (German)	Bp. 1860+	M. 1860+	
St. Bridgid's Church	Bp. 1864+	M. 1864+	
St. Charles Borromeo	Bp. 1887+	M. 1887+	
St. Dominic's	Bp. 1885+	M. 1885+	D. 1887+
St. James'	Bp. 1888+	M. 1888+	
St. Joan of Arc (French)	Bp. 1862+		
St. John the Evangelist	Bp. 1893+	M. 1893+	
St. Joseph's	Bp. 1861+	M. 1861+	D. 1862+
St. Mary's Hospital	Bp. 1887+		
St. Michael's	Bp. 1899+	M. 1899+	
St. Paul's	Bp. 1881+	M. 1881+	
St. Peter's	Bp. 1867+	M. 1868+	
St. Peter & St. Paul's	Bp. 1889+	M. 1884+	
St. Rose's	Bp. 1878+	M. 1878+	
St. Teresa's	Bp. 1880+	M. 1881+	
St. Vincent de Paul	Bp. 1901+	M. 1901+	
Star of the Sea	Bp. 1894+	M. 1894+	

Note: All records for St. Francis (est. 1849), St. Ignatius (est. 1855) and St. Patrick's (est. 1851) were lost in 1906.

Roman Catholic Records

Large numbers of Roman Catholic records have survived and are still held by various churches. Most, including those of defunct churches, are available on film at the Archdiocese of San Francisco Chancery Archives, located at 320 Middlefield Road in Menlo Park.[4] These films were closely examined by CGS volunteers, and the existence of original ledgers was confirmed at extant churches. Death or burial records were rarely found, even though they were mentioned repeatedly in the WPA guide. Original ledgers, however, might indirectly reveal a death in ancillary financial or memorial records. An appointment to examine films at the Chancery Archives is necessary; contact the archivist at (650) 328-6502.

Records from the Roman Catholic Orphan Asylum are now at Mt. St. Joseph's-St. Elizabeth's and are available only by written request to the agency.[5] Some old ledgers and indexes exist, but the earliest books have been lost. Information (beyond lists of names) begins in the 1880s and includes children's birthdates, entry and exit dates, destinations and occasionally some parental background.

Lutheran Records

The detail in Lutheran church records is perhaps second only to Roman Catholic records. Unfortunately, the WPA did not include Lutheran church records in their publication. If information is sought for a German or Scandinavian-speaking immigrant, be sure to check for Lutheran, German Reformed and Evangelical records, as well as records of the Methodist Church, which also served many non-English-speaking San Franciscans.

Following Lutheran congregations through schisms, mergers and name changes is perhaps more of a challenge than with other denominations. Records of early Lutheran churches occasionally are found among records classified as Evangelical or United Church of Christ. The 9.5 million Lutherans in America today belong to twenty-one different Lutheran church bodies. The largest of these is the Evangelical Lutheran Church in America (ELCA), followed by the Lutheran Church – Missouri Synod. The Evangelical Lutheran Church in America (ELCA) was formed in 1988 from the merger of the Lutheran Church in America (LCA) and the American Lutheran Church (ALC). These two denominations encompassed the descendants of most early German, Norwegian and Danish churches, but not the early Swedish. The ELCA maintains archives outside of Chicago and has conducted a filming program of early church registers. The Swenson Swedish Immigration Research Center in Rock Island,

---

[4] Original ledgers of defunct churches are located as follows: All Hallows at Lady of Lourdes, Holy Cross at St. Michael's, Our Lady of Guadalupe at Sts. Peter & Paul, St. Brigid's at St. Vincent de Paul and St. Joseph's at St. Patrick's. For original ledgers of Old St. John's and Sacred Heart, contact the Archdiocese at 445 Church Street, San Francisco 94114.

[5] Write Mt. St. Joseph – St. Elizabeth's, 100 Masonic Avenue, San Francisco, CA 94118.

Illinois, has also swept the country filming extant early Swedish church records. Concordia Historical Institute is the primary archive for Missouri Synod records, but does not appear to have conducted a nation-wide filming program.

Some early German congregations that may have begun as more mainstream Lutheran congregations broke away to join the Evangelical Synod of North America or the German Reformed Church. These two bodies united in 1934 to form the Evangelical and Reformed Church, which in 1957 united with the Congregational Christian Churches to form the United Church of Christ (UCC). The archive that might hold the old records of German churches that fed into this union is known as the Archives at Eden, located in Webster Grove, Missouri. (See Evangelical Church records, following.)

The earliest German-speaking church in San Francisco was First German Lutheran, which had its roots in the Mooshake Mission, informally organized in 1849. In 1866 it changed its name to St. Mark's Evangelical Lutheran Church. St. Mark's is still in existence at 1111 O'Farrell Street. Its earliest records begin in 1860 but are a bit spotty in the early years. The marriage ledger for the years 1895-1912 is missing. The early minister at St. Mark's, the Rev. Buehler, left in 1867 to become the first pastor at St. Paulus Lutheran Church (also German). Its early records were intact until 1995, when all but one register burned in a disastrous fire. The one surviving register covering the years 1867-1872 may be viewed at the church office, located at 930 Gough Street, San Francisco.

San Francisco's Norwegian-speaking Lutherans organized Our Savior Lutheran Church in 1870 and Bethlehem Lutheran in 1901. In 1916 these two congregations merged and underwent a name change to Norwegian Church, which changed its name to Ascension in 1959. In 1978, Trinity Lutheran (organized in 1899) merged with Ascension to form Golden Gate Lutheran, but this church closed in 2007. The Evangelical Lutheran Church of America filmed surviving ledgers of Our Savior (1871-98), Bethlehem (1901-16) and Trinity (1899-1938); this film (#302) can be easily rented or purchased from their archives in Illinois.[6]

A number of other Lutheran congregations that date to pre-earthquake years exist today, including Ebenezer (Swedish, established in 1882) and First United Lutheran (established in 1886). Minutes, membership lists and ministerial acts (presumably baptisms, marriages and burials) dating to 1882/1883 for Ebenezer Lutheran are currently archived at the Swenson Swedish Immigration Research Center in Rock Island, Illinois.[7] Gethsemane, a Finnish congregation established in 1890, and St. Ansgar, a Danish congregation organized in 1903, merged to form St. Francis, which survives today. St. Matthew's Lutheran, formed in 1895, exists at present, but its pre-fire records were lost in 1906.

---

[6] ELCA Archives, 321 Bonnie Lane, Elk Grove Village, IL 60007.

[7] Details for securing information may be found on their Web page or by writing Swenson Swedish Immigration Research Center, Augustana College, 639 – 38th Street, Rock Island, IL 61201-2296.

St. John's (Evangelical) Lutheran, formed in 1887, was completely destroyed in the earthquake and fire; few early records exist today. Whatever records of this church that did survive may be archived at the Missouri Synod's Lutheran Archives at the Concordia Historical Institute in St. Louis.[8] St. Johannes Evangelical Lutheran Mission, established in 1885, lost all records in the 1906 fire, as did St. Paul German Evangelical Lutheran. Some records of defunct churches may possibly be found at the regional ELCA archives at the Pacific Lutheran Theological Seminary, 2770 Marin Avenue, Berkeley.

Evangelical Church Records

The line is somewhat blurred between Lutheran and Evangelical churches, particularly in the case of those churches with congregations that were largely composed of immigrants. Evangelical church records, moreover, may occasionally have found a home in United Church of Christ churches following the 1957 merger of the Evangelical and Reformed Church with the Congregational Christian Church to form the United Church of Christ (UCC). The archives that might hold the old records of German churches that fed into this union are known as the Archives at Eden, located in Webster Grove, Missouri.

Five early San Francisco churches were described as Evangelical in the 1905 city directory: Emmanuel Church of the Evangelical Association, Salem Evangelical Church (German), United Evangelical Church (also German), Alice Hollman Memorial Chapel, and St. John's German Evangelical (see above, Lutheran). St. John's German-speaking congregation later merged with Bethel Evangelical and Reformed and with Congregational Christian of Forest Hill to form St. John's United Church of Christ, which is still in existence.

None of these 1905 evangelical churches exist today by their original names. None of their ministerial records were found except for post-earthquake records for Bethel, held at Eden Theological Seminary in Webster Grove, Missouri. The Archives at Eden also holds records for First Finnish Evangelical Church, organized in 1887 and dissolved in 1990, but only those dating from 1910.[9]

First Covenant Church, an Evangelical Covenant Church (ECC), began in 1877 as Swedish Tabernacle. From the date of founding it would seem that this possibly was the "Swedish Mission Church," classified as Congregational in the 1905 city directory. Although the building was destroyed in the earthquake, minutes and membership rolls dating to 1878 survived and have been filmed by the Swenson Swedish Immigration Research Center.[10]

[8] Contact: Concordia Historical Institute, The Lutheran Church—Missouri Synod; 801 De Mun Avenue, St. Louis, MO 63105.
[9] For further information, contact: The Reverend Dr. Lowell Zuck, Senior Research Consultant for Archives; Eden Theological Seminary, Luhr Library; 475 E. Lockwood Ave., St. Louis, MO 63119.
[10] Write: Swenson Swedish Immigration Center, Augustana College; 639 – 38th Street, Rock Island, IL 61201-2296.

Congregational Records

The 1942 WPA survey did not include Congregational churches. As noted
above, Congregational churches in 1957 joined with churches belonging to
the Evangelical and Reformed Church to form the United Church of Christ.
Some retained the name "Congregational" while others changed their names.
The Congregational Library on Beacon Street in Boston does not hold any San
Francisco records. The old card file at the Graduate Theological Union Library
(2400 Ridge Road, Berkeley) listed as library holdings membership lists, minutes
and financial records for the five early Congregational churches listed below.
The first item likely refers to a rare book in their collection. The UCC archivist
searched school archives for these holdings and found they consist of sermons,
scrapbooks and minutes of church meetings, but no ministerial records.

- First Congregational Church, membership lists 1860, 1867
- Olivet Congregational Church, 1878-1902
- Plymouth Congregational Church (formerly "Second" Congr.), 1854+
- Richmond Congregational Church, 1897+
- Sunset Congregational Church, 1896+

First Congregational Church, established in 1849, and the California Chinese
(Congregational) Mission were destroyed in 1906 and later rebuilt. Membership
lists revealing previous residence, ministers' notes, minutes and a transcription of
baptisms, all from First Congregational, survived and are held at the church. These
were extracted by CGS and are part of the society's online research services.

Few pre-earthquake records were found for other Congregational churches
for which city directories suggest possible mergers and name changes. Pre-
1906 Park Congregational may have been Mission Park Congregational that
merged in 1930 with Grace Methodist. Ocean View Congregational exists
today but is now called Pilgrim. Pierce Street Congregational Church changed
its name to Mayflower Church and seems to have disappeared about 1914.
Transcriptions of some Mayflower records between June 1888 to 1911 are in a
five-page manuscript at the Oakland Family History Center. Three more pre-
earthquake churches disappeared from the city directory in the late 1920s: Fourth
Congregational, which had changed its name to Green Street Church by 1910,
Third Congregational and Bethlehem Congregational.

Episcopal Records

The first San Francisco Episcopal church was Holy Trinity, established in the
summer of 1849. Trinity Church survives today at 1668 Bush Street, and like most
extant early Episcopal churches, still holds its records, which date to 1852. A DAR
abstract of Trinity Church records can be found at Sutro. A number of Episcopal

churches were lost in the fire, as evidenced by holdings the WPA survey denotes as "1905+." The Church of the Advent of Christ the King was totally destroyed and never rebuilt. Episcopal Church holdings that date to before the earthquake and fire, reported in the 1942 WPA survey and modified by several small changes found during the preparation of this guide, are shown below. The churches

Extant Episcopal Church Records			
	<u>Baptisms</u>	<u>Marriages</u>	<u>Deaths</u>
All Saints Church		M. 1905+	D. 1905+
Canon Kip Community House	Bp. 1905+	M. 1905+	D. 1905+
Chinese Mission Church			
(True Sunshine)	Bp. 1903+	M. 1903+	D. 1903+
Church of the Incarnation	Bp. 1905+	M. 1905+	D. 1905+
Community House of			
Sisters of St. Saviour	Bp. 1889+	M. 1889+	
Grace Church/Cathedral	Bp., M. & D. 1850-68, early 1904-06		
Holy Innocent's Church	Bp. 1903+	M. 1903+	D. 1903+
St. Barnabas' Mission Church	Bp. 1905+	M. 1905+	D. 1905+
St. James' Church	Bp. 1890+	M. 1890+	D. 1890+
Church of St. John			
the Evangelist	Bp. 1857+	M. 1857+	D. 1857+
St. Luke's Church	Bp. 1865-87	M. 1865-87	D. 1865-87
(Church of) St. Mary the Virgin	Bp. 1903+	M. 1903+	D. 1903+
St. Paul's Church	Bp. 1875+	M. 1875+	D. 1875+
St. Peter's Church	Bp. 1899+	M. 1899+	D. 1899+
Trinity Church	Bp. 1852+	M. 1852+	D. 1852+

shown, except for St. Barnabas Mission, St. Paul's, Canon Kip Community House, and Community House of Sisters of St. Savior, still exist.

The Episcopal Archives in San Francisco hold records for two defunct congregations, St. Paul's and St. Stephen's. The records of St. Paul's appear in the 1942 survey, but St. Stephen's became defunct about 1930, and its records evidently escaped notice. For the records of St. Paul's and St. Stephen's and for questions regarding records of other defunct congregations, contact the archives.[11]

Presbyterian Records

First Presbyterian Church, organized May 20, 1849, Calvary, organized July 23, 1854, and Chinatown Presbyterian, organized November 6, 1853, all exist today and maintain control of their surviving records. The Presbyterian Archives at San Francisco Theological Seminary, 2 Kensington Road, San Anselmo, holds

---

[11] Archives of the Episcopal Diocese of California, 1055 Taylor St., San Francisco, CA 94108.

Presbyterian Records Found at the Time of the 1942 WPA Survey			
	Baptisms	*Marriages*	*Deaths*
Calvary Presbyterian Church	Bp. 1874+, membership from 1854; some deaths		
Chinese Presbyterian Church	Bp. 1876+	M. 1876+	D. 1876+
First Presbyterian Church	Bp. 1863+	M. 1886+	D. 1888+
First United Presbyterian Church	Bp. 1866-98	M. 1866-98	D. 1866-98
Howard Presbyterian Church	Bp. 1850-96		
Lebanon Street Presb. Church	Bp. 1881+	M. 1881+	
Mizpah Presbyterian Church	Bp. 1890+	M. 1890+	D. 1890+
Olivet Presbyterian Church	Bp. 1869+	M. 1885+	
St. John Presbyterian Church	Bp. 1870-97	M. 1870-97	D. 1870-97
Stewart Memorial Church	Bp. 1892+	M. 1893+	
Trinity Center Presb. Church	Bp. 1871+	M. 1888+	

some registers of the defunct Howard Street Presbyterian Church of San Francisco, which became Trinity Presbyterian in 1892. Holdings include baptisms for the years 1850-1896 and the church ledger covering 1910-13. The archives at the seminary also holds early registers of First United Presbyterian Church (organized January 7, 1866) covering the years 1866-1898 and the registers of St. John Presbyterian (organized March 6, 1870) for the years 1870-1897 and 1919-29.

The Presbyterian Historical Society in Philadelphia holds baptismal records of Lebanon Presbyterian Church (1882-1917) as well as marriages (1894-1914), and some Howard Street records: baptisms (1871-94) and marriages (1888-92). Mizpah Presbyterian merged in 1942 with Trinity Presbyterian (founded in December 1868) under the name Trinity. It more recently became the bilingual Mission Presbyterian Church and is still located in the same building at 3261-23rd Street. Early records, however, were not found. Stewart Memorial Presbyterian Church, founded in 1892, was destroyed by arson in 1972.

Baptismal records for Olivet Presbyterian, along with admissions, dismissals and membership lists for the years 1868-1898, were filmed by the FHL at the Presbyterian Historical Society in Philadelphia. This film of the original register is available as FHL film #505,951 (item 6).

Methodist and Methodist Episcopal (African-American) Records

In April 1906 there were twenty Methodist churches and several small mission groups in the city. As a result of the earthquake and fire, ten churches were totally destroyed, including Central, Howard Street, First, Hamilton, most of the foreign language-speaking churches, and both Bethel African Methodist Episcopal and First African Methodist Episcopal Zion. Many buildings untouched by the fire were nevertheless in such ruins that they had to be rebuilt. This was financially devastating to the local Methodist Church, which never fully recovered. During the ensuing years a number of mergers necessarily took place.

Additionally, as members of non-English-speaking congregations became fluent in English, many churches folded or underwent name changes. Dissolutions, frequent mergers and name changes make following these congregations difficult.

Methodist church organization also underwent change. In 1939 the three existing branches of American (mainline) Methodism—the Methodist Protestant Church, the Methodist Episcopal Church and the Methodist Episcopal Church, South—united under the name Methodist Church. Then in 1968, the Methodist

Methodist Records Found at the Time of the 1942 WPA Survey			
	Baptisms	*Marriages*	*Deaths*
Bethany Mission Park	Bp. 1903+		
Central Methodist Episcopal Church	Bp. 1885+	M. 1885+	
Epworth Methodist Church	Bp. 1880+	M. 1880+	D. 1880+
Grace United Church of the Mission	Bp. M., & D. all covering 1865-1875 and 1878+		
Park-Presidio United Church	Bp. 1898+	M. 1899+	
Simpson Methodist Church [old Swedish]	Bp. 1896+		D. 1896+
Trinity Methodist Church	Bp. 1885+	M. 1885+	
United Methodist Church [incl. St. Paul's German]	Bp. 1862+	M. 1885+	

Church merged with the Evangelical United Brethren Church to form the United Methodist Church, as it is known today. Some churches modified their names accordingly; others did not.

At the time of the 1942 survey the churches listed above held pre-earthquake records, some of which belonged to predecessors. Only two appear to survive under the same or a similar name today: Grace United Methodist and Park Presidio. The Japanese congregation of Pine United Methodist, founded in 1886, had disbanded by the time of the 1942 survey and thus its holdings were missed.

In 1965 Epworth, founded in 1877, and Grace Methodist Episcopal, founded in 1852, merged to form Bethany United Methodist, in existence today. Listings in old city directories suggest that other mergers occurred as well. As new or merged congregations were formed, old ministerial ledgers, some dating to the early 1850s, were often turned over to Methodist archivists. Some of these records may be found in the archives at Pacific School of Religion in Berkeley; others are possibly archived at College of the Pacific in Stockton. If membership in one of the pre-earthquake churches is confirmed, researchers should address inquiries about surviving records to the United Methodist archivist for California and Nevada.[12]

---

[12] Contact: Archivist, Pacific School of Religion; 1798 Scenic Avenue, Berkeley, CA 94080; or e-mail umarchives@psr.edu.

Baptist Records

The Baptists erected the first Protestant church in San Francisco, but no records remain. Records identified in the 1942 WPA survey are shown below.

Baptist churches bearing these names in existence today are Temple Baptist and Hamilton Square. Minutes and membership records for Temple Baptist, which was originally Swedish, date back to 1889 and are on film at both the church and at Swenson Swedish Immigration Center at Augustana College in Rock Island, Illinois. (For address see f.n., p. 34.)

Baptist Records Found at the Time of the 1942 WPA Survey			
	Baptisms	*Marriages*	*Deaths*
Central Baptist Church	Bp. 1905+		D. 1905+
Hamilton Square Church	Bp. 1881+		D. 1881+
Temple Baptist Church	Bp. 1889+	M. 1889+	D. 1889+

Records from Pre-Earthquake Jewish Synagogues

The San Francisco Jewish tradition took its roots in the April 1849 formal establishment of Congregation Sherith Israel, an Orthodox, English and Polish congregation, and soon after, Congregation Emanu-El, a Reform, primarily German, congregation. As San Francisco grew, the number of temples increased; by 1906 there were nine Jewish synagogues in the city.

Although Sherith Israel lay within the fire zone and was heavily damaged, its records, dating to 1850, did not burn. They form part of the Western Jewish History Collection housed at the Bancroft Library. Temple Emanu-El was completely destroyed. Located today at 2 Lake Street, the synagogue has one book of pre-earthquake marriages. Of the remaining synagogues, only Beth-Israel and Ohabai Shalome were not destroyed. Beth Israel, a Conservative congregation organized in 1861, merged with a Reform congregation in the 1960s, took the name Beth-Israel Judea and moved to an outlying area. Its early records, including marriages starting in 1860 and deaths from 1891, are also part of the Western Jewish History Collection, as are the records of Congregation Ohabai Shalome, which had many French members and disbanded in 1934.

Reorganized Church of Jesus Christ of Latter Day Saints

The Reorganized Church of Jesus Christ of Latter Day Saints (RLDS) broke away from the mainstream LDS church in 1860. While informative LDS (mainstream) records from San Francisco did not survive from the pre-earthquake years, at least some, if not all, RLDS records did. This church is now known as Community of Christ and has its headquarters in Independence, Missouri, where surviving records for San Francisco were filmed.

FHL film #1,928,513 (item 7) contains membership lists dating back to 1873. Records for "children blessed" and marriages do not begin until 1900, but the earlier "membership" lists include for every family member: name and when and where born (town and state). Children's "Blessing" records suggest an illness or other major event. Marriage records include names of bride and groom, date and place of marriage, but not parents' names. Additional information may be obtained in some cases by contacting the archives.[13]

RELIGIOUS NEWSPAPERS

The Catholic Archives in Menlo Park, the Graduate Theological Union Library in Berkeley, Temple Emanu-El and the Western Jewish History Collection housed at the Bancroft all hold pre-earthquake religious newspapers and newsletters. Both the Jewish newspaper *Emanu-El* and the Catholic newspaper *The Monitor* are indexed in card files. SFPL holds broken and unindexed runs of both Catholic and Jewish newspapers (see p. 45).

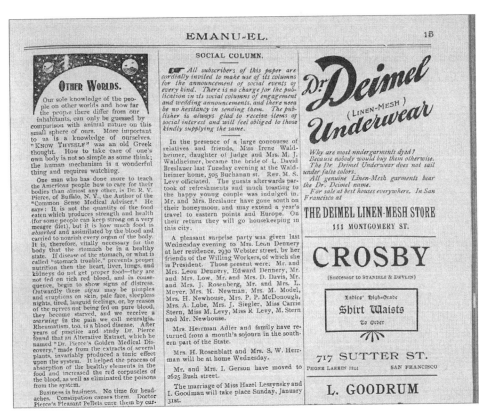

Typical article from Emanu-El *newspaper*
(from Western Jewish History Collection at Bancroft Library, courtesy of Jeremy Frankel).

---

[13] Contact: Community of Christ Archives Division, 1001 W. Walnut, Independence, MO 64050.

upwards was knocked down the other day for $300. The
ground rent had amounted to $1200 per month. The
bulding is now being taken to pieces and removed.

DIED,

In this city, on the 22d inst., MRs. MAGDALENA FAR-
LEY, aged 41 years, relict of the late John G. Farley, for-
merly a member of Col. J. D. Stevenson's 1st New York
Regiment of Volunteers.

The friends of the family are respectfully invited to at-
tend the funeral, from her late residence, Washington
street, above Stockton, at 3 P. M. on Sunday, 24th inst.

Shipping Intelligence.

PORT OF SAN FRANCISCO, MARCH 23, 1850.

Arrived,

March 22—Am brig Malek Adhel, Dolland, 143 ds fm
New York.

Am ship Thomas Dickerson, ——, fm San Diego.

Cleared,

March 22—Am brig Seguin, Mordon, Portland, O.

Fr ship Cachalot, Legrand, Valparaiso.

Eng brig Wm. Hill, Grove, Sydney.

Arg bark Sirena, Lassen, Valparaiso.

BUSINESS NOTICES.

NOTICE.—Consignees by the American bark Mar-

Funeral notice from Daily Alta, *March 23, 1850
(microfilm, Newspaper Room, San Francisco Public Library).*

Newspapers: Films, Indexes, Abstracts and Online Digitizations

Due to the loss of so many original records, historians and genealogists researching early San Francisco have come to depend upon newspaper coverage more heavily than is usually the case. An overwhelming number of San Francisco newspapers were published during the pre-earthquake years. The range of years for which filmed newspapers are available extends from before statehood to the present. Not all publications survived long enough to be filmed, but enough are available that they constitute one of the most important genealogical resources. Newspapers carry information about both rich and poor and provide a historical framework into which family history can be woven. They are worth revisiting as more information about a family surfaces. Once an article of interest is found, other papers over the same time frame should be searched since coverage of an event often differs greatly in detail from publication to publication. Take the time to search the entire paper. Paid obituaries and wedding reports are often scattered throughout a publication wherever fillers are needed; only funeral announcements or government-issued records tend to appear as a single block of text.

The California State Library in Sacramento has a large collection of filmed and bound newspapers from throughout the state, which is convenient if one is trying to unravel a descendancy. Many Bay Area repositories hold films of local publications. The SFPL collection is for most purposes adequate. The newspaper film collection at Doe Memorial Library and bound papers at the Bancroft, both at the University of California (Berkeley) can supplement if an item is not found. Sutro Library holds films of the largest pre-1900 papers. Oakland Public Library holds the *Chronicle* and the *Sacramento Bee*, in which articles about many San Francisco residents and events were published. Doe and the Bancroft are the best source for foreign language newspapers, useful in searching for obituaries of San Francisco's foreign-born. A supplementary listing of holdings at the state library and UC Berkeley appears in the appendix of this guide. For details of holdings at Doe and Bancroft, search the University of California online catalog, *Melvyl*, or the UC Berkeley catalog, *OskiCat*. Researchers can locate institutions holding California newspaper films at both the Library of Congress web page, *http://www. loc.gov/rr/news/lcnewsp.html* and the California Newspaper Project page *http:// cnp2.ucr.edu/cnpsearchdb.html*. Although not identical, together they provide a list of accessible publications covering the appropriate years.

A number of newspaper indexes are available. Those on film start in 1894 but usually index only surnames appearing in titles of articles or of individuals who are the primary subject of the coverage. Instead, they tend to group names under topical headings such as "engagements," "marriages," "elopements," "divorces," "accidents," "suicides," and "deaths." Jim Faulkinbury offers a comprehensive fee-based service, the index of which can be viewed online; see his "Index to the *Call*," below. The *California Information File*, also referenced below and discussed elsewhere in this guide (p. 139), indexes names and events not only from newspapers but also from periodicals and other sources. The file is very large and tends to focus on newsworthy events and prominent individuals; it is, however, a good index to the early paper the *Daily Alta*. It is available on microfiche at SFPL, CGS and at numerous libraries throughout the state.

Despite the growing number of newspaper digitizations available online (see p. 48), abstracts remain an important aid due to the limitations of optical character recognition software. The DAR published twenty-three volumes of vital event extractions from *The Daily Alta*, the *San Francisco Bulletin* and from several other publications covering the years 1854 through 1874, excluding only 1869. They are described more fully on p. 48.

FILMED NEWSPAPERS MOST FREQUENTLY ACCESSED

The filmed newspaper collection in the Newspaper Center on the fifth floor at SFPL contains the most commonly accessed publications. These include:

- *Alta California* (January 4, 1849 – June 2, 1891)
- *California Star* (January 9, 1847 – December 23, 1848)
- *Evening Bulletin, Bulletin,* and *San Francisco Bulletin* (October 1, 1855 to post-earthquake)
- *San Francisco Morning Call* and related titles (December 8, 1863 to 1959)
- *San Francisco Chronicle* (January 1, 1865 to present)
- *San Francisco Examiner* (June 1, 1865 to 2002)

Less used publications found on film or fiche in the sixth floor San Francisco History Center include:

- *Argonaut* (1877 - 1958)
- *Elevator* (Black ethnic, April 1865 - 1895)
- *Evening Post* (1888, 1894-1895); *Weekly Post* (from 1876)

- *Fireman's Journal and Military Gazette* (1855 - 1859)
- *Frank Leslie's Illustrated Newspaper/Weekly* (1855 - post-earthquake, broken run)
- *Golden Era* (December 11, 1859 - December 31, 1871)
- *Hutchings California Magazine* (July 1856 - April 1861)
- *Jewish Progress* (January 15, 1897 - November 18, 1898)
- *Jewish Times & Observer* (January 15, 1892 - February 17, 1911)
- *The Monitor* (Catholic; December 14, 1861 - December 26, 1888)
- *Weekly Gleaner* (January 16, 1857 - December 18, 1857)

The early years of the *Sacramento Bee* noted births, marriages and deaths of San Franciscans. The masthead read *The Daily Bee* from 1857 to 1890 and the *Evening Bee* from 1890 to 1908. Films of this newspaper and the index to its early years on microfiche can be found at the Oakland Public Library. The index, but not the newspaper films, is also at CGS and Sutro. It is somewhat inconveniently arranged in that each year, 1857-1905, is alphabetized separately.

RELIGIOUS NEWSPAPERS

Many religious denominations published newspapers with a San Francisco focus. The Catholic Archives, the Graduate Theological Union Library, Temple Emanuel and the Western Jewish History Collection that has moved to the Bancroft Library in Berkeley all hold filmed newspapers. The films from the Western Jewish History Collection and *The Monitor* at the Catholic Archives are indexed. The 6th Floor History Center at SFPL holds broken runs of the *Jewish Times and Observer* and *Jewish Progress* and *The Monitor*.

FOREIGN-LANGUAGE NEWSPAPERS

The best collection of foreign-language newspapers can be found at Bancroft and Doe libraries on the University of California campus in Berkeley. Holdings include San Francisco newspapers in Chinese, Danish, French, German, Hebrew, Italian, Japanese, Portuguese, Russian, Spanish, Swiss-German and more. These papers usually provide more information on members of their communities than do English language newspapers. A useful guide to locating German language films titled *The German Language Press of the Americas*, two volumes by Karl J. R. Arndt and May E. Olson (Munich: Verlag Dokumentation, 1976, 1980), is available at SFPL. Films of a full run (1887 on) of the Swedish language newspaper *Vestkusten* are available through the Swenson Swedish Immigration Research Center at Augustana College in Rock Island, Illinois.

SPECIALTY NEWSPAPERS

Occupational and union newspapers were published over the years in San Francisco. The Labor Archives & Research Center of San Francisco State University, located in the same building as Sutro Library, owns bound volumes of *The Clarion*, the official journal of the San Francisco Labor Council, from 1902. In addition, there were papers such as the *San Francisco Newsletter* (available at Sutro from 1865 - 1889) that published weekly descriptions of Real Estate Transfers and a newspaper covering fraternal organizations, *The Pacific States Weekly*. Several legal newspapers are described on p. 82.

NEWSPAPER INDEXES AND ABSTRACTS

> *Names in newspaper indexes are often grouped under topical entries, such as "Accidents," "Deaths," "Suicides," "Divorces," "Engagements," "Elopements" or "Marriages," as opposed to being directly indexed by surname.*

- *Index to the San Francisco Call, 1894-1903*: available on film at CGS for the years 1894-1903 and at SFPL for 1894-1898. This index includes names in news articles only and not the names in the official vital records sections. Names are often grouped under topical entries such as "Accidents," "Deaths," "Suicides," "Divorces," "Engagements," "Elopements" and "Marriages," as opposed to being indexed directly by surname.

- Post-1903 indexes: a microfiche collection covering 1904-49 is available at SFPL, Sutro and CGS. Pre-earthquake coverage is limited to the *San Francisco Call*; later years include the *Examiner* and the *Chronicle*. A separate index to the *San Francisco Chronicle*, 1950-1980, useful for working out descendancies, can also be found at SFPL, Sutro and CGS.

- *An Index of Births Marriages and Deaths Appearing in the Sacramento Bee* can be found at CGS, Sutro and Oakland Public Library. Only Oakland and the state library in Sacramento hold the corresponding newspaper films.

- Jim Faulkinbury's online "index" of vital events that appeared in the *Morning Call* currently covers the years 1869 - 1899. Faulkinbury is a nationally certified genealogist (CG) who, for a modest fee, will provide either full text transcriptions or newspaper photocopies of events listed in his online index. His index, formerly housed in space provided by the Continental European Family History Association, has recently moved to its own site at *http://www.jwfgenresearch.com*.

- *DAR Vital Records from Newspapers*: this collection of abstracts covering various years between 1854 and 1906 is at the state library in Sacramento and on FHL films #844,447, #844,422-430, and #874,354 (items 4-5). SFPL holds the publications covering the years 1854-7 and 1861; CGS holds the full set of films (BMD 1855-74 and births only 1900-01 and 1904-06). Sutro Library also holds some of this collection. Newspapers abstracted include *The (Daily) Alta California*, *San Francisco Bulletin*, *San Francisco Daily Evening Bulletin*, *San Francisco Daily Bulletin*, *Wide West* and *Golden Era*.

- CGS volunteers prepared a paper and an electronic index to the *San Francisco Call* that includes births, marriages and deaths from July 1, 1898 through March 31, 1900, and July 1, 1904 through June 30, 1905. Original indexes to marriage licenses covering July 1, 1904 through April 17, 1906 somehow survived (see p. 4). A paper publication compiled by Barbara Close and published by CGS in 2003, *San Francisco Deaths 1902–1904*, indexes approximately 27,000 deaths reported in the *Call* and in surviving city records. It is available from the society.

- Three indexes–one to births, one to marriage licenses and the third to deaths–all for the year 1900, were prepared from the three major San Francisco newspapers–the *Examiner, Chronicle* and *Morning Call*–by Maggie Fujii (privately published, Sparks, Nevada, 1995-1996). These indexes are not available in local libraries but were filmed by the FHL on microfilms #1,598,392 and #1,598,394. Her index to deaths also covers entries in the surviving "Book P" (of city death registers) covering March 17, 1900 through October 22, 1901 (see p. 4).

- Shipboard deaths occurring in 1850, either in or on the way to San Francisco, were included at the beginning of a DAR publication titled *Annual Compilation of Births, Marriages, Deaths in the Sacramento Union, 1859-1886*, available on FHL film #844,431 (item 2).

- *California Information File*: this enormous card file can be found at the California State Library and on microfiche at SFPL, Sutro, the FHL, CGS and some smaller libraries. Fiche do not circulate, however, from the FHL to Family History Centers. It indexes newspapers and periodicals, biographies and histories, manuscript collections and pioneer records, but is not comprehensive. Material cited dates from the 1840s to the earthquake and beyond and consists of over 721,000 cards representing about 1.4 million citations. Material indexed since 1985 is available electronically only at the state library in Sacramento.

- Mary Dean Alsworth, *Gleanings from Alta California–Marriages and Deaths Reported in the First Newspapers Published in California 1846 through 1850* (Rancho Cordova, California: Dean Publ., 1980): available at Oakland Public Library (OPL), CGS and the state library in Sacramento.

- Mary Dean Alsworth, *More Gleanings from Alta California–Vital Records Published in California's First Newspaper–Year 1851* (Rancho Cordova, California: Dean Publ., 1982): available at OPL, CGS and the state library in Sacramento, it includes vital records, details from published probate proceedings and coroner's inquests, and other facts of possible interest.

- Kathleen C. Beals, *Index to San Francisco Marriage Returns, 1850–1858* (Oakland: California Genealogical Society, 1992): some original indexes to land records survived (FHL films #967,466-9 and #973,627-30). They also indexed marriage licenses and contracts and occasionally naturalizations, all of which were recorded in ledgers that did not survive. The dates shown in the indexes reflect the recording date, however, and not the date of the ceremony or court transaction. About forty percent of the extractions were amplified with information from DAR newspaper abstracts, indexes to the *Sacramento Bee* and extracts from the *San Francisco Call* reprinted in the short-lived *San Francisco Historic Genealogical Bulletin*.

- *California Fatalities from Sacramento Daily Union*, by Lois A. Dove (Sacramento: self-published, 1988): these abstracts, available at Sutro, cover the years 1860-1879 and include many San Francisco deaths by accident, murder, etc.
- *Vital Records from Early Newspapers of Stockton, California, 1850-1852* (1962 DAR publication, available on FHL film #844,432, item 2, and at the state library in Sacramento): early Stockton papers included some San Francisco vital records. The San Joaquin Genealogical Society also extracted Stockton newspaper records over the years 1850-72, publishing nine volumes collectively known as *Gold Rush Days*, available in part at Sutro and SFPL and on FHL film #844,432 (item 1).

SFPL will respond to obituary/death notice lookup requests by mail at no charge provided no more than three requests are made per month and the exact date of death is submitted.[14]

Newspaper Digitization Projects

Searchable newspaper digitization is perhaps the most important tool developed over the past five years to help locate pre-earthquake events. The California Digital Newspaper Collection (CDNC), a project within the Center for Biographical Studies and Research at the University of California at Riverside is by far the largest of these projects. With support from the National Endowment for the Humanities, the project archive has grown to over 100,000 master film negatives extending from 1846 to the present, copies of which may be purchased. Scanned images of selected publications have been and are being placed online at *http://cdnc.ucr.edu/cdnc*. The number of available publications currently includes twelve pre-earthquake Northern California newspapers. Those most important to San Francisco research are the *Californian; California Star; California Star & Californian* (August 15, 1846 - December 23, 1848); the *Daily Alta* (December 10,

[14] Mail request, along with a self-addressed, stamped envelope to: Obituary requests, Newspapers and Magazines Center, San Francisco Public Library, Main Branch; 100 Larkin Street, San Francisco, CA 94102-4733.

1849 - June 2, 1891); the *San Francisco Call* (April 1, 1890 - October 15, 1912); the *Sacramento Transcript* (April 1, 1850 - June 5, 1851); and the *Sacramento Daily Union* (March 19, 1851 - December 31, 1895).

Similar digitization projects are offered as links through paid subscriptions or as a membership benefit of a number of genealogical societies. Increasing numbers of large libraries and county library systems hold institutional subscriptions and often make them available remotely to card holders. SFPL, for example, makes Proquest-created images of the *San Francisco Chronicle* over the years 1865 through 1922 available to its card holders both onsite and remotely. The subscription service *Footnote.com*, searches issues of the *Chronicle* that were digitized at Allen County Public Library, Ft. Wayne, Indiana. Negative results do not justify conclusions, however, since success is limited by both the quality of the software used and the clarity of the digitized material. The determined researcher should search creatively, using a variety of terms, even unrelated words that appear similar in print.

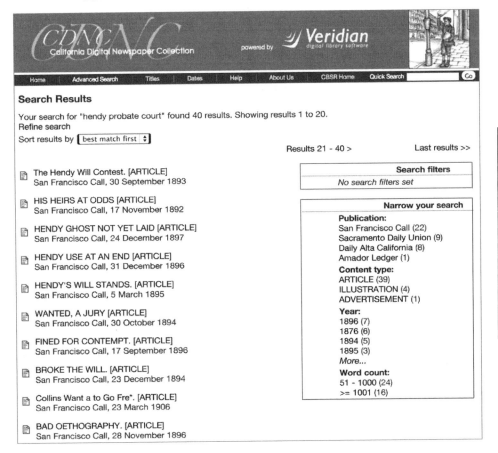

Searchable newspaper digitization is perhaps the most important tool developed over the past five years to help in pre-earthquake research.

Typical results obtained from searching for probate articles at the California Digital Newspaper Collection website, cdnc.ucr.edu/cdnc.

In the 1852 census, the use of initials in place of given names was frequent. Note that previous residence is given but is only occasionally detailed.

Page from 1852 state census, San Francisco County
(filmed at the California State Library by the Family History Library; available on FHL film #909,231
and as digitizations by subscription at Ancestry.com).

*D*ue to the widespread loss of records in the earthquake and fire, federal and state census records are of greater importance for tracing San Francisco ancestry. Pre-statehood censuses, which date to 1790, are covered in the section dealing with pre-statehood Spanish records (p. 121). The first federal census enumeration for the state of California took place in 1850. The census rolls for San Francisco, Santa Clara and Contra Costa counties, however, do not exist. The only state census ever conducted by the State of California took place in 1852 and must, for these counties, serve as a substitute.

1852 STATE CENSUS

This state census differs from the 1850 federal census in that previous residence, before arrival in San Francisco, is noted. Many of those enumerated were identified only by initials and surname, which may make identification less certain. Filmed copies of the original records, which are in the state archives, are available at SFPL, CGS, NARA, the California State Library, through Family History Centers (FHL films #909,231-232) and as digitizations on Ancestry. The script is very faint, almost impossible to decipher in some parts. The researcher may find it easier to start with the typewritten index and transcript that were prepared by the DAR and then move to the original if relevant information is found. The DAR index and transcripts are available at SFPL, Sutro, CGS and on FHL films. Volumes 6-8, the transcriptions for San Francisco County, are on FHL film #558,286. The DAR transcript, while easier to read, is incomplete: Chinese and Native Americans were omitted, and close to half the names in San Francisco were marked as "unreadable." The index, moreover, refers to page numbers in the transcript and not to page numbers in the original census. An index to both the DAR transcript and the original census films was prepared by the Southern California Genealogical Society and is sold by that society on a CD.

Federal Population Schedules 1860–1930

The federal census records for California, including Soundex (1880, 1900 and 1920) and Miracode (1910) indexes, as well as commercially published paper indexes, can be found at the NARA regional facility in San Bruno, at Sutro Library, and in part at CGS and SFPL. Most researchers use the online images available by paid subscription from *Ancestry.com* and Heritage Quest (ProQuest). A growing number of libraries and genealogical societies hold subscriptions; some may make them available by remote access.

Electronic indexes, such as exist for census images, are convenient, particularly when they can be searched by a number of fields, such as birthplace, age range, given name or by wildcard variations of surname. *Ancestry.com* offers every-name indexes to all digitizations for all censuses. However, the indexing was not performed by those familiar with the material or with abbreviations. Thus, when a name is not found, even with the inspired use of wildcards and field searching, it is advisable to use other available indexes, including the older published, paper indexes and soundexes when available. Sponsored by the FHL, volunteers across the country have been indexing all decennial censuses as part of the FHL digitization project and website remodeling; at this writing it is a work in progress. A number of years ago the FHL *abstracted* the 1880 enumeration, which can be searched by a variety of fields on the FHL website, *http://www.familysearch.org*.

Some errors in census information may arise from the fact that the NARA films of the 1860 and 1870 enumerations and the online digitizations that were made from them are not necessarily the enumerator's originals. (Recall that the 1850 San Francisco enumeration either was not taken or did not survive.) In 1850, 1860 and 1870 what one normally sees in these enumerations may be twice removed from the original. The instructions to the enumerator specified that each census taker was to prepare three copies, one of which was to be sent to the federal government and one to the Secretary of State. The third (often the most reliable) was normally kept at the county level, although it was not stated where it should be archived. Researchers have found both more and less information in state-retained copies, but for California only the 1860 state copy is available. The California State Archives holds a non-federal, bound copy of the 1860 enumeration, which evidently has not been filmed.[15] Tips for circumventing other recording and indexing errors appear in Part III of this guide (pp. 169-172).

---

[15] Enumerator instructions may be viewed at the IPUMS (Integrated Public Use Microdata Series) website, presently located at *www.ipums.org*. The California State Archives also holds the bound originals of 1850 and of the 1852 state census, but 1870 appears to have been lost. A second copy prepared in 1880 is abbreviated.

Non-population Schedules

Non-population census schedules consist of mortality (1850-1880), agricultural (1850-1880), industrial/manufacturing (1850-1880), social statistics (1850-1870) and Defective, Dependent and Delinquent classes (1880 only). As noted, the 1850 schedules for San Francisco were lost. All but social statistics contain individuals' names. Mortality schedules record the usual personal (census) information as well as the month and cause of death for anyone who died from June 1 of the previous year through May 30 of the census year.

Films of the originals of California's non-population schedules are held at the Bancroft Library and the California State Library and are now also available at *Ancestry.com*. The most convenient way to search is at *Ancestry.com*, but the location is difficult to find. The current address of agricultural, industrial and manufacturing schedules is *http://search.ancestry.com/search/db.aspx?dbid=1276*, where all years 1850-1880 (1860-1880 for San Francisco) may be searched. The schedules for "Defective, Dependent and Delinquent Classes" may be searched at *http://search.ancestry.com/search/db.aspx?dbid=1634*.

Mortality schedules were transcribed, indexed and published in book format by the Sacramento Genealogical Society, available at Sutro, the California State Library at Sacramento and CGS. The FHL filmed some of the original non-population schedules: the agricultural, manufacturing and mortality schedules for 1850 and 1860 (FHL film #1,549,969), the agricultural and mortality schedules for 1870 (FHL film #1,549,970) and the mortality schedule for 1880 (FHL film #1,549,971).

The Defective, Dependent and Delinquent schedules are interesting because they include not only the names of deaf, mute, blind or homeless residents classified as such in the regular census, but also include grouped enumerations of a prison, the city jail, at least one reform school, several orphanages and indigent institutions, such as one simply noted as "Old People's Home." Although names included here do appear also in the regular population schedules, some additional information, such as the cause of a disability, is included.

Although almost all of the 1890 census did not survive, half of the 1890 Union Veteran Schedules did. Sadly, California's schedules did not.

Census Searching

In Part III of this guide, the point is made that every available census from 1852 through 1930 should be checked for every member of a San Francisco family, including all descendants, no matter how distantly related. In the event of a stubborn problem, check for those related by marriage and for friends and even business acquaintances. The 1890 *Great Register of Voters* (p. 88) can be used as a substitute for the missing 1890 federal census. Enumerations when found should be reproduced, including not only the page in question, but also the two pages before and following. Complete descendancies should be worked out from this data and from other sources in order not to miss clues to previous residence and parentage and so that all family records can be located. When a person cannot be found in one index, search every paper and electronic census index available. In electronic indexes, use wildcard options to bring up alternate spellings and search on other fields with the surname and/or forename omitted.

Many of San Francisco's residents were immigrants with unusual surnames. This makes census searching a challenge, if it weren't already difficult enough. The ins and outs of census searching in a big city are described in greater detail on pp. 169-171, where attention is given to information that is often ignored, to naming problems and to ways of locating enumerations when indexes fail.

When the enumerator's script is difficult to read, it isn't surprising that people known to have been in certain locations are not found, even using multiple indexes. An excellent example is Malinda Tansey (line 11, p. 274 of the LaSalle County, Illinois, 1860 census) who has been indexed in a number of ways from "Fanzg" to "Krugg." Names in the San Francisco enumeration, particularly ethnic ones, are likely also misindexed.

SAN FRANCISCO CITY DIRECTORIES

*T*he first San Francisco directory was published in 1850, a rather small volume compared to the much larger publications just two decades later. There were several competing directory publishers, especially in the early years. Henry G. Langley was the dominant publisher from 1858 until 1895. H.S. Crocker & Co. assumed this role until 1906. In some years competing firms published directories that may or may not contain the same information.

Directories should be searched for every year that a family lived in San Francisco. While it is clear that some people were missed each year, the directories can be extremely helpful in determining the length of residence of an individual and in tracing the movements of families, which were often frequent since so many urban residents did not (and still do not) own their residences. Following a family through all available directories can also suggest spelling variations in a name or reveal a middle name. Occasionally directories provide indirect evidence of a divorce or death. A woman, however, would often list herself as a "widow" when in fact she had been divorced or was separated from her husband. City directories often reveal a head-of-household's occupation as well as address. As children came of age they frequently warranted their own listings, even when remaining in the family household.

In searching a directory, note the informational pages, usually at the beginning but occasionally at the end. These, too, change from year to year and can be extraordinarily useful. Among other things, these pages normally list names and addresses of churches and synagogues a resident may have attended and may in some years offer detailed church histories. Used in conjunction with maps and surviving church records, this information can possibly lead to birth, baptismal, marriage and burial records. Church listings usually include the name of the minister; that may then identify the church holding baptismal, marriage or burial records if the minister's name was included in a newspaper account. In addition to churches, other institutions such as orphan asylums, schools and fraternal societies are listed, often with descriptive paragraphs relating founding dates.

> *City directories should be searched for every year that a family lived in San Francisco.*

Directories also commonly describe voting ward boundaries, which can shorten census searches when the name of a known resident can't be found in a census index. Some early directories include chronologies of events from the previous year, including newsworthy deaths. Chronologies from the 1868, 1871 and 1879 directories have been posted at *www.sfgenealogy.com*. One can determine when a business came into being by searching for the first listing year. Comparing the 1905 and 1907 directories may indicate whether a residence, church or business was destroyed in the earthquake and fire. Directories also include descriptions of street names and their cross-streets. This can help determine streets that may have undergone a change in name, although this information may be more easily found in Gladys Hansen's *San Francisco Almanac* (San Rafael: Presidio Press, 1980; various editions available at SFPL, Sutro and CGS). Listings of street names and cross-streets over a span of years also can serve to sort out confusing residence re-numbering or to pinpoint exactly on a map where an ancestor lived.

Scans and links to scans of a number of directories, both city and telephone directories, are available at *www.sfgenealogy.com*. Also posted there are convenient links to the multitude of city directories digitized at *Archive.org*, beginning in 1850 and running through 1982. Searching at this website has recently become much faster than in the earlier version of the site, and will probably become necessary to use as paper copies are withdrawn from library shelves. The FHL purchased and makes available copies of pre-earthquake city directory films and fiche, as well as films of several business directories and the first telephone book (1878). They can be located in the FHL catalog by searching by locality. The early years are on microfiche, beginning with fiche #6044471; starting in 1861/62 they appear on film, beginning with #1,377,422 (until 1902) and #1,606,004 (1902 on). Directories over the same years can be found at local repositories. Microfiche of those from 1850-1860 can be found at Sutro and SFPL and also at the Oakland Family History Center. Directories covering 1861-1905 are on both microfilm and in bound form at CGS, Sutro and SFPL. Searching paper copies over a span of years, if this is possible, remains faster but perhaps less convenient than searching the online directories. CGS holds two 1906 business directories, which may be useful since a residential directory was not published that year, as well as the first city directory and the first telephone book.

The *San Francisco Blue Book* and *Pacific Coast Elite Directory* contain names and addresses for prominent or wealthier residents. Copies for most of the years 1888-1906 are at SFPL and Sutro; those for several years are online at *www. sfgenealogy.com*. The directories for 1890-1892 are available on FHL films #1,000,133 (item 5) and #374,938.

CHRONOLOGICAL HISTORY OF PRINCIPAL EVENTS,

From July 1st, 1867, to September 1st, 1868.

JULY 1. A fire broke out on Jackson Street, near Drumm, destroying a number of frame buildings....A building on Post Street, near Stockton, also took fire, but was extinguished with trifling damage.

JULY 3. Generals Halleck and McDowell with their respetive staffs visited the British Admiral on board the iron-clad "Zealous"....The Japanese Embassy arrived on the steamer "Sacramento" on their way to Japan....A little girl named Marsh was fatally burned by her clothes taking fire from a lighted match.

JULY 4. The Anniversary of American Independence was celebrated with great enthusiasm throughout the State. In this city it was observed by a grand military and civic parade with literary exercises at the Metropolitan Theatre, and concluding with a magnificent display of fireworks in the evening....The body of a Mulatto boy, named John Brown, was found in the Bay at the foot of Fourth Street....The steamship Continental arrived from Mazatlan, bringing $230,600 in treasure....Two fires occurred in the evening; the one destroying a frame building at 615 Mission; damage, about $2,000; the other at 608 Bush, damage about $1,800 ....Two soldiers belonging to the Second Regiment of Artillery, were blown to pieces at Fort Point by the discharge of a cannon before which they were standing.

JULY 5. A man was killed by the falling of the chimney of a building near the corner of Hyde and O'Farrell Streets....A man named Harrington was suffocated by impure air in a sewer on Howard Street....A fire broke out on Essex Street; damage, about $300....The steamers Idaho and Contra Costa collided, damaging the former to the amount of $1,000.

JULY 6. Extremely hot weather, the mercury standing at 94° in the shade....The British iron-clad Zealous sailed for Vancouver's Island.... Daniel Clark, Esq., a well known member of the Bar, died aged 33 years.

JULY 7. A fire broke out at 515 Merchant Street, but was extinguished with but slight damage.

JULY 8. The Captain of the ship Royal Saxon and two passengers were arrested on a charge of smuggling. A large quantity of valuable goods, found in possession of the latter, was seized.... Two fires occurred: one at 4 A.M., at 517 Bush Street, estimated loss $2,500; the other at 1 P.M., on Stewart Street; damage about $800.

JULY 9. James Spruance, a prominent merchant of San Francisco and a pioneer Californian, died at Warm Springs....News received of the death of Thomas Francis Meagher, Acting Governor of Montana, at Fort Benton....The annual election of the California Pioneer Association was held at Pioneer Hall, resulting in the choice of Wm. R. Wheaton, Esq., as President.

JULY 10. At 3 o'clock, P.M., a fire broke out at No. 8 Commercial Street, doing slight damage.... The Pacific Mail Steamship Sacramento sailed for Panama with passengers and treasure amounting to $1,533,668.55....Pierre Lombat, a patient in the French Hospital, committed suicide by cutting his throat.

JULY 11. A woman known as Selina Bouclet was murdered in her house on the corner of Washington Street and Waverly Place....A fire broke out at 10¼ P.M., at 50 Second Street, doing trifling damage.

JULY 12. C. A. Ehrenpfort a native of Hanover, aged 63 years, was crushed to death at the corner of Fremont and Mission Streets.

JULY 13. Two fires broke out during the evening, which were extinguished with but slight damage... The Bay View Water Company filed a certificate of incorporation in the office of the County Clerk.... A man named John Sullivan was killed by falling from a wall at Lake Honda.

JULY 14. At 2 A.M., a dwelling house in the rear of 1412 Powell Street took fire and was totally destroyed. A fire also occurred at 5 P.M., near the corner of Folsom and Spear Streets, doing slight damage....Three noted Indian Chiefs from the northern portion of the State visited San Francisco in company with B. C. Whiting, Superintendent of Indian Affairs for California.

JULY 15. A man named Edward C. Phillips was killed by falling under the wheels of a sand car on Market Street....At 12 M., the Merchants' Exchange was thrown open to the public for the first time and formally inaugurated with appropriate ceremonies. A sumptuous collation was served to two hundred and fifty invited guests including the leading merchants of the city.

JULY 16. A man named Samuel Trask died very suddenly at 39 Clay Street from disease of the heart.

JULY 17. At 9 P.M., a fire broke out on Broadway, near Stockton Street; damage, about $1,000 ....A man named Christian Graf was drowned in the Bay near Point San José.

JULY 18. Col. James Miller, who served with distinction during the war, was found dead in his bed at the What Cheer House, aged 25 years.

JULY 19. The P. M. Steamship Golden Age sailed for Panama with a number of passengers, and treasure amounting to $907,824.61....Edward Devlin was run over by a coal cart on Howard Street, and instantly killed.

JULY 20. The boiler of the Capital Mills exploded, destroying the mills and doing much damage to the adjoining buildings.

JULY 21. The City Gardens on Folsom Street were opened to the public for the first time.....At 9¼ P.M., a fire occurred corner Beale and Howard Streets; damage about $1,000.

JULY 22. About 4 A.M., a small building on Filbert Street was destroyed by fire; loss trifling. Fires also occurred at 2 P.M., on Fremont Street, destroying three or four frame buildings, loss about $10,000; and at 9¼ P.M., in a store on Montgomery Street near Sutter, which was extinguished with but little damage....The body of a man named John Byorkman was found in the bay near Washington Street Wharf ....The ship David Crockett arived at New York, after a passage of one hundred and ten days.

JULY 23. At 2 P.M. a fire broke out in the Shamrock Saloon, Market Street, doing considerable damage....The body of an unknown man was found in the bay off pier 24 Stewart Street....Daniel Bryan fell from the yard of the bark Arva into

"Chronological History of Principal Events" from Langley's
San Francisco City Directory, 1868-69
(California Genealogical Society Library).

Raking the Ashes

46   CORONER'S REPORT.

TABLE No. 4—Continued.

DATE.	NAME.	PROPERTY AND TO WHOM DELIVERED.
1898—May 4.............	Mrs. L. Kampos....	Yellow-metal ear-rings. May 19th, to City and County Treasurer.
May 5...............	Mrs. Murphy..	Yellow-metal ring (two white and one red stones), key. May 9th, to Alice McGrath sister.
May 5...............	John H. Heffing..............	Seven and 55-100 dollars, German Savings and Loan Society bank book No. 39,081, Hibernia Savings and Loan Society bank book No. 93,683. May 5th, to Public Administrator.
May 5.............	Frank L. Smith....	Forty-five cents, purse, keys, papers. pistol, fifteen cents, white-metal watch, yellow-metal chain. May 17th, to Public Administrator.
May 5.........	Mary L. Smith.................	Two yellow-metal rings. May 7th, to Public Administrator.
May 6..............	Nicholas Schwartz...........	Twenty-one and 40-100 dollars, white-metal watch, yellow-metal chain and charm, letters, valise. May 8th, to Mrs. Bella Schwartz.
May 6	Claus Wohltmann............	White-metal watch, book, papers, yellow-metal ring. May 13th, to Emma Wohltmann.
May 7................	William Kroeger.,...........	Nine and 20-100 dollars, white-metal watch, yellow-metal chain, matchbox, key, wallet, account book, tax receipts, papers. May 7th, to Fred Kroeger, son.
May 9	Richard Murphy....	Knife, beads. May 19th, to City and County Treasurer.
May 11............	Joseph Grant...................	Memorandum book. May 19th, to City and County Treasurer.

Typical "Coroner's Report" in an Annual Municipal Report *(here 1898) (California Genealogical Society Library).*

Note that some entries provide the name and relationship to the deceased of the person receiving the personal effects. A full run of these reports is at San Francisco Public Library.

MUNICIPAL RECORDS:
ANNUAL REPORTS AND TAX RECORDS

SAN FRANCISCO MUNICIPAL REPORTS

While most city records were destroyed, the year-end abstracts and reports that were prepared from various departmental records are available to us. They were bound and widely distributed each year as the *San Francisco Municipal Report*. Copies are available at SFPL in the San Francisco History Center for the years 1861/2 through the earthquake and are available at *www.archive.org*. Use the links in the SFPL catalog. Many are at CGS, which has one of the few copies of the 1859-60 publication, but in that early year content was minimal. Much in these reports is statistical. Those parts particularly useful to genealogists include, although not for all years, Health Department reports (deaths), city hospital reports (deaths), mortuary statistics (occasionally detailed), abstracts of the Coroner's Report, and abstracts of parts of the Public Administrator's Report. Report subsections are also described in the sections of this guide titled "Vital Records" (p. 3) and "Court Records" (p. 69). Many reports contain Police Relief and Pension Fund summaries, which occasionally carry dates of death for policemen and names of various city employees, such as members of the Fire Department. In later years, the "Report of the Chief of Police" included details of extraditions.

Coroners' Reports

A coroner is charged with the investigation of unexpected, sudden, violent or unexplained deaths. Unfortunately, all coroners' records with the exception of one ledger and some records from the Office of the Medical Examiner (1903-1906) were destroyed in the earthquake and fire. Abstracts from the coroner's reports, however, appear in issues of the *Annual Municipal Report*. Some of these have been abstracted at *www.sfgenealogy.com*. A typical report contains the following information: date, name (if known) and description and disposition of property. Frequently the entry will include the name of the person to whom personal effects were delivered and even his or her relationship to the deceased. While any death in which the cause was not known would have been referred to the coroner's office, the referral may not have been accepted or a report may not have been produced. Some deaths may have occurred under newsworthy circumstances. If a name of interest is found among these abstracts, all newspapers for that date and the several days following should be checked for additional details.

Public Administrators' Reports

The Public Administrator served in a fiduciary capacity to distribute assets of estates of deceased residents when no administrator was appointed. Some of the indexes to pre-earthquake probates described elsewhere in this guide (pp. 76-9) were or may have been prepared in part from the reports of this office appearing in the *Annual Municipal Report*. Information abstracted usually included the names of estates settled and occasionally unsettled, letters of administration issued, the approximate value of the estate, administrative expenses and possibly a page reference to the missing records. Some reports included nativity, date of death and residence of heirs. Finding names of interest should lead to a search of filmed newspapers or at least of newspaper indexes.

SURVIVING TAX RECORDS

A fair number of ledgers from the office of the County Treasurer somehow survived destruction. It is unlikely that they will do more than establish the presence of a given person. These ledgers are described more fully in the 1940 *Inventory of the County Archives of California*, volume II, number 39: *The City and County of San Francisco*, prepared by the WPA and available at SFPL and as FHL film #908,267. Nine ledgers consist of unindexed tax lists, receipts and receipt stubs dating to one or two-year periods in the mid-1850s. Forty-seven surviving ledgers contain receipts for delinquent taxes over the years 1850-1906, but no names are included. Three more unindexed ledgers contain receipts or refer to real estate sold to the state due to delinquent taxes in the 1870s and 1880s. Some twenty-three ledgers account for personal property tax overpayments at the turn of the century; names are included. Finally, four unindexed ledgers containing poll tax receipts and accounts over many years do not include names; three more for non-consecutive years in the early 1850s do.

Federal Internal Revenue Service assessments for 1862-1866 are on FHL films beginning with #1,534,664. Arranged by surname within districts and divisions, it is not quickly evident which districts and divisions pertain to San Francisco.

Ledgers containing dated receipts for money collected in conjunction with probates, containing the name of the deceased or providing the relationship of legatees and divisees, will be described in the section on probate.

ARREST AND PRISON RECORDS

Also surviving the fire were the index to and the records of arrests for 1905-1906 and the index only for the years 1896-97. The indexes contain only name, date and reference, while the one year of more complete pre-earthquake records includes name, date, age, occupation, nativity, place of arrest and names of witnesses. The 1940 inventory of county records placed these records in the Hall of Justice, but many, if not all, have since been transferred to the archives at SFPL and will be made available in the coming year.

Convicted felons may have been sent beyond San Francisco, perhaps to Folsom Prison or perhaps to San Quentin. The State Archives holds records from both prisons beginning in the 1880s.

Extracts of these records over the years 1879-1903 were published by Lois A. Dove in 1988. Information included: dates served, county where convicted and charge on which convicted.

Convicted felons often were sent to Folsom Prison, for which records are available. Lois Dove extracted these records in California State Prison, Folsom, California, 1879-1903: Numerical Register *(Citrus Heights, Calif.: Sacramento Genealogical Society, 1988, also available on FHL film #1,533,716, item 4).*

San Francisco in 1848 (from Hubert H. Bancroft, History of California,
7 vols. (San Francisco History Company, 1886], 5: 677).

San Francisco land records, dating to both before and after statehood, were not all destroyed in 1906. Unfilmed federally-held land entry files were not destroyed and are at the National Archives facility in College Park, Maryland. With the exception of two ledgers of early records, all surviving ledgers were filmed by the FHL and are archived at SFPL. Although they may be tedious to search, land records can provide useful information about those who acquired or unsuccessfully sought to acquire land. In urban areas many residents were financially unable to purchase real estate or perhaps not dependent upon property ownership for their livelihood. The researcher must judge, according to each individual research problem, at what point it becomes worth the time and energy required to search for those wonderful gems that occasionally lie hidden within property records. After statehood, city directories may help in this decision. Families that moved frequently likely were not property owners.

SPANISH AND MEXICAN SETTLEMENT AND LAND CLAIMS

Early History

San Francisco land was first settled in 1776 with the establishment of Mission Dolores (San Francisco de Asis a la Laguna de los Dolores) by the Franciscan padres and, at the entrance to the bay, a Spanish military reservation ("presidio"), built to protect the mission. Lands outside the mission were used for livestock grazing and farming, while the padres and mission Indians lived within the walls. Soldiers' families and other new arrivals were given small parcels of land near the presidio by its commandante. Beyond these jurisdictions, grants of land ("ranchos") were given to encourage agriculture and industry or as service or political rewards. At that time the nearest rancho lay outside of what today is San Francisco.

The Spanish government oversaw the mission and presidio settlements until 1821, when Mexico gained independence and acquired the territory. Under existing law, upon reaching a certain population, a settlement was to become a "pueblo" and various officials were to be appointed. In 1834, the territorial assembly created the pueblo of San Francisco, which then also included today's San Mateo County and parts of Contra Costa and Alameda counties. A civil government was formed consisting of one alcalde (magistrate), two regidores (councilmen) and one sindico-procurador (attorney). The alcalde had the authority to lay out and distribute additional land within defined boundaries. In the mid-1830s, settlement had begun near the harbor on the east side of the peninsula. The first accurate survey was performed by Jasper O'Farrell in 1839, but was confined to the harbor area. By 1846 over sixty lots had been granted. Thus the settlement called "Yerba Buena" slowly came into being.

In July 1846, shortly after the outbreak of the Mexican War, the United States took possession of California. The existing government was allowed to continue, and a proclamation was issued that those holding title to real estate would be allowed to retain their title. The war ended in 1848 with the signing of the Treaty of Guadalupe Hildalgo, which reaffirmed the rights of previous landholders to titles within the conquered territories. Meanwhile, the alcalde continued to grant and later sell land to newcomers. Whether or not the alcalde had this power was the subject of debate for a number of years. At the same time, others claimed that the city territory belonged to the federal government and was open to preemption. Squatters descended upon unoccupied property, and at the same time land speculation on the lots O'Farrell laid out became rampant.

Pre-existing claims to land were a continuing problem; in 1851 Congress established the Board of Land Commissioners to adjudicate them. The burden of proof was placed upon individuals seeking confirmation of their claims, a process that was costly and time-consuming. The average length of time for a final patent to be issued after the filing of a petition was seventeen years, but some claims took much longer. Mission Dolores, for example, was patented in 1858, but the Presidio of San Francisco was not patented until 1884.

Records

The state archives holds most records for the years 1833-1845; some transactions may cover land within what later became San Francisco County. These records, which encompass the state, are indexed by surname and by the name of the property grant. Records and indexes are on FHL films #978,888-901.

Early records, including grants, transfer deeds and lot sales by the alcalde, dating to 1838, are held at SFPL. Some are available on film, which can be accessed in the FHL catalog by entering film numbers #974,651-664 and 974,036-043. Many of these records are in Spanish; some volumes are indexed at the end. Three previously unfilmed ledgers known as miscellaneous records of the alcalde were digitized by the FHL several years ago but have not yet been indexed. They contain not only deeds dating as early as 1847, but also petitions, leases

Preemption claim of Jacob Harman, 1847, found in original records of the alcalde at the San Francisco Public Library.

and mortgages, partnership certificates, declarations of intent and certificates of citizenship, several preemption claims, a death and one manumission.

Two publications, *Spanish and Mexican Land Grants in California* by Rose Hollenbaugh Aviña (1932; reprint, New York: Arno Press, 1976), and *Ranchos of California, A List of Spanish Concessions, 1775-1822, and Mexican Grants, 1822 - 1846* by Robert G. Cowan (Fresno, California: Academy Library Guild, 1956), discuss the history of land distribution and list pre-1847 "ranchos." Both are available at SFPL. *San Francisco Land Titles 1852 in San Francisco and the Laws Affecting the Same, with a Synopsis of All Grants and Sales of Land within the Limits Claimed by the City* was compiled by Alfred Wheeler in 1852, following by several years his appointment to study rights and titles to lands within city boundaries. Available at SFPL and online at *www.sfgenealogy.com*, it consists of ten schedules summarizing pre-statehood transactions from September 1835 through November 5, 1852.

Records of the court proceedings involving claims to pre-existing land grants are housed at NARA, both at Washington and at the regional branch in San Bruno, and have been filmed by the FHL. They are indexed in a publication by J. N. Bowman titled *Index to the Spanish-Mexican Private Land Grant Records and Cases of California* (1958; reprint Berkeley: Bancroft Library, University of California, 1970), also available as FHL film #833,343. The records for both circuit and district court cases, excluding cases from 1852 to 1910, comprise NARA micropublication series T1207 (FHL films #1,549,359-386). This series includes indexes to plaintiffs and defendants. An index and calendar to cases heard in the District Court, Northern District of California, 1853-1904, which would probably include its predecessor, the Circuit Court, is available as NARA micropublication T1214 and FHL film #1,415,714. NARA micropublication T1216, which indexes cases for both Northern and Southern District courts, is arranged differently, by county and rancho name, and is available on FHL film #1,415,716. How many of these claims related to land in San Francisco County is not known.

PRE-STATEHOOD FEDERAL LAND TRANSACTIONS

Unclaimed land normally became part of the public domain and was sold or perhaps offered free by the U.S. government through land offices. However, land acquisition in the new settlement was chaotic for a number of years. Early San Francisco deed indexes, available on FHL film and at SFPL, occasionally contain a homestead entry, which should alert the researcher that there likely exists an informative land entry file at NARA. Land entry files, both homestead and cash entry, have not yet been filmed. "Blacks" and immigrants who had not begun naturalization were not eligible for entry land.

Securing copies of land entry files from the Archives is a lengthy process and until recently required the completion of NATF form 84. It is now possible to order a file online at the NARA website and pay for the copies with a credit card. One must provide the name of the homesteader or person who purchased the entry, the approximate date of entry, the land entry file number and either the legal description of the land, which can usually be obtained from a subsequent deed, or the name of the land office, which was Benicia until November 1857, then San Francisco. Files exist for both successful and unsuccessful applications and often contain immigration, military and family information.

Successful land entries resulted in a patent, which does not contain genealogical information but which can simplify the file application process. Patents for successful (called "proved") homestead entries and cash entries are indexed by surname in the California Land Patents Database, which is available online or by writing the California State Office of the Bureau of Land Management in Sacramento.[16] The San Francisco portion, including location and patent number, can be found at *www.sfgenealogy.com*. Tract books are available at NARA in San Bruno, at Sacramento and on FHL films. To locate the correct book one must provide the legal description of the property, which probably lay in Township 1S[outh] or 2S and Range 5W[est] or 6W of the Mt. Diablo Baseline and Meridian. FHL film #1,444,605 (volumes 147-149) covers this area.

Post–Statehood Land Transactions

Land entries continued well past statehood (1850). Once land left the public domain, records of transfer became a local responsibility, in this case the responsibility of the County Recorder's Office. About one-third of all locally-held land records from about 1850 through the earthquake and fire survived; indexes fared better. Original ledgers are in the city archives at SFPL. Grantor indexes exist through all of the decades; grantee indexes are only partly available. Following the earthquake and fire, many missing land records were reconstructed in the court actions known as the McInerney lawsuits.

Indexes

All *grantor* indexes survived and have been filmed through April 1913. Combination *Grantee/grantor* indexes are missing from 1853 to May 1868, and from June 1869 to May 1885. *Grantee* indexes, if they ever existed, did not survive. Obtain film numbers for indexes and deeds by entering #966,122 in the FHL online catalog.

---

[16] The Bureau of Land Management is located in the Federal Building, 2800 Cottage Way E-2845, Sacramento, CA 95825-1889. Phone (916) 979-2900.

Deeds

As is usually the case in land record research, culling through less related material can be tedious, but there are genealogical gems, such as family relationships, to be found. Years for which filmed deeds survived are:

- 1850 - 1854 (volumes A-39, with vols. C, I and J missing; series starts with FHL film #974,859)
- 1859 (part) - early 1860 (includes vols. 91 through 98 on films #975,101 through #975,104)
- 1861 (most of) - 1864 (vols. 141-226 with 168 incomplete and 224-5 missing; series starts with film #975,105)
- 1894-1900 (vols. 1627-1895, but missing vols. 1658, 1701-1745 and 1787; series starts with film #975,323).

The gaps over which indexes but not corresponding deeds survived, except for a few volumes, are roughly: part of 1854 - part of 1859; parts of 1860 and 1861; 1864 into 1894; parts of 1896 - 1898; and part of 1900 to the earthquake.

Occasionally descendants donate old family deeds to the state library, to the Bancroft Library or to the California Historical Society. If one enters *Real property, California, San Francisco* into the subject area search box of the online catalog *Melvyl*, or an unusual family surname as a keyword search, a surprising number of these archived records will be presented.

Liens, Mortgages and Other Documents in Land Records

Liens, mortgages, preemptions, leases, certificates of sale, powers of attorney, releases, bonds, sheriff's certificates, distributions, partnership dissolutions and various other records were indexed in land indexes, although many of the corresponding records may have been kept separately in non-deed ledgers. Of non-deed ledgers, a few volumes of attachments (property seizures to furnish security for debts) survived: part of 1850 (FHL film #974,856) and 1869-1872 (films #974,856-857).

Marriage certificates and marriage contracts were also indexed in the early deed indexes from 1850 to 1858, but the ledgers that were referenced in the indexes were lost. Over two thousand indexed entries were extracted by Kathleen C. Beals and published as *Index to San Francisco Marriage Returns 1850 - 1858* (Oakland: California Genealogical Society, 1992). Entries represent the date of posting and not the date of marriage. Some forty percent of the entries are amplified with information found in various newspaper indexes.

LAND RESEARCH AIDS

Maps and Block Books

Sanborn Fire Insurance maps can be found at SFPL for the years 1886–1893, 1899-1900 and 1905. Most are on film, and a few are available in ledgers; they are currently being digitized. The six volumes and indexes to them for 1899-1900 have been scanned and placed online at *www.sfgenealogy.com*. Sanborn maps are also available on microfilm at the Earth Sciences Library at the University of California at Berkeley. They do not bear the property owners' name but do include block and lot number, which may simplify locating deeds. Block books, on the other hand, do include the name of the property owner. Pre-earthquake books are at SFPL and have been placed online at *www.Archive.org*. While they may not provide any genealogical information, they may help to locate ethnic or family groupings.

Pre-statehood records often included maps that give a picture of the extent of settlement at a given time. Occasionally street layouts and names of adjacent land owners are shown. The records which contain these maps are tedious to sort through, but if one is researching early land acquisitions, particularly among Spanish settlers or by wealthy developers and ranchers, they may be useful.

RECONSTRUCTED LAND RECORDS

Civil actions to re-establish ownership of real estate in instances where records had been lost were carried out in Superior Court and are known as the McInerney [sic] Actions.[17] They were filmed by the FHL and are indexed according to plaintiff surname on four rolls of film starting with #1,403,292.[18] Claimants were required to identify their property by lot and block number and to describe how it was acquired. If there were no other claims to the property, the matter could be settled within a reasonably short period of time. A few cases dragged on for years and even decades. The judgment rolls, as they are known, can contain valuable genealogical information in those cases where any of the owners or legal claimants died before the claim was settled.

---

[17] Garret McEnerney was a key figure in planning of order and reconstruction after the earthquake. Although he was one of the state's great lawyers, his name was and will likely remain misspelled.
[18] The original records appear to have been archived in the off-site storage facility of Bancroft Library. A finding aid is available as a link at the *Melvyl* catalog website. Access it there or at the Online Archive of California under the title "Complaints to establish title following the 1906 earthquake."

McInerney claims in which the property owner had died required legal heirs to establish identity. Family relationships and maiden names can thus be learned.

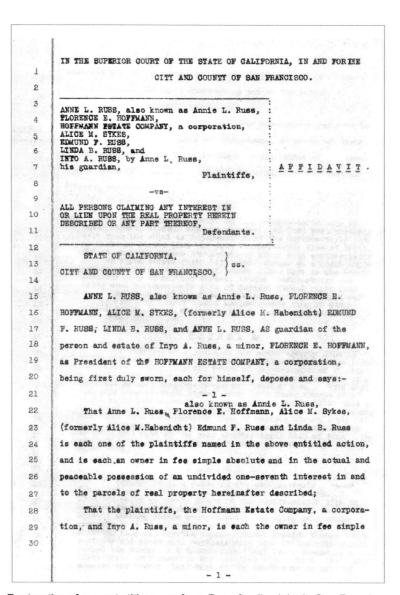

IN THE SUPERIOR COURT OF THE STATE OF CALIFORNIA, IN AND FOR THE
CITY AND COUNTY OF SAN FRANCISCO.

ANNE L. RUSS, also known as Annie L. Russ,
FLORENCE E. HOFFMANN,
HOFFMANN ESTATE COMPANY, a corporation,
ALICE M. SYKES,
EDMUND F. RUSS,
LINDA B. RUSS, and
INYO A. RUSS, by Anne L. Russ,
his guardian,
                                    Plaintiffs,   A F F I D A V I T .

                              -vs-

ALL PERSONS CLAIMING ANY INTEREST IN
OR LIEN UPON THE REAL PROPERTY HEREIN
DESCRIBED OR ANY PART THEREOF,
                                    Defendants.

          STATE OF CALIFORNIA,   )
) ss.
          CITY AND COUNTY OF SAN FRANCISCO,   )

          ANNE L. RUSS, also known as Annie L. Russ, FLORENCE E.
HOFFMANN, ALICE M. SYKES, (formerly Alice M. Habenicht) EDMUND
F. RUSS, LINDA B. RUSS, and ANNE L. RUSS, AS guardian of the
person and estate of Inyo A. Russ, a minor, FLORENCE E. HOFFMANN,
as President of the HOFFMANN ESTATE COMPANY, a corporation,
being first duly sworn, each for himself, deposes and says:-
                              - 1 -
                    also known as Annie L. Russ,
          That Anne L. Russ, Florence E. Hoffmann, Alice M. Sykes,
(formerly Alice M. Habenicht) Edmund F. Russ and Linda B. Russ
is each one of the plaintiffs named in the above entitled action,
and is each an owner in fee simple absolute and in the actual and
peaceable possession of an undivided one-seventh interest in and
to the parcels of real property hereinafter described;
          That the plaintiffs, the Hoffmann Estate Company, a corpora-
tion, and Inyo A. Russ, a minor, is each the owner in fee simple

                              - 1 -

Restoration of property title: page from Russ family claim in San Francisco Superior Court, 1908 (McInerney Actions, case no. 11949).

Original and Appellate Court Records: Naturalization, Probate, Land, Divorce and Adoption

*D*uring the earthquake and fire most records in the San Francisco City and County Courthouse, were lost. They would include Superior Court records, where one might hope to find divorces, probates, some naturalizations and other civil records, and possibly some records from four earlier courts that were dissolved by 1879: the "court of sessions," the "probate court," the early "district court" and the "county court." *Federal* court records, including naturalizations, criminal litigation, land grant records and appellate cases, were not lost. They evidently were housed in court offices located on the upper floors of the main Post Office building at 7th and Mission, where postal workers managed to beat back encroaching flames. NARA San Francisco, located at 1000 Commodore Drive in San Bruno, now holds early district and circuit court naturalization records, as well as some related records of other types, primarily Chinese immigration and emigration-related records (pp. 132-134). California Supreme Court records that originated in or involved litigants from San Francisco also escaped destruction and are housed in the state archives.

When information in lost files was necessary for ongoing litigation or for proof of citizenship or land ownership, the files were reconstructed. This included ongoing probates and naturalizations still in process. Reconstruction of lost land records is covered in the previous chapter, along with attachments (seizures of property to cover debts) for some years.

Thus, the loss of ancestral information with respect to court records need not be taken for granted. Much is still to be found in federal cases and in cases that were appealed to higher courts. These sources are discussed on p. 82. Court proceedings have always been of interest to the public, particularly criminal cases and cases involving bankruptcy and divorce. The careful researcher should always check newspaper indexes and digitizations and, if something of interest is found, examine other publications over the same range of dates. For more detailed examination of original records held at NARA San Francisco, examine the description of Record Group 21 holdings at the website and proceed from there. Records for cases adjudicated in the California Supreme Court and now housed in the state archives are also described in considerable detail on the NARA website.

Naturalization

California achieved statehood in September 1850; most naturalization records for California residents date from this time. The lure of the gold fields attracted miners from all over the world. Clues to their origins may lie in naturalization-related records, but in the case of San Francisco residents, rarely with the detail one might hope for.

State and U.S. District Courts and the U.S. Circuit Court had jurisdiction over naturalizations starting in 1850. In 1862 county courts were also given this responsibility, and a greater proportion of San Francisco residents appear to have been naturalized through the Superior Courts. While superior court records were destroyed by the 1906 fire, district and circuit court records survived. Pre-statehood naturalizations existed as well, and can be found scattered within three ledgers of miscellanous records of the alcalde, archived at SFPL (p. 64).

There are a number of reasons other than loss of records in 1906 to explain why expected naturalization papers for San Francisco aliens cannot be found. Naturalization may have taken place elsewhere, and the process may, moreover, have been spread across a number of courts as a person moved from area to area. Citizenship for the foreign-born at times was conferred by virtue of military participation or after serving a number of years on a U.S. merchant vessel, in which cases records may be minimal. Some acquired citizenship as a result of treaties with Mexico or Russia. Naturalization for underage children likely was automatic when their father acquired citizenship. Papers for women are rarely found dating to pre-earthquake years, since a married woman's status until 1922 depended upon that of her husband, even if he was deceased. Nonetheless, despite the obstacles and lack of detailed information, we continue to search for naturalization information as a clue as to immigrant origins.

Evidence of citizenship can be found in the 1870 census enumeration; more detailed information is provided in the 1900 - 1930 enumerations. The Immigration and Naturalization Service, recently renamed the U.S. Citizen and Immigration Services, was formed in September 1906. Records since then have been archived in Washington, D.C.; prior to that time they were retained locally. Early records, however, often contained little more than name, signature and country of origin; this was the case for most early San Francisco records. After 1906 papers included occupation, residence, date and place of birth, date and place of emigration, date and port of arrival, name of the ship or transportation company if arrival was by other means, a physical description, and names and ages of spouse and children. Post-earthquake records for relatives and friends, therefore, are useful when records for the person in question cannot be found or was deceased.

If a Declaration of Intent (usually the most informative document) was filed in another state,some proof of this would have to have accompanied an immigrant. Occasionally these papers were deposited locally when the final application for citizenship was made. Those deposited with the District Court were filmed at NARA San Francisco and are available also on FHL films 977,767-70. The final petition, the Petition for Naturalization, usually included court name and location, book and page number where the Declaration of Intent was filed. Affidavits of two witnesses and the Naturalization Certificate number were generally also documented. In the absence of original papers, naturalization details before 1900 may appear in voter registrations. (See pp. 85-8.)

Records and Repositories

Superior Court Naturalizations: Superior Court records were lost. FHL films #1,405,752-754 and #1,405,833 (items 1-4) cover the post-earthquake restoration of naturalization records for aliens that occurred over the years 1870-1942. Some volumes appear to be missing, records are not always in sequence and the information in most appears to be quite minimal. These films consist of both indexes and records and are available at both SFPL and CGS. Information includes name, country of birth, date naturalized and date restored.

U.S. District and Circuit Court Naturalization Records (Northern California): The National Archives regional branch at San Bruno holds both District and Circuit Court indexes and records. The indexes, which are located in Record Group 21, have been filmed in two publications:

- Micropublication T1220, Selected Indexes to Naturalization Records of the U.S. Circuit and District Courts, Northern District of California, 1852-1928; available as FHL films #940,177-8, at CGS, through Family History Centers and at *Ancestry.com*.

- Micropublication M1744, Index to Naturalizations of the U.S. District Court for the Northern District of California, 1860-1989. This card index is now available in digitized form by browsing at the FHL website, *www.familysearch.org* and is also available at *Ancestry.com*.

A chronological, unindexed listing of naturalizations containing (only) names recorded in minutes of the District Court and predecessor courts over the years 1851-1950 was filmed as NARA micropublication T717.

Surviving *original* records dating to pre-earthquake years for these federal courts are at the NARA facility in San Bruno. Because they are rarely detailed, they tend to be very disappointing. Surviving pre-earthquake records include:

- Circuit Court Declarations of Intention, 1855-1911
- Circuit Court naturalization petitions and affidavits, 1903-1906
- Circuit Court certificates of naturalization, 1855-1906
- District Court records of naturalization, 1852-1906.

Other Naturalization Sources

Legislation enacted in 1866 in California to control voter registration created the Great Registers (see p. 85-8). Voters who had been naturalized were required to provide information about when, where and by what court they had become citizens. A compilation of naturalization data appearing in the *Great Register* of 1872, and when necessary from the registers of the several years following, was published in 1994 by Jim W. Faulkinbury, CG, and is titled *The Foreign-Born Voters of California in 1872: Including Naturalization Dates, Places, and Courts of Record.* Prepared on six microfiche, this publication can be found at Sutro and in the collections of various genealogical societies, including CGS. The Family History Library in Salt Lake City has not been allowed to prepare copies for local Family History Centers. Mr. Faulkinbury offers an index to the compilation online at *http://www.jwfgenresearch.com* and will send copies of entries for a modest fee.

The CGS publication, *San Francisco, California, 1890 Great Register of Voters,* is another excellent source document, perhaps more convenient than poring through Great Register films. It contains an integrated index of all voters of the various precincts of the city and county of San Francisco in 1890 and provides some information that a similar paper publication covering the entire state does not. This book is now out of print, but CGS performs lookups in it. Copies can be found also at the California State Library and Sutro Library.

The *San Francisco County Index of Naturalized Voters* is a record compiled in 1898 of only those registered voters who had been naturalized. This index is in the form of an alphabetized card file. It consists of naturalizations occurring over the years 1850-1898 and lists the name of the voter, date naturalized, voter precinct and ward, and the city and state where the voter was naturalized. It is also available on six reels of FHL film (#1,378,779-784), copies of which are available at SFPL.

A later compilation prepared by the San Francisco County Department of Elections abstracts naturalization data of all persons registering to vote in San Francisco for the time period 1906-1923. This compilation is available as FHL film #2,641, but pertains only to those registered to vote in San Francisco in the years following the earthquake and fire. Name, address, country of birth, and date and place of naturalization are provided. Consider, however, the possibility that post-earthquake naturalization data for family members and friends may provide clues to pre-earthquake problems.

Typical restoration of naturalization record
(San Francisco History Room, San Francisco Public Library;
also available on FHL film #1,405,752).

Even though the court proceeding took place at a time when more information would normally have been required, only the minimal detail appearing in the original record was recorded.

Ordering Documents by Mail

Copies of federal court naturalization documents can be ordered from the regional NARA branch in San Bruno.[19] In the event that a name may have been misspelled, it is advisable to direct a request to the U.S. District Court in San Francisco and ask for a check of the indexes under various spellings.[20]

PROBATE

The destruction of Superior Court offices in 1906 resulted in the loss of all probate files, including wills, guardianships and administrations. Usually those searching for pre-fire probate files are seeking evidence of death, of the nature of family relationships and names of family members, reasons for disinheritance, or for clues to the chain of land ownership. Most of this information can be found in workarounds, in newspaper accounts and notices, in deeds and other land records and in surviving or reconstructed indexes and abstracts.

Abstracts, Indexes, Case Reports and Receipt Books

Each year the Public Administrator's office published as part of the *San Francisco Annual Municipal Report* abstracts of probate proceedings in which that office was involved. Genealogically useful information included file names of estates settled (or occasionally unsettled), the value of settled estates, and frequently names of those issued Letters of Administration in intestate cases. Occasionally reports included nativity of the deceased, date of death, and residences of heirs. Surviving issues of the *Annual Municipal Report* dating to 1859-60 are at SFPL. Many are also held by CGS, and some transcriptions have been placed online at *www.sfgenealogy.com*. Relationships of family members to deceased individuals, which one might seek in probate proceedings, can sometimes be found in the section of the municipal report prepared by the Coroner's Office that names those to whom personal effects of the deceased were delivered. (See p. 59.)

In 1880, Probate Judge Milton H. Myrick published 122 detailed case studies selected from contested probate cases adjudicated in his court between January 1, 1872, and December 31, 1879. This publication has been placed online at Nancy Pratt Melton's "Golden Nugget Library" website hosted by Rootsweb. Copies are also available at the Bancroft Library and the state library in Sacramento.

Several unindexed receipt books for payments in conjunction with probate actions in Probate and Superior Court over the years 1874-1894 survived and

---

[19] Direct requests as follows: Attention: Historical Naturalizations; National Archives and Records Administration San Francisco; 1000 Commodore Drive, San Bruno, CA 94066.

[20] Write: Attention: Naturalizations, Office of the Clerk; U.S. District Court, Northern District of California; PO Box 36060, San Francisco, CA 94102.

are available on FHL film #1,405,831, with copies at CGS and SFPL. A number of unindexed collateral inheritance tax receipt ledgers dating from November 1893 to 1921 also survived and are available on FHL film #1,405,832. These films are at CGS and SFPL. The books are chronologically arranged and include date, estate of ___ and by whom paid (administrator or executor). One ledger (August 1905 - June 1906) lists all heirs at law and their relationship to the deceased.

   Probate abstracts based upon newspaper articles appearing in 1867, 1869, 1873, 1887 and 1892 were published over the years 1963-5 by Louis Rasmussen in the *San Francisco Historic Record & Genealogical Bulletin*. This publication is shelved at Sutro Library, SFPL and CGS and is available on FHL microfiche #6048001-003.

Reconstruction of ongoing probate from 1906 Register of Actions
(California Genealogical Society research services).

Digitizations of the Register of Actions ledgers are available from CGS.

   A book titled *Index of All Estates in Probate in the City and County of San Francisco, Calif. from 1850* was published in San Francisco by P. J. Thomas in an unrecorded year. A micro-reproduction of this publication was made in 1974 by W. C. Cook Co. of Tucson, Arizona, and is available on FHL film #1,000,133. Indexed information includes name, original file number and the register and page on which the data appeared. The source of this data may have been in part three volumes of indexes to wills covering the years 1851-1907. The will indexes were itemized by the WPA in the 1930s, but can no longer be found. The Thomas book indexes Probate Court ledgers 1-14 and Superior Court ledgers 1-11 and was probably published in the decade before 1900. Probate Court existed through 1879, after which its functions were assumed by the Superior Court. A survey of names contained in the last indexed ledger of Superior Court suggests that it indexed files up to shortly before 1890. The original files were lost in 1906, but newspaper coverage may possibly be found by searching digitized newspaper websites using as search terms the surname and some combination of the terms "probate," "superior"and perhaps "will."

Reconstructed Probate Files

Considerable information about probates filed before the earthquake and fire can be found in reconstructed files of probates still unsettled in April 1906 or in pre-earthquake probate proceedings reopened for varying reasons at later dates. Kathleen Beals compiled over 10,000 names appearing in pre-1906 probates from various "Report[s] of the Public Administrator" that appeared in the *San Francisco Annual Municipal Report[s]*; from surviving collateral inheritance tax and probate receipts; from newspaper-based abstracts published in *San Francisco Historic Record & Genealogy Bulletin*; and from reconstructions found in volumes 1-10 and 12-40 (covering 1906-1915) of the *Register of Actions* ledgers. This compilation was published as *San Francisco Probate Index 1880-1906, A Partial Reconstruction* (Oakland: California Genealogical Society, 1996) and is available at SFPL, Sutro Library and CGS.

Register of Actions ledgers reference all proceedings found in a probate file. Arrangement of entries in them is chronological according to initial filing date, or the date of reopening of pre-earthquake proceedings. An index to the *Register of Actions* volumes 1-179, covering April 12, 1906 through March 27, 1942, with the exception of volume 11 (January 9 -March 17, 1908), arranged by surname and representing over 100,000 probate proceedings, was compiled by Vernon A. Deubler and published in two volumes as *San Francisco Probate 1906-1942: Register of Actions* (Oakland: California Genealogical Society, 2010). References to pre-earthquake proceedings have been found in ledgers as late as 1925, and some files were not closed until the mid-1980s. Digitizations of the contents of the *Register of Actions* for these years are available as part of the fee-based lookup services offered by CGS. The researcher can then judge whether a file will be useful and can either use the docket number to request the complete file or have CGS volunteers look at the file and request copies of useful parts. Retrieving a file from storage takes several days. There is a fee charged for the pull, and copying charges currently run fifty cents per page.

References to pre-earthquake probates have been found in Register of Actions ledgers as late as 1925 .

When ongoing pre-earthquake probates were reopened, papers relevant to earlier proceedings that had remained in the possession of families or attorneys were copied and placed in the reopened file, which was then assigned a new docket number. The original docket number was noted in the *Register of Actions*. In instances where dates of original actions were known, it was possible to establish a rough correlation between original docket numbers and dates of opening of probate. The chart given in the appendix of *San Francisco Probate Index 1880-1906, A Partial Reconstruction* can be used to correlate old docket numbers which might be found to a range of dates corresponding to the original opening of probate. This time frame, if sufficiently narrow, can help to focus a search of old newspapers where additional information might be found.

DIVORCE RECORDS

Pre-earthquake divorce proceedings took place in Superior Court, and the records therefore were lost in the earthquake and fire. A divorce action with colorful or scandalous testimony, however, was likely covered to some extent in one or more local newspapers.

At the ends of many years, compiled divorce lists were published in various newspapers. The lists generally included names, arranged alphabetically by surname, and the grounds upon which the divorce was granted, but usually not the date of the decree. Lists have been found in the following newspapers:

- *San Francisco Bulletin*, December 31, 1856, p. 3
- *San Francisco Bulletin*, December 29, 1857, p. 2
- *San Francisco Bulletin*, December 24, 1858, p. 3
- *Daily Alta California*, January 1, 1859, p. 2
- *San Francisco Bulletin*, December 30, 1859, p. 3
- *Daily Alta California*, December 24, 1860, p. 1
- *Daily Alta California*, December 24, 1861, p. 1
- *Daily Alta California*, December 25, 1862, p. 1
- *San Francisco Morning Call*, December 25, 1882, p. 1
- *San Francisco Morning Call*, January 1, 1884, p. 5
- *San Francisco Daily Examiner*, January 1, 1884, p. 7
- *San Francisco Chronicle*, January 1, 1885, p. 11
- *San Francisco Examiner*, January 1, 1885, p. 3
- *San Francisco Chronicle*, January 7, 1886, p. 14
- *San Francisco Morning Call*, October 26, 1887, p. 3 (void divorces)
- *San Francisco Chronicle*, December 31, 1887, p. 3
- *San Francisco Chronicle*, January 1, 1890, p. 5
- *San Francisco Chronicle*, January 7, 1890, p. 5
- *San Francisco Morning Call*, January 4, 1892, p. 3

The 1863 through 1881 gap in the above list indicates only that year-end lists were not easily located. They may have been published outside of the expected late December – early January period or not have been published at all. Many have been placed online at *www.sfgenealogy.com*. Only a small number of divorces appear to have merited more newspaper coverage than a brief accounting of superior court actions. However, if the year of the divorce was late enough to be covered by newspaper indexes (pp. 46-8), these indexes should be checked. Search digitized newspapers online and, for the years 1869 and 1870, check Jim Faulkinbury's online index to the *San Francisco Call* (p. 46). The *California Information File* (p. 143) indexes some divorces, and lists of divorces over some years appeared serially in the *San Francisco Historic Record and Genealogy Bulletin*. The latter, short-lived periodical is available at Sutro, SFPL, CGS and on FHL microfiche #6048001-003.

Divorce records may often supply previously unknown information about the date and place of marriage. Thus, a post-earthquake record may pinpoint a pre-earthquake marriage. To search for a *post-earthquake* record, consult the civil indexes of the Superior Court. They are partially alphabetized—by the first two letters of the surname of the plaintiff and/or defendant—and are easily recognized because in the indexes both the plaintiff and defendant will be listed under the same surname. Civil indexes are on microfilm in the public viewing room at the building housing the Superior Court. The full case files to about 1942, however, have been destroyed. CGS holds indexes from the time of the earthquake to 1913.

COURT NOTES.

Anna Kreite yesterday obtained a divorce from Henry Kreite in the Third District Court.

Willie Cook, the lad who snatched a purse from an elderly gentleman's hand on Pacific street on Sunday, was yesterday committed to the Industrial School.

The suit of Rose Ann Shaw vs. William Shaw, an action for divorce, was submitted yesterday in the Fifteenth District Court on report of the Court Commissioner.

In the Third District Court yesterday a writ of habeas corpus was granted on the application of F. H. Adams on behalf of Ah Cheum. The writ was made returnable to-day.

Jane Britton, administratrix of the estate of George Britton, has brought suit against Michael Cumberford, the Hibernia Savings and Loan Society and others, on a promissory note for $2,800 75.

In the United States Circuit Court yesterday Judge Field granted a perpetual injunction in favor of plaintiff in the case of James Gillispie vs. James H. Cummings. This was an action upon a patent fastening for brooms.

William Watson, who was arrested early yesterday morning for assisting a couple of ruffianly companions in garroting and robbing James McDougall, an engineer in the Pacific Mail service, was yesterday held to answer the charge before the Grand Jury, with bail set at $5,000.

The following gentlemen were yesterday impaneled as the United States Grand Jury: Horace Hall, John Shirley, Alpheus Bull, Samuel Lewis, George C. Boardman, Isaac Upham, W. H. Coddington, Joseph Perkins, E. S. Farnsworth, R. J. Trumbull, John Heuston, J. B. Hitchcock, James C. Collins, A. E. Head, Henry Mackie, C. L. Dingley, J. H. Withington, N. G. Kittle, Isaac E. Davis; Alfred L. Tubbs, Foreman.

"Court Notes" from San Francisco Chronicle *September 14, 1875 (microfilm, Newspaper Room, San Francisco Public Library).*

SEVERED TIES.

Twelve Months' Record of Matrimonial Wrecks.

Why the Galling Chains Were Cut, and Who Wore Them—Warnings from the Divorce Courts which Will not be Heeded.

"Whom God hath joined together, let not man put asunder." Notwithstanding this clinching adjuration to the Christian marriage ceremony, the play of moral forces to which many who are conjugally united are subjected brings every year a procession of penitents into the divorce courts. Some married in haste and repented at leisure; some mistook an irrational infatuation for love, and under the delusion took the vows from which they wish to be absolved. Some loved—not wisely, but too well—and incompatibility or obliquities of character, hidden at first, later on becoming revealed, they clamor for a separation. In some instances poverty came in at the door and love flew out of the window, and pretexts were not wanting upon which to supplicate a dissolving decree of the divorce court. There should be another tense in conjugal conjugation, and properly an additional mood, and we would have disgusted mood, preterite-delusion tense—I thought I loved (but didn't); and in the same mood there might also be added the repentant tense—I wish I never had loved. The record of the divorce courts of San Francisco for the past year discloses the debris, so to speak, of frail barks that have been wrecked on matrimonial reefs, and that ought to be a warning to those who are dreaming dreams of happiness, without studying the philosophy of cause and effect, or the economy of ways and means.

THE UNFORTUNATES.

The causes that have led to these disasters are classified as follows: Extreme cruelty, 61; neglect and failure to provide, 66; wilful desertion, 93; habitual intemperance, 31; adultery, 27. Following is the list:

Abel—Rosa from Lewis; failure to provide.
Arota—Catherine from David; extreme cruelty.
Archey—George M. from Henrietta; adultery.
Abrams—Nettie L. from Thomas C.; failure to provide.
Anderson—Elizabeth from Albert; neglect and intemperance.
Appum—Elizabeth from Alphonso; failure to provide.
Atkinson—Annie K. from George W.; desertion.
Beck—Robert L. from Eliza; cruelty and habitual intemperance.
Bucklin—Kate from William E.; desertion.
Brown—Theodore A. P. from Charlotte E.; desertion.
Bell—Lucy Jane from Wm. M.; failure to provide.
Berry—Sarah from Peter; desertion and adultery.
Beel—Bertha Kahn from Philip S.; desertion.

INDEX SAN FRANCISCO CALL 1899-1903.

384

DIVORCE (Continued)—	—Date—	P	C
Coburn, Jockey William, secures	6 19 1903	7	4
Colby, Mrs. Arthur E., sues for..9-21, 31: 7; 10-22, 8: 7	11 23 1902	33	1
Cole, Amos A., sued for	6 12 1902	9	1
Cole, Mrs. Louisa M., sues for	10 1 1902	14	6
Coleman, Charles, sues for	5 10 1903	14	3
Colorado Judge's charge in Richards case	11 24 1901	30	7
Colorado Judge's plan	4 26 1902	7	5
Colson, Henry W. P., secures	9 27 1903	38	2
Commins, Mrs. Anna, sues for............8-16, 8: 7	10 22 1902	8	6
Commissioners on uniform laws	8 20 1901	9	1
Conger, Mrs. Lillie M., sues for	8 16 1902	8	2
Constitutionality of new law argued	8 6 1903	13	6
Cook, Mrs. Ella, secures	4 5 1902	7	3
Coombs, Rev. J. C., sues for	1 27 1903	14	2
Cooper, Mrs. Sarah M., asks for final decree	6 26 1903	9	3
Corcoran, Mrs. H. J., asks for	1 25 1901	11	4
Cordt, John L., sues for	9 17 1902	7	5
Covell, Lottie A., secures	11 15 1901	2	4
Cowell, Mrs. Clara D., asks for	12 9 1903	16	3
Cox, Leander, sues for	5 14 1902	7	6
Cox, "Tommy," sued for	5 16 1901	13	7
Craig, Mrs. Harriet, sues for	3 28 1903	4	4
Craig, Mrs. Maria, sues for	4 1 1902	9	1
Craven, Julia and Peter, denied to	10 11 1902	14	1
Creagh, Dr. J. W., sued for	9 24 1903	7	5
Crist, Gussie Fuegel, sues for	8 6 1899	15	3
Crooks, Frank H., sued for	11 22 1902	5	4
Crossett, Mrs. Minnie B., asks for	4 23 1902	8	7
Crowdy, William S., sued for	11 11 1903	13	5
Crowley, Mrs. Maggie J., sues for	1 27 1903	14	2
Culver, Mrs. Everett Mallory, secures	12 11 1903	1	1
Cumberson, Mrs. Flora J., secures	7 25 1902	13	4
Cutting, Minnie Seligman, secures	5 22 1900	11	6
Cutting, Robert L., sues for	5 24 1899	3	6
Dailey, Edward C., sues for	3 21 1900	12	5
Dailey, Mrs. Luella, denied	12 19 1899	9	3
Dakota, invalid in Great Britain............7 30, 6: 5	8 11 1903	2	1
Dales, George B., sued at Redding	3 13 1903	1	5
Dalton, Charles R., sued for	4 26 1903	32	2
Danaher, Mrs. Bridget, files answer	10 21 1903	2	4
Daneri, Officer John B., secures	11 19 1902	8	1
Danz, John H., sued for	6 24 1903	7	3
Davenport, Mrs. Helen, sues for	9 25 1903	16	1
Davies, Mrs. Elizabeth Montague, sues for	6 25 1903	7	1
Davies, William, sued for	12 1 1901	33	3
Day, B. F., sued for	7 12 1903	31	1
Day, Mrs. Ethel P., sues for	12 17 1902	9	4
Deaf mutes sue for	10 18 1903	25	1
Decision of Judge Hall in Noy case..1-25, 10: 3; (ed.)	1 26 1902	22	3
Decision of United States Supreme Court	4 16 1901	2	1
De Leon, Mrs. Matilda, sues for	9 27 1902	14	2
Dell, Mrs. Virginia, sues for	2 7 1902	7	2
De Moro, Rafael Jr., sues for..............3-26, 9: 1	3 29 1902	10	5
Deuprey, Mrs. Eugene N., secures	12 24 1899	20	5
De Witt, Mrs. Florence, asks for	11 18 1903	7	7
De Wolf, Mrs. Emma Waters, secures	2 27 1902	11	5
Dexter, Mrs. Libbie, sues for	9 22 1903	7	2
Diamond, Jacob, sued for	7 1 1903	9	4
Dierdorff, Mrs. Libbie M., secures	3 28 1900	5	6
Dierssen, Mrs. Frances R., sues for	3 30 1901	3	6
Dinmore, Mrs. Walter, secures	5 9 1899	9	3
Dinslage suit..................10-28, 11: 4; 11-3, 9: 3	11 11 1899	11	5
Dodson, Mrs. George K., secures	2 25 1900	17	9

At the left is a year-end divorce list printed in the Morning Call, *December 25, 1882 (microfilm, Newspaper Room, San Francisco Public Library). Divorces over the years 1894-1903 appearing in the* Call *were indexed under the letter "D" in the* Call *index covering 1894-1903 (above right).*

RESEARCHING CALIFORNIA FEDERAL COURT RECORDS

Statehood brought an established federal court system, consisting of a district court and a circuit court subordinate to the U.S. Supreme Court. Jurisdiction in these courts varied during the early years, but ultimately the U.S. Circuit Court (today called the U.S. Ninth Circuit Court of Appeals) assumed appellate responsibility. Federal courts addressed the areas of immigration, naturalization, land claims, customs, bankruptcy, maritime issues and patents. Following the 1906 earthquake, federal court records remained undamaged. Original files are at the State Archives in Sacramento, with holdings described at the Online Archive of California website, *http://www.oac.cdlib.org*. Films are available at NARA San Francisco (located in San Bruno) and on loan at Family History centers. Cases deemed significant have been published in *West's Federal Supplement* and the *Federal Reporter*. These publications can be found at public, private and academic law libraries and also through the online legal services Westlaw and Lexis, which are available to the public at county law libraries.[21]

RESEARCHING STATE COURT RECORDS

Files of cases that took place in non-federal courts located in San Francisco were all lost in 1906. Our only access to them is through newspaper coverage or summaries of those cases that were appealed and deemed "reportable." The names and jurisdictions of the courts in which proceedings originated varied considerably over the years and included District Court, Superior Court, County Court, numerous Justice of the Peace courts, Police Court, Probate Court and the short-lived Court of Sessions. Eventually the District Court assumed intermediate appellate responsibility between the lower courts and the state Supreme Court. Summaries of "reportable" District Court and Supreme Court procedings back to 1851 have been published in *West's California Reporter*, the *Pacific Reporter*, in *California Reports* and *California Appellate Reports*. Titles of these publications vary slightly from series to series. Many unreported cases over the years 1855 through 1883 were later gathered and published in seven volumes titled *California Unreported Cases*. Digitizations of these publications are available at several publicly accessible websites, including Google Books, and through the online legal services Westlaw and Lexis, which can be accessed by the public at county law libraries.

---

[21] The San Francisco County Law Library has two branches. The main branch (across from City Hall) is located in the Veterans War Memorial Building, 401 Van Ness Avenue, Room 400 (phone 415-554-6821); the Financial District branch is located in the Monadnock Building, 685 Market Street, Suite 420 (phone 415-882-9310). Check for current hours.

April, 1872.] McLERAN *v.* BENTON. 471

Opinion of the Court — Rhodes, J.

by a decree of the Court of First Instance which was rendered October, 1849, and affirmed in 1850 by the Supreme Court. By the decree it was adjudged that Eleonora was entitled to the one half of the community property; but it does not appear that a partition thereof was ever made. In November, 1850, Harmon died, leaving a last will and testament, by which he devised the undivided two thirds of the land to his son Jacob, and the remaining third to his executors in trust for his daughter Mary Ann. Soon after the divorce, Eleonora married Michael Foley, and in 1850 they entered into possession of the land; and on the 16th of August, 1852, they executed a lease of the land to Commerford, for a term to expire January 16th, 1856, describing the land as a part of the Harmon estate. Immediately after the execution of the lease, Foley and wife removed from the land, and Commerford entered and occupied, under the lease. In June, 1853, Foley and wife entered into a contract in writing with Brannan and others — under whom defendants claim title — by which Foley and wife agreed to sell and convey to Brannan and others one hundred and sixty acres of the Harmon tract; and in the same month the purchase money, six thousand dollars, was paid; and Foley and wife executed to them a deed for the land. The contract and deed will hereafter be alluded to. In December, 1853, Commerford sold and assigned his lease to Brannan and others, but he remained as the tenant of Brannan and others until October, 1854, and for the period of ten months thereafter he remained on the premises as their agent or servant. In 1854 Mrs. Foley, with her two children, Mary Ann and Jacob Harmon, removed to the County of Santa Clara, and thereafter neither she nor the children had possession of the premises. In October, 1859, Jacob died a minor and unmarried, and in November, 1859, Mrs. Foley, his mother, died. In May, 1861, Mary Ann, who before that time had married Roussel, conveyed the premises to

During the several decades following statehood, lawsuits over land flooded the courts. If the decision was appealed, details of settlement, ownership and family relationships often can be found in online publications.

Page in Appellate summary from Reports of Cases Determined in the Supreme Court of the State of California *(commonly called "Cal. Reports" (43 Cal. 467)) available on Google.*

The Recorder

The Recorder, a legal newspaper first published toward the end of 1900 and now published weekly, has been the official newspaper for the U.S. District Court of Northern California, the Superior Court of the City and County of San Francisco and the San Francisco Municipal Court. Details and summaries appear here that do not necessarily appear in other newspapers or publications, in some instances constituting the only record of a case tried in Superior or Municipal Court from 1901 to the earthquake. The library at Hastings College of the Law, located at 200 McAllister Street, holds films of *The Recorder* starting in 1901.

Adoptions

Access to adoption records in the state of California is similar to that in other states—quite limited. The first adoption statutes were passed in 1870. California in 1935 became one of the earliest states to seal birth certificates of adoptees from the individuals themselves; records were already sealed to the general public and remain so to this day. The names of birth parents are replaced on birth certificates with the names of the adoptive parents after the adoption is finalized. Court orders to open records can be obtained only in the most unusual of circumstances. According to the 1940 WPA Northern California Historical Records Survey, San Francisco had at that time in sealed archives 3,657 court adoption case files covering the years 1897-1905 and four registers that could serve as an index to them, all of which somehow escaped destruction in 1906.

Shortly after the year 2000, Edgewood Children's Home, a private orphanage known in the past as Edgewood Children's Orphan Asylum or the San Francisco Protestant Orphan Asylum, reviewed their older records and released many of them covering the years 1851-1958 to SFPL. Included in the collection are numerous business records, an extensive history of the institution, admissions and discharges, correspondence (1881-1915) and adoption case files (1867-1916). The adoption files do not contain information on birth parents. The History Room website (www.sfpl.org/sfhistory) provides a finding aid to this collection.

SFPL also holds records obtained from the Family Service Agency of San Francisco, founded in 1889 as Associated Charities. Included in the collection are two volumes of admissions and discharges (in early years primarily deaths) from the San Francisco Foundling Asylum covering 1869-1918. Information on these abandoned infants includes not only dates but also sex, weight, real or presumed age and occasional information if known on the parent(s). Records dating from 1889 are more detailed, but names of adoptive parents are not included. Also in the Family Service Agency collection are three alphabetical indexes to placing-out (fostering) data of the Children's Agency (1900-1908), consisting in some instances of information on families with whom children were placed.

VOTING RECORDS

*E*arly voting records provide a very important source of information about adult male San Francisco citizens, especially those for whom more definitive information has been lost. These records supplement what can be learned from the federal decennial census enumerations and are particularly useful over the years 1881-1899, during which no census survived.

Organized, recorded and published voter registration was instituted in 1866 to reduce the incidence of voter fraud that inevitably seems to accompany sudden population growth. California's population started to explode following the discovery of gold in January 1848 and continued to grow at an almost undiminished rate until 1870. The pre-Gold Rush village of Yerba Buena with a population of about a thousand non-native inhabitants grew to become by 1860 San Francisco, the "Queen of the West Coast," a bawdy city boasting a population approaching sixty thousand. It became necessary to create some semblance of voting order out of the chaos that reigned.

GREAT REGISTER OF VOTERS COMPILATIONS

The Registry Act of 1866 required that all males at or over twenty-one years of age (with ethnic-based exceptions) register and provide the following information: full and complete name; age, occupation and native country; address down to ward or district level; and if naturalized, the date, place and court that awarded citizenship. This information along with the voting precinct name or number and an indication that the registrant attested to the accuracy of the information was compiled annually as the *Great Register of Voters*. Occasionally if a voter moved or died before the next register was prepared, the clerk would indicate this and even, in rare instances, record a date of death or the fact that the voter was no longer mentally capable of voting. In 1872 it was mandated that alphabetized indexes to these registers be printed every other year, but unfortunately not all of these have survived. In the mid- to late 1890s, additional information, including physical description and literacy, was required, but previously required naturalization information was dropped by 1896.

While the 15th Amendment gave African-American men the right to vote in 1870, they were frequently disenfranchised on the basis of literacy until well into the twentieth century. Women were not given the right to vote in California until 1911. Native Americans, unless they surrendered all tribal affiliation and underwent a naturalization process, were denied the right to vote in California until 1924. Natives of China did not receive the right to vote in California until 1926. Thus, except for voters of Hispanic heritage, researchers will not find ethnic minorities represented in the registers and no women at all until 1911.

The California State Library at Sacramento holds the surviving registers through April 1942, although some years are incomplete. The state library also holds *indexes* for 1866, 1888-1892 and 1896-1904. Films of the registers, but not the indexes, are available from Sacramento through interlibrary loan. The filming was done by the Family History Library; thus, the same material (but also including filmed indexes) is available on loan through local Family History centers.

The San Francisco Public Library holds filmed registers for the early years through 1873, for 1876-1878, and part of 1879, 1880, 1884, 1899 and 1901 through the earthquake. The library also has a very limited number of registers and indexes in paper format. The register for 1867 has been extracted and placed online at *www.sfgenealogy.com*. CGS has films of the 1866, 1867, 1869 and 1870 registers, as well as a paper copy of its own publication, an abstract of the San Francisco portion of the *1890 Great Register of Voters*. (See p. 88.)

The filmed indexes are an excellent starting point. You should record both name and district number for every year possible for the person of interest. The voting district number is necessary in order to locate the record itself within the correct filmed register. FHL film numbers of indexes for the following years and surname ranges are as follows:

FHL Filmed Indexes to the Great Registers

1866	film #1,001,665-667	(surnames A - Z);
1888-1904	film #1,001,507-526	(Aa - Dunton, C.);
	film #1,001,551-568	(Dunton, C.- Kearns, G.);
	film #1,001,570-591	(Kearns, G. - Potee, R.);
	film #1,001,644-664	(Potee, R. - Zuzulich).

The registers themselves are organized alphabetically for the entire city and county from 1866-1873 and within voter districts from 1875 on. Indexes are not available for the surviving registers between the last citywide alphabetized register and 1888; thus, one will have to search each district.

Film Numbers for Great Registers of Voters

1866-1878	film #977,096-100;
1880	film #977,101 and 977,194-200;
1882	film #977,201-208;
1886	film #977,209-214; 977,476; 977,622;
1888	film #977,623-631; 977,475;
1890	film #977,632-642;
1892	film #977,643-646; 977,598-610;
1896	film #977,611-621; 977,257-263;
1898	film #977,264-280.

Ancestry.com has placed online various printed registers over the years 1900-1968, although few go beyond 1944. Naturalization information was not included in these years, but to a certain extent they can supplement online city directories. The searching software is somewhat imperfect at this point since adjacent surnames and forenames are often merged as though they are one name.

FOREIGN-BORN VOTERS IN 1872

Jim W. Faulkinbury has compiled an abstract of voter information for foreign-born voters throughout the state, based upon the 1872 *Great Register*, and to a lesser degree those of 1873 and 1875. His index to this compilation (which he calls an "abbreviated finding aid") is currently available online at *http://www. jwfgenresearch.com*. There is a working link to it at *www.sfgenealogy.com*. The index includes full name, age and place of birth. Mr. Faulkinbury will provide a copy of all the information for an individual in his database for a modest fee. Additional information in the full records includes date and place of naturalization, court of record and first year registered. He claims that among his nearly sixty-two thousand records, about seventy percent have complete or partial naturalization details. The full publication is available in microfiche format at CGS and at the State Library in Sacramento. The FHL also has a set of fiche, but they do not circulate to individual Family History Centers.

San Francisco, California
1890 Great Register of Voters

The California Genealogical Society's publication, *San Francisco, California 1890 Great Register of Voters*, Jane Billings Steiner, ed. (North Salt Lake, Utah: Heritage Quest, 2001), integrates and indexes all voters of the various precincts of the city and county of San Francisco in 1890, and thus serves as a partial substitute for the lost 1890 federal census. Data includes name, address, age, birthplace (state or country), occupation, date and location of naturalization and a volume/page reference to the original record. Now out of print, it is part of the online lookup service offered by CGS and can be found there, at SFPL, at the California State Library in Sacramento and at Sutro.

San Francisco, California						ABRAMS - ADAMS	
1890 Great Register of Voters							
Name	Age	Orig	Occupation	Address	Date/Location of Naturalization	Date	Vol./Pg.
Melville Samuel	22	CA	Bookkeeper	507 Lombard		24 Sep 1890	D34/P3
Nathan	30	POL	Merchant	1811 Baker	Father's Nat.	16 Oct 1890	D41/P18
Samuel	23	CA	Clerk	356½ Clementina		22 Sep 1890	D36/P10
Thomas	35	NY	Printer	625 Bush		24 Sep 1890	D32/P16
Walter Samuel	21	CA	Bookkeeper	507 Lombard		17 Oct 1890	D34/P3
ABRAMSON							
Edward	45	PRU	Merchant	219 Grant Ave.	31 Aug 1869, S.F. Ca, 4th Dist.	17 Oct 1890	D35/P1
ABRE							
John Erie Peter	30	DEN	Maltster	226 Francisco	17 Jan 1884, S.F. Ca, Sup.	15 Oct 1890	D34/P1
ABREGO							
George Abernial	22	CA	Barber	2016 Hyde		16 Aug 1890	D34/P7
ACAPOLEO							
Pietro	31	ITA	Bootblack	738 Vallejo	23 Jul 1890, S.F. Ca, 11th Sup.	16 Sep 1890	D32/P7
ACH							
Henry	33	CA	Lawyer	2419 Webster		14 Aug 1890	D41/P13
Julius	32	CA	Traveler	2015 Bush		15 Oct 1890	D42/P10
ACKER							
Frank Valentine	22	CA	Molder	407 Sutter		18 Oct 1890	D36/P1
Franz	35	GER	Tailor	307 Leavenworth	8 Jul 1889, S.F. Ca, Dept. 11 Sup.	18 Aug 1890	D39/P4
Frederick	28	CA	Boiler Maker	611 Howard		17 Oct 1890	D30/P6
Nicholas Alexander	26	DC	Attorney	1502 Jones		5 Sep 1890	D33/P10
Valentine	57	GER	Tailor	407 Sutter	19 Aug 1861, Placerville Ca, 11th Dist.	16 Oct 1890	D36/P1
William Henry	22	CA	Sail Maker	5 Washington		18 Oct 1890	D31/P3
ACKERMAN							
Charles	70	NY	Capitalist	650 Jessie		11 Aug 1890	D39/P7
Charles Henry	68	GER	Baker	636 Commercial	17 Oct 1848, Phil. Pa, Sup.	12 Aug 1890	D31/P8
Charles Lewis	40	LA	Lawyer	423 Eddy		27 Aug 1890	D39/P4

Page from California Genealogical Society publication, San Francisco, California, 1890 Great Register of Voters.

San Francisco County Index
of Naturalized Voters (1898)

The *San Francisco County Index of Naturalized Voters* is a record of those registered voters who were naturalized anywhere over the years 1850-1898. It lists name, date naturalized, voter precinct and ward, and the city and state where the voter was naturalized. This, along with Jim Faulkinbury's database, can be helpful for locating those who were naturalized outside of San Francisco. Filmed by the Family History Library, it is available on films #1,378,779-784.

IMMIGRATION AND EMIGRATION: OVERLAND ARRIVALS, PASSENGER LISTS AND PASSPORTS

S an Francisco, or as it once was called, Yerba Buena, grew very slowly until the Gold Rush changed everything. In 1776 the first non-native immigrants arrived. Two far-flung settlements were established at that time: a Spanish mission located two and a half miles inland and a fortified Spanish military post, the Presidio, located at the entrance to San Francisco Bay. The small cove that would eventually grow into the settlement called Yerba Buena received no immigrants until 1835. By 1844, perhaps a dozen houses and tents hugged the shore; Yerba Buena then consisted of about fifty permanent residents, not counting those who lived at the outlying mission and the Presidio.

In July of 1846 following the outbreak of the Mexican-American War, the United States took possession of the area when Captain John Montgomery of the sloop *Portsmouth* raised the American flag at what is now Portsmouth Square. Several weeks later the *Brooklyn* arrived from New York with about 240 Mormon passengers, some of whom stayed but most of whom moved to inland areas. In March of 1847, three shiploads of soldiers and their families arrived from New York. Known as Stevenson's Regiment of New York Volunteers and ostensibly recruited to fight in the war, their true role was to establish an increased American presence in order to bolster chances for statehood. By 1847, when the sleepy village of Yerba Buena was renamed "San Francisco," its population had grown to barely over eight hundred, of which only about half were Americans. That ended with the discovery of gold near Sutter's Mill in January 1848. Within a year there began an explosive population growth that did not begin to tail off until the 1870s.

We can find mention of many early, pre-Gold Rush arrivals in Hubert Howe Bancroft's *History of California* and other compilations. (See pp. 139-40). Passenger lists for the *Brooklyn* and for the six ships bearing Stevenson's New York Volunteers are available. Lists of gold seekers arriving in 1849 have been published in C.W. Haskins' *The Argonauts of California* (p. 140). However, until 1882, when Chinese immigration records begin, or 1893, when government-held passenger ship records begin, establishing the arrivals of most of those who came is problematic. In general, fewer early San Franciscans came overland than by the sea. Passenger lists for the early years have been reconstructed from various sources, primarily newspapers. They are described below and on the following pages. By the time the transcontinental railroad began operation in 1869, however, there were tens of thousands of San Franciscans who had made their way west for whom we have no arrival records.

General sources for western overland immigration will contain the names of some San Francisco settlers, and there are a number of pioneer compilations and biographical collections discussed in Part II that may help.

National Archives Passenger and Crew Lists

Immigration Passenger Lists, as opposed to the less informative Customs Passenger Lists that preceded them (1820-1891), were instituted in 1882, but most surviving lists begin in 1891 or later. Immigration Passenger Lists include last legal residence (as opposed to country of origin), place of birth, final destination, name of relative (if any) at final destination, and, beginning in 1906, a personal description. Both record types contain name, age, sex and occupation.

Only the lists for Chinese immigrants date to 1882. Whether lists for non-Chinese arrivals were lost or were never kept at all is not known. NARA San Francisco in San Bruno holds these federally-kept passenger lists. Publications M1413 (returning Chinese laborers, 1882-1888), M1414 (Chinese-born arrivals, 1882-1914) and M1476 (Chinese-born immigrants applying for admission, 1903-1947) contain only lists of Chinese immigrants.

Non-Chinese arrivals are contained in publications M1389 (index to arrivals 1893-1934), M1410 (arrivals 1893-1953), M1412 (Customs Passenger Lists 1903-1918), M1438 (arrivals from insular possessions 1907-1911) and M1494 (arrivals from Honolulu 1902-1907). The FHL has filmed the following NARA publications of non-Chinese arrivals and indexes: M1389 (first film in series is #1,430,959); M1494 (misidentified as M1440) on film #1,454,998; and M1410 (access series by entering film #1,465,571).

NARA holds alien crew lists from vessels arriving 1896-1921 (M1436, available on FHL films #1,578,399-406) and crew lists (not otherwise defined) of vessels arriving 1905-1954 (M1416, available also on FHL films #1,534,450-84). The FHL also filmed ships articles and crew lists (not passenger lists) that were kept at the United States Customs House for 1854-6 (films #976,992-6); 1861-62 (films #976,996 and #977,761-5); and 1883, 1886 and 1892 (film #977,765).

NARA films are being digitized in a partnership with the subscription websites *Ancestry.com* and *Footnote.com*. Availability is tabulated at *http://www.archives.gov/digitization/digitized-by-partners.html*. Whether the acquisition of Footnote by Ancestry will change this is not yet clear.

NARA Immigration Passenger Lists include last legal residence (as opposed to country of origin) and also place of birth, final destination and name of relative at final destination.

SHIP PASSENGER LISTS FROM OTHER SOURCES

Since most original arrival records did not survive, it is necessary to turn to other sources, such as lists published in newspapers, journals and diaries or departure lists from foreign ports.

Some immigrants arriving by ship, particularly from Australia or New Zealand, put into port first in the Hawaiian Islands, where arrival and departure records were kept. Many of these records can be accessed on FHL films. Look for film numbers in the FHL catalog under the location topic, Hawaii--Emigration and Immigration.

As part of its Maritime Heritage Project, the J. Porter Shaw Library, located in the San Francisco Maritime National Historic Park, has placed online transcriptions of a few lists that have been found.[22] Directors of the project once hoped to place online contents of *The California Gold Rush Fleet Encyclopedia,* eleven volumes that comprise part of a large archive at The Huntington Library in San Marino originally collected by John B. Goodman, III, but this did not happen. The volumes consist of over 5,000 pages of data on 762 ships that sailed from the eastern U.S. seaboard around Cape Horn to San Francisco between December 7, 1848 and December 31, 1849. Passenger names are not included, but data does include, besides ship name, the name of the owner and master and frequently other key crew members, date and city of departure, date of arrival in San Francisco, numbers of crew and passengers aboard, ports of call and details about the ship.

Some lists of passengers departing from eastern or gulf coast ports were extracted from newspapers at departure or at stops along the route west. A number of these lists were donated to *www.sfgenealogy.com* and may be viewed at that website by clicking on the link "California Bound."

The names of soldiers who came as members of Stevenson's New York Volunteers in the spring of 1847, but not the names of their accompanying family members, are detailed in transcriptions of several old manuscripts and a more recent publication:

- *Stevenson's Regiment in California,* or, as on the title page, *The First Regiment of New York Volunteers 1846-1848* by Francis D. Clark (published in 1882 by George S. Evans & Co., New York). Sutro Library holds a microfiche of an earlier version (1874) of Clark's list in addition to the 1882 publication.
- *With Stevenson to California* by James Daniel Lynch (a manuscript in the California State Library originally published in 1896). In 1970, this and the Clark manuscript were republished together by the Rio Grande Press, Glorietta, New Mexico, as *The New York Volunteers in California.*

---

[22] The library is located on the third floor of Building E at Fort Mason Center, near the intersection of Buchanan and Marina Blvd.

- Also: *California Expedition: Stevenson's Regiment of First New York Volunteers* by Guy J. Giffen (published in 1951 by Biobooks, Oakland).

The New York Volunteers books are shelved at SFPL, CGS and Sutro; the combination of the two manuscripts is available on microfiche through the FHL (fiche 6100686). A compiled list of the Mormon passengers on the *Brooklyn* is available on FHL film #2,055,477, at SFPL and at *www.sfgenealogy.com*.

Ancestry.com makes available transcriptions of San Francisco lists, 1893-1953, and data from the Rasmussen "lists" described below. Few other early passenger lists have been transcribed onto various Internet sites, but considering the hundreds of thousands of gold seekers that arrived, these lists touch upon only a few arrivals. The following publications are available at SFPL and Sutro. CGS has the Rasmussen books but only part of the Carr collection.

- *San Francisco Ship Passenger Lists*, four volumes by Louis J. Rasmussen (Colma, California: San Francisco Historical Records, 1963-1965) consists of information culled from various old newspapers, books, letters and journals. Volume 1 covers the years 1851-1864 and includes information on about 13,500 persons; volume 2 includes the records of another 16,500 arrivals; volume 3, containing lists dated November 7, 1851-June 17, 1852, holds records for about 25,000 persons; volume 4 covers June 17, 1852 - July 6, 1853. Compilations in many instances include names of those who died en route for whom place of residence and date of death is stated. Volumes 1, 2 and 3 were

Newspaper lists of passenger arrivals may not include those traveling in steerage.

Passenger arrival list from the Alta California, *July 16, 1850 (microfilm, Newspaper Room, San Francisco Public Library).*

reprinted by Genealogical Publishing over the years 1978-2003. Volume 4 has not been reprinted.

- *San Francisco Departure Lists*, by Peter E. Carr (San Louis Obispo, California: TCL Genealogical Resources, 1991-1996), available in five volumes, names passengers who left San Francisco by ship headed for Panama and San Juan del Sur over the period September 30, 1850 to December 31, 1852. The data was extracted from the newspaper *Alta California*.

OVERLAND ARRIVALS

California Wagon Train List, 5 April 1849 - 20 October 1852, by Louis J. Rasmussen (Colma, California: San Francisco Historic Records, 1994), provides names in parties leaving St. Joseph, Missouri, or passing through intermediate points. Information is based upon many types of sources, including newspaper accounts and diaries, although none are cited. Occasionally there are notations of deaths along the route. It is available at SFPL, CGS and Sutro. Other sources of overland pioneer arrivals and pioneer biographies are discussed on pp. 148-150.

Rasmussen also wrote *Railway Passenger Lists of Overland Trains*, two volumes published in 1966 and 1968. Volume 1, based upon journals, diaries, magazines, letters and newspaper lists, covers July 28, 1870 to November 13, 1871. It provides names and previous residence of those arriving in Oakland and San Francisco, and of passengers leaving Ogden, Utah, or Omaha, Nebraska. In May 1869, at Promontory, Utah, the Central Pacific tracks from the west were symbolically joined to the Union Pacific tracks from the east, completing a transcontinental train route. The first year the tracks ended at Sacramento. The system was extended to Oakland by July 1870; San Francisco-bound passengers were then ferried across the bay. The lists are generally limited to first and occasionally second class passengers and rarely include those holding "emigrant" tickets. Volume 2 covers November 14, 1871 to April 23, 1873 and includes passengers passing through or transferring at Carlin, Nevada, and Ogden, Utah. These lists include passenger origins and destinations. Although not stated, presumably the sources were similar to those of volume 1. These publications may be found at SFPL and Sutro; the wagon train book, but not the railway book, is at CGS. The FHL filmed the railway lists on FHL film #1,000,138 (items 10-11).

GENERAL IMMIGRANT SOURCES

Several large compilations, although not original records, are so widely used they are listed below. They, along with descendant-submitted pioneer records, suggest that more information is probably available elsewhere. Both are discussed more fully in Part II of this guide. Immigration compilations of ethnic groups to eastern ports, which would prove useful in the instance of identifiable family groups or immigrants with unusual names, are discussed on p. 181.

Argonauts of California, Being the Reminiscences of Scenes and Incidents That Occurred in California in Early Mining Days by Charles W. Haskins was published in 1890, more than fifteen years before the earthquake and fire, a time when original records must still have existed. The last 141 pages of the book consist of data on 27,000 people who arrived in California by the end of 1849, arranged in alphabetized lists according to general source. A number of these sources may have been either ship passenger lists or newspaper accounts of arriving vessels, but the larger part of the data was obviously abstracted from membership data of pioneer organizations. This publication is shelved at SFPL, CGS and Sutro.

The *California Information File*, mentioned earlier, is an enormous card file indexing names and information gleaned from early California newspapers, periodicals, biographies, histories, manuscript collections and pioneer records. Material cited dates from the 1840s to 1986, when the file was microfilmed, and represents about 1.4 million citations. Indexing has continued since 1986, but is available only at the state library. More than half the indexed entries are personal names, but among the indexed subject categories is a large section on "Vessels."

PASSPORTS

Passport applications often bear information not easily found elsewhere, such as exact birthplace and naturalization details. Passports were not required in the pre-1906 years except during the Civil War from August 1861 to March 17, 1862. Citizenship was a requirement except from March 3, 1863 through May 30, 1866, when the right was extended to aliens having filed a Declaration of Intent. Naturalized immigrants wishing to protect themselves from military conscription or guarantee their re-entry often applied for them when visiting their homeland.

The responsibility for issuing passports fell to a number of federal agencies, each of which created a set of records. There are a number of passport types as well, and New York City and Boston kept separate records at various times. In addition to "Basic Passports," there were "Emergency Passports" issued by U.S. officials in a foreign country and "Special Passports" issued to military personnel and government employees. Varying record types, multiple offices and multiple agencies involved make it easy to overlook an entire group of records.

Access to digitized passport applications from some record groups is available online to *Ancestry.com* and *Footnote.com* subscribers. Over 1,000 passports of San Francisco-born citizens are in the Ancestry collection.

Passport index searches can be made at NARA San Francisco (located in San Bruno), at other regional branches or by using FHL film. Most applications and indexes for 1850-1906 are part of NARA micropublications, M1371 and M1372.

Additional indexes covering the pre-earthquake years 1850-1852 and 1860-1881 are available as part of micropublication M1848. The FHL holds films of indexes covering all years of interest except 1853 through 1859 and most, but not of all of the corresponding application files. The complete array of FHL holdings can be viewed by entering film #1,429,876 into the online catalog. If an entry is found, search indexes for all the years of the person's life. Passports were only valid for a few years, and multiple applications do differ from one another.

In the event that an indexed entry is found on an FHL film for which there is no filmed application, a copy of the file can be obtained by writing NARA.

Passports can be a wonderful source, particularly when searching for immigrant origins

This 1903 passport application of John Abramovich of San Francisco provides both date and place of birth.

Page from Mary D. Burd widow's pension file, no. w. o. 1695006, for service of William Burd (Private, Co. F, 6th Reg't. New York Cavalry), Case Files of Approved Pension Applications, RG 15, National Archives (courtesy of Michael Burd). Subsequent documents in the file provide date and place of marriage and Mary's maiden name (p. 203).

MILITARY RECORDS

San Francisco's military history began with the establishment in 1776 of a Spanish fortification, the Presidio of San Francisco, located on the south side of the entrance to San Francisco Bay. Spanish soldiers and their families, along with the Spanish padres who established Mission Dolores that same year, were the only residents in what would become San Francisco until 1835, when settlers began to drift in to form the small village of Yerba Buena.

Spain did not particularly value the small garrison at the Presidio and allowed it to deteriorate over the years. Under Mexican occupation, which began in 1821, the facility continued to fall into ruin and eventually was staffed by only a few soldiers. The strategic importance of the garrison changed when the United States declared war on Mexico in May of 1846. Two months later the United States took possession of Yerba Buena when Captain Montgomery of the sloop *Portsmouth* arrived in the bay and planted the flag at what later became Portsmouth Square. Most Presidio records begin at this point. The garrison was further revived when eight months later, after a long voyage around the tip of South America, Col. Jonathan Stevenson's Regiment of New York Volunteers arrived in three ships. Ostensibly sent to fight in the war, Stevenson's Regiment in actuality had been recruited to establish an increased American presence in California in support of and fulfillment of the philosophy of Manifest Destiny.

Military presence steadily increased during the war, and many soldiers remained as permanent settlers after they were mustered out. The explosion in population that accompanied the discovery of gold soon afterwards brought additional veterans, some from wars dating as far back as the War of 1812. The records of all these men and those of veterans with later service through the Philippine Insurrection (1899-1902) contain useful genealogical information often found nowhere else. Because these records were archived outside of San Francisco, they were unaffected by the earthquake and fire and undoubtedly offer solutions to countless ancestral puzzles.

Military records and veteran records were never intended to serve as genealogical source material, and many consist of little more than name, rank and unit, squadron or ship name, and perhaps the dates of service. A full exploration of available records is far beyond the intended scope of this guide. This section deals with only those easily obtained records likely to answer the most common genealogical questions, such as date and place of birth, date and place of death, current and previous residences and spouse or survivors' names. The NARA website is an excellent starting place, *http://www.archives. gov/genealogy/*. A useful article by Trevor K. Plante on researching military personnel that appeared in *Prologue* (vol. 34, Fall 2002) can be downloaded there. Two comprehensive government-published guides provide fuller, detailed descriptions of military records and their use: *Guide to Genealogical Research in the National Archives* (available at many genealogical libraries) and a continually updated version of the 1995 three-volume publication by compilers Robert P. Machette, et al., *Guide to Federal Records in the National Archives of the United States* (available under the topic "publications" at the NARA website).

OVERVIEW

Records of value exist for both federal and state service. Those for *state* service, as opposed to federal service, are housed at the California State Archives. Many of these records have been filmed by the FHL, and a number of compilations and abstracts are available at Sutro Library and at the state library.

The two main repositories for records relating to *federal* military service are the National Archives and Records Administration (NARA) and the National Personnel Records Center (NPRC). With respect to pre-1906 research, the NARA facility in Washington, D.C., currently holds records relating to:

- Volunteer enlisted men and officers whose military service was performed during an emergency and whose service was considered to be in the federal interest, 1775 to 1902
- Regular Army enlisted personnel, serving 1789 - October 31, 1912
- Regular Army officers, serving 1789 - June 30, 1917
- U.S. Navy enlisted personnel, serving 1798-1885
- U.S. Navy officers, serving 1798-1902
- U.S. Marine Corps enlisted personnel, serving 1798-1904
- Some U.S. Marine Corps officers, serving 1798-1895
- Those who served in predecessor agencies to the U.S. Coast Guard (i.e., the Revenue Cutter Service (Revenue Marine), the Life-Saving Service, and the Lighthouse Service, 1791-1919).

Military personnel files concerning veterans from pre-earthquake San Francisco that may be held at the NPRC in St. Louis, Missouri, include:

- U.S. Navy officers separated after 1902 and enlisted personnel separated after 1885.

- U.S. Marine Corps officers separated after 1895 and enlisted personnel separated after 1904.

Army records at NPRC generally date to after 1906. Occasionally federal records may still be retained at the Department of Veterans Affairs. Useful information may also exist at a veteran's home retirement facility or military cemetery. Some copies, compilations and abstracts of federal service records were provided to the appropriate state adjutant general's office and may be found there or at state archives.

An ever-increasing number of digitized NARA films are being placed online by the subscription websites *Ancestry.com* and its subsidiary *Footnote.com*. A continually updated list of these digitized publications can be found at *http:// www.archives.gov/digitization/digitized-by-partners.html*.

Most *indexes* to federal records, both government-created and privately published, can be found at the NARA branch in San Bruno and on FHL films. The National Park Service created and placed on the Internet an index to Civil War army service; it does not include Confederate servicemen, career servicemen and most members of the Navy. The federal government periodically published lists of those receiving federal pensions. Most of them pre-date 1850; a very useful compilation, however, was published in 1883. (See p. 101.)

Very few *original* post-Revolutionary federal *records* (as opposed to indexes) dating to the years after the American Revolution have been filmed; photocopies usually must be ordered from the National Archives. Except in the instance of very uncommon surnames, or unless you can supply considerable detail about pre- and post-service residences and the unit name and number in which a man served, it is advisable to check indexes and pension lists before ordering a search. There may have been many men with the same name who served, and names are often misspelled. For these reasons clerks filling orders may easily overlook the record that was requested.

Start your search by determining in what time period or conflict the man or woman in question might have served. Anyone settling in San Francisco would have been unlikely to have served in the Revolution but may have seen federal service in any of the following conflicts: the War of 1812 (1812-1814/1815), the Indian Wars (throughout the 1800s to the 1890s), the Mexican War (1846-1848), the Civil War (1861-1865), the Spanish American War (1898) and the Philippine Insurrection (1899-1902). A man may, on the other hand, have served in the California State Militia. The most genealogically informative federal records are pension records. Service files, enlistment records, correspondence files and veteran headstone records, if they can be found, may also help untangle puzzling problems. Records of state and local service are usually less detailed, one important exception being the original ledgers of Civil War enlistments that, at least in the case of California, were retained by the state.

Except in the instance of very uncommon surnames, or unless one can supply considerable detail regarding pre- and post-service residences, it is advisable to check existing indexes and pension lists personally before ordering records.

RECORD TYPES

Pension Records

Pensions were awarded to the disabled and to survivors of those killed in action during or soon after the war in question, but generally many years passed until veterans qualified on the basis of past service alone, even if destitute. Pensions to surviving veterans based on War of 1812 service were not authorized until 1871. If a man qualified for a military pension, his complete pension file will normally provide birth and death data, and names of dependents and possibly other relatives. If a man's wife applied as a widow, the papers that were added to the file to establish their marriage may not be found anywhere else. Applications by a veteran's minor children had to include proof of the children's births.

Pension files for those who served in the Indian Wars and in the Mexican War can contain much family information. Pension files based upon Civil War Union service average 126 pages and are a genealogical bargain. Civil War Union pensions are particularly important because such a large percentage of eligible men served and because the pension laws were such that most Union soldiers, their widows or their minor children eventually applied.

Pensions were not awarded by the federal government for Confederate service in the Civil War, but most states in the confederacy eventually were able to fund them, though not for all veterans or widows and a few not until after the turn of the century. These files are housed in the archives of the state that issued them. The FHL filmed indexes to Confederate pension applications found at state archives. One can access the film numbers through the online FHL catalog by selecting "place search," entering the appropriate state, and then selecting "military records, Civil War, pensions." Recently most of the Confederate indexes and even some digitizations of the records themselves have been placed online. This includes the indexes to applications from Oklahoma (Department of Libraries website), Louisiana (Secretary of State website), Georgia (Georgia State University website), Tennessee (State Library and Archives website), Texas (State Library website) and Virginia (The Library of Virginia website). Digitized applications for Florida are available at the website for the Florida Bureau of Archives and Records Management, while those for South Carolina are digitized at the website of that state's Department of Archives and History. Joe Beine hosts an Internet website with up-to-date links to online records. You can locate the site by searching on his name, in quotes, plus "military."

Pensions for naval service were funded differently, and the records were not turned over to the Veterans' Administration until 1932. The files are indexed separately except for the consolidated index T288, "General Index to Pension Files, 1861-1934," which does contain the names of naval pensioners, although they are very difficult to read. Surviving files for pensions awarded before the Civil War are interfiled with Army files.

If you know where a possible pensioner lived in 1883, search the publication *List of Pensioners on the Roll, January 1, 1883: giving the name of each pensioner, the cause for which pensioned, the post-office address, the rate of pension per month, and the date of original allowance, as called for by Senate resolution of December 8, 1882*. This can be found in the U.S. Serial Set microfiche at libraries serving as government depositories and as a five-volume Genealogical Publishing Co. reprint in large genealogical collections. Names are segregated by state and county; California is in volume 4. CGS has alphabetized the California list. The search may take time, but as the official list of those actually receiving pensions, it includes those who may not have applied through the usual channels and thus may not be found in the regular indexes. A review of the pages for San Francisco (vol. 4, pp. 788-95), reveals a number of possibly misspelled foreign surnames, such as Drwinheller, Ralinkalbro, Whaites, Gardenousky and Fregea. If one were to request a NARA search for such a surname, the response might be that no record was found under the submitted name, whereas by first locating the name in the list, one can supply the pension file number and the service claim on which it was based.

NARA films and a number of books list names of those for whom regular pension application files exist. However, they do not include the names of those who obtained pensions through congressional appeal, nor do they include files that were lost or pulled and never restored before indexing. Entries are always under the name of the veteran, even if it was a widow or other family member who applied. The FHL purchased the National Archives indexes, and most are available online at one or both of two subscription sites, *Ancestry.com* and *Footnote. com*. Book indexes must be sought in large genealogical libraries. (See p. 103.) Family History Library film numbers refer to the number of the first film in a series, the full range of which can be accessed by entering that number in the film/fiche selection box in the online library catalog.

National Archives Pension Index
Publications for the War of 1812 and Later

- M313, Index to War of 1812 Pension Application Files (FHL film #840,431 and ff.).
- T316, Old War Index to Pension Files, 1815-1926 (FHL film #821,603 and ff.). This indexes the applications of many career servicemen and officers and also indexes some claims based upon service in the War of 1812 and some based upon service in the earlier Indian Wars.
- T317, Index to Mexican War Pension Files, 1887-1926 (FHL film #537,000 and ff.). This index contains some cross-references to files in other series.

- T288, General Index to Pension Files 1861-1934 (FHL film #540,757 and ff.). These file cards were digitized by Ancestry, but are only available with an Ancestry subscription. Accompanying pension requests with a copy of the file card shortens response time.
- T289, Organization Index to Pension Files of Veterans Who Served between 1861 and 1900 (FHL film #1,725,491 and ff.). This index includes U.S. Army only and is grouped by state, then branch of Army, then regiment, then finally by name. It is a fallback when National Archives staff cannot locate in T288 a name for which the necessary information has been provided.
- M1784, Index to Pension Application Files of Remarried Widows Based on Service in the War of 1812, Indian Wars, Mexican War, and Regular Army before 1861 (FHL film #2,155,462).
- M1785, Index to Pension Application Files of Remarried Widows Based on Service in the Civil War and Later Wars and in the Regular Army after the Civil War (FHL film #2,155,463 and ff.).
- T1196, Selected Pension Application Files Relating to the Mormon Battalion, Mexican War, 1846-1848 (FHL film #480,129 and ff.; NARA does not list this one roll of film as being available at regional archives).
- T318, Index to Indian War Pension Files, 1892-1926 (FHL film #821,610 and ff.); applications based upon participation in Florida Seminole Wars.
- M1408, Case Files of Disapproved Pension Applications of Civil War and Later Navy Veterans, 1861-1910 ("Navy Survivors' Originals").
- M1469, Case Files of Approved Pension Applications of Civil War and Later Navy Veterans, 1861-1910 ("Navy Survivors' Certificates").
- M1274, Case Files of Disapproved Pension Applications of Widows and Other Dependents of Civil War and Later Navy Veterans, 1861-1910 (FHL microfiche 6,333,813 and ff.; indexed on 6,333,805-812).
- M1391, Lists of Navy Veterans for Whom There Are Navy Widows' and Other Dependents' Disapproved Pension Files.
- M1279, Case Files of Approved Pension Applications of Widows and Other Dependents of Civil War and Later Navy Veterans, 1861-1910 ("Navy Widows' Certificates.")

Most of the above publications are available at *Ancestry.com* and *Footnote.com* through digitization partnerships with NARA. An up-to-date list of where to find them is currently available at the NARA website, currently located at *http:// www.archives.gov/digitization/digitized-by-partners.html*. The recent acquisition of Footnote by Ancestry, however, may change locations.

Printed Pension Indexes and Lists for the War of 1812 and Later

The following publications were transcribed from the National Archives filmed indexes by Virgil D. White and published by the National Historical Publishing Co. in Waynesboro, Tennessee. Each includes information on applicable pension laws and describes the data that can be found in the indexes.

- *Index to War of 1812 Pension Files* (published 1989 and 1992; at Sutro Library and CGS). The book, like the filmed index, also contains names of many of those applying for bounty land but not for a pension. Names of wives and widows (including some maiden names) and other family members are cross-indexed.
- *Index to Old Wars Pension Files, 1815-1926* (published 1993; at Sutro and CGS).
- *Index to U.S. Military Pension Applications of Remarried Widows for Service Between 1812 and 1911* (published 1999; at CGS).
- *Index to Pension Applications for Indian Wars Service between 1817 and 1898* (published 1997; at Sutro Library and CGS).
- *Index to Indian Wars Pension Files, 1892-1926* (published 1987; at Sutro). Indexes pensions based on participation in Florida Seminole Wars.
- *Index to Mexican War Pension Files* (published 1989; at CGS).
- *Index to Volunteer Soldiers, 1784-1811* (published 1987; at CGS).

White also compiled lists of Confederate applications using information at several state archives:

- *Index to Georgia Civil War Confederate Pension Files* (published 1996; at CGS).
- *Index to Texas CSA Pension Files* (published 1989).
- *Register of Florida CSA Pension Applications* (published 1989; at CGS).

Federal Service Records

Service records as a whole are less genealogically informative than pension records. Civil War Union service records, however, can be rich. Since enrollment was done by the state and service was for the most part in state-identified units, these records (or duplicates) are normally held at the state level. They often include age, place of birth and occupation, as well as summaries of promotions, discharges, desertions, war-related injuries, deaths and imprisonments.

For California personnel, two publications at Sutro Library direct the researcher to the existence of NARA service records, but the abstracted information in these is minimal:

Frequent detail regarding place of birth makes this compilation valuable.

Page (above and facing page) from state-held compilation of Civil War volunteers (filmed at the California State Archives and available on FHL film #981,530).

- *Records of California Men in the War of the Rebellion 1861 to 1867* (originally published by the government in 1890, reprinted at various times by various publishers; also at CGS) and
- *Official Army Register of the Volunteer Force of the United States Army* for the Years 1861, 1862, 1863, 1864, and 1865. (Reprinted in 1987 in eight volumes; California records are in vol. 7, available at CGS.)

One state-held compilation of data for California volunteers holds additional information regarding birthplace that may be difficult to find in full files. The records found in it are often so complete that it is more than worth the search to see if similar compilations for other states have been retained in their respective archives. The California ledgers were filmed by the FHL at the California State Archives and cataloged as "California Volunteers, Civil War 1861-1865" (FHL film #981,530). This film is available at CGS. An example of a ledger page is shown on the previous two pages. Names within an alphabetical group appear to have been entered by company, which makes the search somewhat tedious if the company is not known. Note that "Place of Nativity" often includes town, county and state for both the U.S. and foreign countries. This is particularly valuable with respect to San Franciscans, since so many of them were born abroad.

Most other records filmed by the FHL at the state archives were found to be less informative, except for the "Veterans General Register," which includes data on those who received veterans' services. See "State and Local Records."

National Archives indexes to compiled service records exist only for volunteer soldiers and not for regular U.S. Army units or officers. The indexes are available at subscription websites (p. 99) and have also all been filmed by the FHL. Locate film numbers in the online FHL catalog by entering as the title, using quotation marks, "Index to Compiled Service Records of Volunteer Soldiers," "Index to Compiled Service Records of Volunteer Union Soldiers" or "Index to Compiled Service Records of Confederate Soldiers." Others may be found by searching in the catalog under either "United States" or the appropriate state and then selecting "Military Records" and the appropriate war or conflict. NARA San Francisco (located in San Bruno) holds some, but not all of the indexes.

NARA micropublication M233, "Registers of Enlistments in the U.S. Army, 1798-1914" (available on FHL films starting with #350,307) abstracts enlistment records for soldiers, not officers, serving in the *Regular Army*. Information includes civilian occupation, place of birth, age at enlistment, personal description and possibly other comments. Records before 1820 are arranged chronologically and by leading letters of the surname. The organization of later records varies. The search can be confusing and take time, but the detail in these records often leads to solutions to difficult research problems.

The Army did not compile personnel information for officers until midway into the Civil War. The best source for early information is found in Francis B. Heitman's *Historical Register and Dictionary of the United States Army from Its Organization, September 29, 1789, to March 2, 1903* (multiple editions). Heitman is available in most genealogical libraries, on FHL film #2,229,899, and online at Ancestry, Footnote and the website of the U.S. Army Military History Institute.

Personnel information for Navy enlisted men separated after 1885 and for Marine Corps enlisted men separated from 1906 is held at the NPRC in St. Louis, Missouri. Record requests should be made on NATF Form 180, available at the NARA website or at any Department of Veterans Affairs office. Requests may also be submitted online by following the instructions at *http://www.archives.gov/ veterans/evetrecs*. Earlier service records for *enlisted men* that can be easily accessed (called "Rendevous Reports") do not as a rule contain much genealogical information. Presumably non-released records of *officers* at the NPRC will be made available to descendants. Filmed abstracts of pre-1902 officers' service records contain useful genealogical information such as birthdate, birthplace, date and place of death and spouse's name. Check the following two NARA publications: M330 "Abstracts of Service Records of Naval Officers, 1798-1893" (FHL films #1,445,969-987) and M1328 "Abstracts of Service Records of Naval Officers, 1829-1924" (FHL films #1,579,079-096). Some Confederate naval records are available in NARA publication M0260 "Records Relating to Confederate Naval and Marine Personnel" (FHL films 191,662-8).

The U.S. Coast Guard falls under the aegis of the Treasury Department, though records for war years are generally found with naval records. Requests submitted on NATF Forms 85 and 86 should result in pension and service records of more recent Coast Guard personnel; information at the NARA website suggests that records of Coast Guard predecessor agencies are too fragile to copy.

State and Local Records

State military records housed in the state archives in Sacramento have been filmed by the FHL. Locate them by entering "California" into the "Place Search" option in the FHL online catalog and select military records. Included are papers of the California Militia covering the years 1850 to 1916, registers of volunteers in the Civil War and Spanish American War and records of National Guard units. However, very few contain more than names and chronologies of service. An exception to this is the series of ten indexed volumes titled "Veterans General Register," which covers the years 1884 to 1917, on FHL films #981,559-561 (also at CGS). Comprising a record of those admitted to veterans' hospitals and similar facilities, each volume contains in addition to name and regiment or branch of naval service, age and place of birth (county and state or foreign country), dates of enlistment and discharge, cause of discharge, residence at time of admission, married or single, description of disease or disability, pension (if any), rate of pension, estate or income and remarks.

One fairly informative set of local records bearing more than minimal information is *San Francisco Cadet Company, 2ⁿᵈ Artillery, N.G.C., San Francisco, California: Applications to Enlist, 1882-1883* (Margaret A. Wilson, compiler). This publication also includes lists of veterans of the Mexican War and muster rolls of the National Guard (1869-1872) and can be found at SFPL, CGS and at the state library in Sacramento. Genealogical information in the cadet applications includes birthdate, birthplace, name of parent or guardian and residence.

The Walter P. Story Memorial Library and Research Center associated with the Military Museum in Sacramento holds more than ten thousand volumes of military history writings, including biographical material and personal recollections that may provide information not found elsewhere.[23]

Bounty Land Records

The offering of bounty land in the public domain served as an inducement to potential recruits until 1855, at which time it was discontinued. For men who might later have settled in San Francisco this would probably include service in the War of 1812, the Indian Wars and the Mexican War. Successful applicants received a warrant, a certificate not bearing any genealogical information, for a specified number of acres, which could then be exchanged for a land patent, or in most instances be sold. Applications from the earlier years often included more genealogical information than those in the later years. Over the years 1976 through 1984 in volumes 64-72, the *National Genealogical Society Quarterly* published an alphabetized list of Northern California bounty land grantees compiled by Keith Lingenfelter, "Northern California Bounty Land Grantees under Acts of 1847-1855." Copies of this periodical are at Sutro Library; a photocopy of the series is available at CGS. The data was compiled from records at county courthouses and is therefore incomplete. No records for San Francisco survived, but some San Francisco residents may have applied for land elsewhere in Northern California.

Civil War Draft Records

Civil War draft records contain the nativity (rarely exact) of a man born between the years 1818 and 1843. They are not always available for a given geographical area, and only two of the five record types can be obtained by writing. Consider them only when more easily obtained records such as pension records or volunteer enlistment records fail to provide needed information.

Much of the following information is taken from a booklet titled *Civil War Draft Records, An Index to the 38ᵗʰ Congressional Districts of 1863* by Nancy Justus Morebeck (Vacaville, California: privately published, 1997). A copy of this publication can be found at Sutro and CGS. In her book Morebeck provides the

---

[23] The Walter P. Story Library is located at 1119 – 2ⁿᵈ St., Sacramento 95814; phone (916) 442-2883.

congressional district numbers that are required to obtain several types of Union draft records from NARA. These numbers were obtained from the *Congressional Directory for the Second Session of the Thirty-eighth Congress of the United States of America* (Washington, D.C.: Philip & Solomons, 1865), which can also be viewed on FHL film #1,425,543 (item 6).

The first draft in U.S. history was enacted in April 1862 by the Confederate Congress, affecting men aged eighteen to thirty-five. The act was amended five months later to include men up to forty-five, and five months following that to men seventeen to fifty. For the first year exemptions could be purchased, and substitutes could be engaged. Few Confederate records have survived.

On March 3, 1863, President Lincoln authorized a Union Army draft by signing the Enrollment Act. Under it all eligible white males between twenty and forty-five, both citizens and aliens having filed declarations of intent, were eligible. Single males twenty to forty-five were to be drafted first, followed by all married men between the ages of thirty-six to forty-six. Males seventeen to twenty could serve with the permission of a parent or guardian. Six drafts were held between June 1863 and December 1864, with varying lengths of service commitment. Originally the bill allowed for few exemptions, most based upon physical or mental disability or family hardship. Any drafted man could, on the other hand, either pay a $300 commutation fee or provide a substitute to serve in his place. It was later estimated that sixty-five percent of the men identified in the 1863 draft were released because of disability or hardship.

The very unpopular Union draft was not applied in any locality that had met its quota of recruits. The various congressional districts across the country were assigned quotas that, if met, relieved a district from the draft. Clearly it was in the interest of local officials to recruit men vigorously in order to keep the draft from applying in their areas. This resulted in a great many men volunteering who probably would not have enlisted if left to their own devices.

There are five types of Union draft records: Descriptive Rolls, Consolidated Lists, Statements of Substitutes, Medical Records of Drafted Men, and Case Files of Drafted Aliens (those who had not declared their intent to naturalize). Unfortunately, one must go to the Archives in Washington to research a name in the Descriptive Rolls, Medical Record of Examinations and Statement of Substitutes. The remaining two record types can be obtained by writing.

The Consolidated Lists, part of Record Group (RG) 110, provide the person's name, age, state or country of birth, place of residence, occupation, previous military participation and marital status, all as of July 1, 1863. Although the staff at the Archives does not usually copy the page from the tightly bound volumes, they will transcribe the information found. The records are arranged by state and by Congressional or Enrollment District. To access a man on the consolidated lists, it is necessary to identify the Congressional District in which he lived in 1863. In 1863, Morebeck writes that San Francisco was in the "Southern District."

However, there are no consolidated enrollment lists for either the "Middle" or "Southern" district of California; records for the rest of the state are fairly complete.

The descriptive rolls, also part of RG 110, add a physical description and a place of birth (rarely more than state or country) to the information found on the consolidated lists. You must know the congressional district number in order to locate them and they must be obtained onsite in Washington.

The Medical Record of a draftee must be researched in person. It contains a date, record number, name, where drafted, occupation, age, nativity (state, country), present residence, physical description, race (white or colored), marital status, and result. These records are organized by state and then by congressional district and are also part of RG 110.

The Case File of a Drafted Alien, for 1861-1864 only, contains name, district from which drafted, country of citizenship, age, length of time in U.S., and physical description. These records are part of RG59, records of the Department of State. It is not necessary to provide the congressional district number, and a transcription of the information can be obtained by writing.

To obtain those records available by mail, write Old Military and Civil Branch (MWCTB), National Archives and Records Administration, Seventh & Pennsylvania Ave. NW, Washington, DC 20408.

Cemetery and Gravestone Records

Roll of Honor, twenty-seven volumes published over the years 1865-1871 by the U.S. Quartermaster's Office (FHL films #1,445,832 and ff.), documents dates of death and other data for Union soldiers who died during the Civil War. These volumes were indexed by Martha and William Reamy as *Index to the Roll of Honor* (Baltimore: Genealogical Publishing Co., 1995). Both publications are shelved at Sutro Library. CGS holds the California records and the index.

Since 1879, the Department of Veterans Affairs has furnished upon request headstones for gravesites of Civil War Union veterans buried in private or public, non-military cemeteries. Genealogical information in applications is generally limited to date and place of death and burial. NARA publication M1845 (on FHL film #2,155,576 and at *Ancestry.com*) consists of a card index to these records for the years 1879-1903. In 1996 the Genealogical Publishing Co. released *The Unpublished Roll of Honor* by Mark Hughes, described as including government headstone application records not previously found, many at military posts. Hughes's publication is available at CGS. NARA publication M2014, "Burial Registers for Military Posts, Camps, and Stations, 1768-1921," covers many of these records. Available at NARA San Francisco (in San Bruno) and at *Ancestry.com*, it is arranged by post and covers regular Army only.

The San Francisco Bay Area has several military cemeteries: San Francisco National Cemetery, which was formed from several existing cemeteries on the grounds of the Presidio in 1884 and was closed to new burials in 1990, the now buried U.S. Marine Hospital Cemetery also once located on the grounds of the Presidio (for reconstructed records, see p. 27) and Golden Gate Cemetery in San Bruno, which did not receive interments until 1941. Records for those buried at San Francisco National Cemetery are available on the cemetery premises and on the Internet at *http://www.interment.net*. Tombstone inscriptions from San Francisco National Cemetery and from the Veterans' Home in Napa County, where many veterans from San Francisco spent their final years, are available on FHL film #874,359 and at *www.findagrave.com*. Information includes birth state, death date and age at death.

Retirement Home Records

The California Veterans Home at Yountville in Napa County was founded in 1884. Records of veterans who once lived in San Francisco but later lived there presumably should be available to descendants.[24]

Early Records of the San Francisco Presidio

Erwin N. Thompson of the National Park Service wrote a detailed and well-annotated history of the Presidio, *Defender of the Gate: The Presidio of San Francisco, A History from 1846 to 1995* (Golden Gate National Recreation Area: National Park Service, 1995). This book can be accessed online at the National Park Service website. Primarily historical in focus, it contains very little genealogical information. Most records of the Presidio are under the care of the U.S. National Park Service at the Army Records Center. They consist primarily of maps, historical background, photographs and clippings, including a fair amount on the earthquake and fire in which Gen. Frederick Funston, the temporary commander of the post, played a prominent part. Military and civilian deaths that occurred at Letterman Hospital on Presidio grounds from June 1898 through April 1910 are available as textual records at NARA San Francisco as "Registers of Deaths and Interments of Patients" (Record Group 112).

OBTAINING RECORDS FROM NARA

Until recently, it was necessary to fill out NATF Form 85 for copies of federal pension or bounty land warrant applications and NATF Form 86 for copies of military service records. These forms are still available from NARA, but it is considerably more convenient to place (and receive) an order directly online using a charge card at *https://eservices.archives.gov/orderonline/*. [25] All ordering options are described at *archives.gov/order*.

In sending for a pension application file, it is necessary to provide enough information for NARA clerks to locate the correct serviceman. Unless the name is

---

[24] Contact the California Department of Veterans Affairs, 1227 O Street, Sacramento, CA 95814, or the Veterans Home at PO Box 1200, Yountville, CA 94599.

[25] Postal address: National Archives and Records Administration, Attn: NWDT1, 700 Pennsylvania Avenue NW, Washington, DC 20408-0001.

very unusual, the serviceman's official service designation and unit are essential. Try also to provide (if known) year of birth, places of residence before and after the war and name of spouse. In the Army, there were three types of soldiers who served: militia, volunteers and the regular army. Most units, except for those in the regular U.S. Army, were associated with the state from which they served, which occasionally was a state just over the border from a man's residence. If a man's pre-war residence is known, check county histories for lists of participants. It is best to start with NARA micropublication T288, "General Index to Pension Files," which is readily available at all regional archives branches, as FHL film #540,757, and at *Ancestry.com* by subscription. Once the correct pensioner is located, accompany the request with a photocopy of the index file card.

The exception to this is the case where the pension file card bears an XC (deceased) or X (active) pension number. These indicate a file was still active about 1928 and may not have been returned to NARA by the Veterans Administration. Nonetheless, check first by submitting a request to NARA in Washington, D.C., and be sure to enclose a photocopy of the pension file card. If the file remained with the Veterans Administration, NARA will return a FOIA (Freedom of Information Act) form, which can then be submitted with a request to the Department of Veterans Affairs.

In requesting a NARA pension file, it is best to request the "full file" rather than the less expensive (current charge $25) "Pension documents Packet," a set of selected records that does not include all supporting testimonies and correspondence, some of which may provide clues to other relatives. If a full Civil War file ($75) or pre-Civil War file ($50) exceeds 100 pages, you will be informed and given the option of paying a per page charge over the basic fee. Recall that Civil War *Confederate* pensions, if they were awarded, were handled through the state. Not every state had the funds to do so, and veterans, in order to qualify, had to live in the state in which they had served at the time of application. For those records, contact the state archives of the state in which a man enlisted.

Compiled Civil War service files for those serving in Union forces, although they are smaller and less expensive ($25) than pension files, are interesting in that they contain records of injuries and imprisonment. NARA holds service records of Civil War Confederate units as well as of Union soldiers and sailors, but the Confederate records are not as varied. Pre Civil War service files, as well as bounty land applications cost $25. Bounty land files typically provide a description of service, but only if a widow applied will they normally contain desired family information.

Records of Fraternal Organizations and Benevolent Societies

*O*ld city directories attest to the large numbers of fraternal associations and societies that existed in San Francisco over the years. Most of these organizations existed for the purpose of (or included in their activities) the funding of orphanages, maternity homes and homes for wayward youths, and help for members who might find themselves in financial need. Occasionally a benevolent society evolved into an insurance company. Fraternal organizations also played an important role in fulfilling the social needs of San Francisco's residents. Some were ethnic-based. Among the largest societies were the Independent Order of Odd Fellows (IOOF), the Free and Accepted Masons (Freemasons), the Knights of Pythias, the Knights of Columbus (Catholic), the Ancient Order of Hibernians (Irish Catholic) and the GAR. Many had auxiliary branches for women, generally under a different name.

The original records of these societies probably held information on each member's birthplace, residence, family members and occupation. What remains of those records, however, are for the most part capsule histories, articles in old newspapers and brief member rolls or officer lists and photographs that appeared in membership books occasionally to be found in used bookstores or libraries. Many of these organizations exist today. If evidence of membership is found, such as in an obituary or among personal effects, the researcher should at least inquire if old organizational records have been retained.

Ethnic Organizations

Ethnic-based societies were particularly important to members of San Francisco's large immigrant population. Some records of Jewish welfare organizations are archived in the Western Jewish History Collection now at the Bancroft Library, but whether they contain genealogically useful information is not known. Two archives, the Immigration History Research Center, associated with the University of Minnesota, and the Balch Institute for Ethnic Studies, now part of the Historical Society of Pennsylvania in Philadelphia, maintain collections of ethnic business and society records. The pre-1906 San Francisco holdings of the former appear currently to be limited to records of the Estonian Veterans Union. The only pre-earthquake holding at the Balch Institute, an 1866 German newspaper film, will soon be made available as a digitization by Readex.

IOOF

The Independent Order of Odd Fellows attracted large numbers of San Francisco German immigrants, although it was not limited in any way to a particular ethnic group. The IOOF maintains a website that is linked to contact information for the Grand Lodge of California. The amount of genealogical information that might have been retained by the Grand Lodge is probably limited to a date of death. Fortunately, the IOOF turned over many of their older cemetery and crematory records (to about 1930) to CGS. These records are very complete and have been discussed elsewhere in this guide (pp. 24-25).

MASONIC LODGES AND AFFILIATED ORGANIZATIONS

The fraternal organization Free and Accepted Masons dates back to 1717. Many allied organizations have grown out of or have since become affiliated with Masonry, including Shriners of North America, Scottish Rite of Freemasonry, York Rite of Freemasonry, Knights Templar and affiliated women's and youths' organizations. Member applications, if they can be found, should include date of birth and date of death. Additional information possibly can be gleaned from John S. Yates' pamphlet, *Researching Masonic Records, A Guide for Genealogists* (Wichita Falls, TX, 1998), available as FHL film #1,425,198, item 4. Two books at SFPL provide additional color but not personal member information: *One Hundred Years of Freemasonry in California* (Leon O. Whitsell, ed., 1950) and *California Freemasonry, 1850-2000: the Past Fifty Years* (Masonic Grand Lodge of California, 2000). Some local material can be found at the California Masonic Memorial Temple, a library and museum located at 1111 California Street in San Francisco.

KNIGHTS OF PYTHIAS

Founded in 1864 during the Civil War, this organization also exists today. The earliest chapters in San Francisco date to 1869, but since there appears to have been no centralized or duplicate record keeping, it is unlikely records from early years survive. Some information may appear in the early fraternal publication *Illustrated Pacific States*, filmed copies of which are at SFPL.

ANCIENT ORDER OF HIBERNIANS AND THE KNIGHTS OF COLUMBUS

These two organizations restricted their membership to Roman Catholics, the Hibernians to those of Irish descent. San Francisco chapters were not formed until 1901 and 1902. Both organizations raised enormous amounts of money to aid victims of the 1906 earthquake and fire.

OTHER RELIGIOUS-AFFILIATED SOCIETIES

Most benevolent societies required some type of religious affiliation or statement of belief. The Ladies' Protection and Relief Society, founded in 1853 by women of the Presbyterian Church, survives today as The Heritage, a retirement community located since 1925 at the corner of Bay and Laguna streets. One might check the Presbyterian archives for early records of this group. Records of other societies with a religious affiliation may lie buried in regional church archives or even within the written records of the churches that sponsored them. Organizations that existed nationwide may have kept centralized records. Inquiries can be made through national and regional offices, the addresses of which can be located through Internet searches or by contacting local branches.

G.A.R.

Following the Civil War, Union veterans formed an organization known as the Grand Order of the Army of the Republic to provide benefits and support for veterans and their families. This organization finally ceased to exist in 1949, but some of its records live on. Several publications provide easily obtained evidence that a man belonged to the GAR: *Register of the Department of California, Grand Army of the Republic, 1886* (FHL film #394,396 with copy at Sutro library); *Roster, By-laws and Roll of Deceased Members* (1927 publication of San Francisco Geo. H. Thomas Post no. 2; copy at California State Library); and *Records of Members of the Grand Army of the Republic, with a Complete Account of the Twentieth National Encampment* (ed. by William H. Ward, 1886; copy at SFPL).

Occasionally GAR sketchbooks, which contain personal accounts of members, surface. The detail in these books is often quite experiential and not necessarily limited to military recollections. Some books are held at the U.S. Military Institute at Carlisle Barracks, Pennsylvania, while others are archived at the GAR Civil War Museum and Library, located at Ruan House in Philadelphia. Each of these two organizations has a website where contact information can be found.

SOCIETY PERIODICALS

SFPL holds filmed copies over the years 1887, 1888 and 1889 of *Illustrated Pacific States* and *Illustrated Pacific States Weekly*, publications that include information on members and activities of Freemasons, Independent Order of Odd Fellows and Knights of Pythias. Occasional obituaries and biographies are quite detailed, but the paper is not indexed and must be searched by hand.

Records of pioneer societies and a number of patriotic lineage societies, all of which can be particularly helpful, are covered in Part II of this guide.

INSTITUTIONAL, BUSINESS AND OCCUPATIONAL RECORDS

*A*t one time records that were held by employers, professional organizations, schools, hospitals, jails and so forth would have provided some of the genealogical information we seek. Not only was this information received from the person in question (or from his or her parents), making it primary, but it was often detailed and would have added considerable color to our family histories. Unfortunately, this is not the type of data that normally survives for one hundred years, even without the intervention of an earthquake and fire. What has survived, for the most part, are just lists of names—lists found in films of old newspapers and lists that appeared in municipal reports. To know that one's ancestor checked in at a hotel, graduated from nursing school or was a member of a fire department does not usually tell us when or where a person was born and to whom, although hotel arrivals, extracted from old newspapers, often list last previous residence.

Exceptions, however, do exist. A number of early businesses have gathered historical material and will make it available to interested parties if contacted. An excellent resource for locating such businesses and institutions is the *Directory of Archival and Manuscript Repositories in California*, published by the Society of California Archivists. The fourth edition, published in 1996, can be found at SFPL and CGS and appears to be the most recent edition available. This publication, while an excellent source, is not comprehensive, so it is always wise to check directly with the business or organization of interest. Some businesses may have undergone a name change or have been acquired by a larger firm and yet still retain records. The old Hendy Iron Works, for example, moved to Sunnyvale following the earthquake and fire and was later acquired by Westinghouse. A museum containing much historical material is maintained on the Westinghouse premises in Sunnyvale. Another source for locating old business and institutional records is the Online Archive of California (OAC), a website providing the location of archived records in contributing repositories throughout the state.

Orphanage and Children's Home Records

A publication titled *Record of Orphans, Half-Orphans, etc. on State Aid, 1907-1910: City and County of San Francisco,* available as FHL film #1,412,658 through Family History centers and at CGS and as digital links at *sfgenealogy.com,* consists of original documents containing the child's and parents' names, the age of child in years and months, the place and date of birth, the death date of parent or parents, the dates of aid and the society receiving the funds. The ledger from which it was prepared is archived at SFPL.

| | NAME OF CHILD | AGE | | SEX | PLACE AND DATE OF BIRTH | DATE APPLICATION WAS FILED | |
| | | Year | Month | | | | |

Record of Orphans, Half Orphans, Etc., on State Aid

Entries often include death date of parent(s) and year of arrival in California.

Typical page from Record of Orphans, Half-Orphans, Etc., on State Aid 1907-1910: City and County of San Francisco *(FHL film #1,412,658).*

Orphans of California and Children on Aid, 1883-1889, compiled by Lois A. Dove and privately published in three volumes in 1989, is based upon records of the Board of Examiners at the California State Archives. Both Sutro and CGS own copies of this publication. Despite its broader scope, there are many San Francisco entries. Typical entries include the child's name, age, birthplace (often exact), admission date (and dismissal if any) and some parental information. Orphan homes were licensed by the state, and presumably periodic reports were required. Those in search of additional orphan record abtracts or those from other years might inquire at the California State Archives.

Children living in institutions, not only orphanages but also maternity homes and correctional facilities, were individually enumerated in the censuses. Enumerations may have been recorded in the geographical district in which the facility was located or at the end of a voting ward or other political district. A number of these enumerations have been transcribed at *www.sfgenealogy.com*.

Many institutions underwent name changes over the years. Mount St. Joseph Orphanage opened in 1852 and continues today as Mt. St. Joseph–St. Elizabeth, although it now provides a broader range of services. Some early records may be available, as the 1906 fire did not reach the facility.[26] Very detailed records starting in 1872 from the Jewish orphanages, Pacific Hebrew Orphan Asylum and Eureka Benevolent Society, and from Homewood Terrace (which resulted from their merger), are contained in the archives of the Jewish Family and Children's Services, part of the Western Jewish History Collection at the Bancroft Library.[27]

Records from the Edgewood Orphanage, 1851-1958, are archived at SFPL.[28] Included are admissions and discharges, baptisms, some adoption information and indexed correspondence. SFPL also holds records from the Family Service Agency, 1869-2004, including placing-out (fostering) information covering the years 1900-1908 and foundling admissions back to 1869 (see p. 84).

SCHOOL RECORDS

Original school records likely contained student age, birthdate and parental names. At the primary and intermediate level within the public system, however, this information rarely has been preserved. San Francisco Unified School District records are archived at San Francisco Public Library. Surviving original, student records more often are from private schools, however, particularly at the post-secondary or graduate level. The California Historical Society holds some records for Lick Wilmerding, Lux and Girls' High School. From school yearbooks one can approximate a year of birth and perhaps find alumni notes. Some enrollment and graduation lists are posted at *sfgenealogy.com*.

Pre-earthquake graduate institutions surviving today include Hastings College of Law, which was founded in 1879 and exists today under that name, and Stanford School of Medicine, which had its roots in the Medical Department of the University of the Pacific from 1859-1864 and 1870 to 1882, and then changed its name to Cooper Medical College. The University of California School of Medicine began as Toland Medical College in 1864 and affiliated with the University of California in 1870. The University of San Francisco opened as St. Ignatius Academy in 1855; its records, and those of San Francisco State College, which opened in 1899, were lost in the earthquake and fire.

---

[26] Contact them at 100 Masonic Ave., San Francisco, CA 94118.

[27] In 2010 this collection was in the process of being moved. It should be available in 2011.

[28] Address: 101 – 15th Street, San Francisco, CA 94103.

HOSPITAL RECORDS

Some hospital records from the pre-earthquake years survive, and ledgers from some institutions are archived at SFPL. Summaries of hospital admissions and deaths appeared in some issues of the *Annual Municipal Report* (p. 59); several of these have been posted at *www.sfgenealogy.com*. For reconstructed records of the State Marine Hospital, once located on the grounds of the Presidio, see p. 27. Records for the much older Marine Hospital for the year 1852 were published by the Pomona Valley Genealogical Society in 1991. Old records of Mt. Zion Hospital and Medical Center are part of the Western Jewish History Collection at the Bancroft Library, where early records of Children's Hospital and the French Hospital Benevolent Society may also be found. Those for San Francisco General Hospital are at the Kalmanovitz Library at the University of California at San Francisco. Death records from Letterman Hospital at the Pesidio are discussed on p. 111.

OLD AGE HOMES AND POOR RECORDS

The San Francisco City and County Almshouse, built in 1867 to house the indigent sick, later became the Laguna Honda Home. Today as the Laguna Honda Hospital and Rehabilitation Center, located at 375 Laguna Honda Blvd., it is under the wing of the city Department of Public Health. Pre-World War II WPA county record inventories describe detailed patient records, most of which begin in 1913/1914.[29] Pre-earthquake records found include six to seven unindexed volumes beginning in 1897 titled "Register of Inmates," described as containing name, nativity, occupation, case number, disease and disposition. Several unindexed death registers beginning in 1895 detail name, age, sex, color, nativity, attending doctor and date, time and cause of death. It is not known, however, whether disclosure policies allow access.

In addition to her orphanage publication, Lois Dove privately published in 1989 two volumes of abstracts from California old-age institutional reports found in records of the State Board of Examiners at the state archives. *California Old Age Homes and County Hospitals, 1883-1889* is available at Sutro and on FHL film #1,597,643. San Francisco institutions include the San Francisco City and County Alms House, the Protestant Episcopal Old Ladies Home, the Lick Old Ladies Home, Old Ladies Home and Old Peoples Home. Typical entries include name, age, admission date, date of discharge or death, date of arrival in California, residence, birthplace (occasionally exact) and minimal previous history.

---

[29] See *Inventory of the County Archives of California,* prepared in May 1940 by the Northern California Historical Records Survey Project. The survey of San Francisco records is subtitled No. 39, Vol. II, and is available at SFPL and on FHL film #908,267.

OTHER INSTITUTIONAL RECORDS

Records of maternity homes and homes for wayward youths for the pre-earthquake years do not appear to have survived. Sheriff's records for some years are archived at SFPL; plans are to bring them online in the next few years. Researchers can access old records of San Quentin State Prison and Folsom State Prison at the California State Archives in Sacramento. San Quentin (1851-1939) and Folsom records (1880-1942) have been indexed by the Sacramento Genealogical Society; Folsom records for 1879-1903 have been abstracted with some detail by Lois Dove. These publications can be viewed at CGS or purchased through the Sacramento Genealogical Society.

BUSINESS, LABOR AND PROFESSIONAL RECORDS

It may be possible to locate archived records of a local business that still exists by contacting the firm. Usually it is photographs and historical vignettes rather than personnel records that survive. Some early businesses such as Wells Fargo maintain small company museums. Old personnel records for the Central Pacific Railroad and the Western Pacific do not appear to have survived, but both the Central Pacific and the Union Pacific Railroads have historical websites where short accounts and photographs of both trains and old schedules are posted. The data in the Southern Pacific Railroad personnel card file at the California State Railroad Museum in Sacramento (1900-1930) is limited to name, dates of employment, position or job assignment and record of former employment. It is available on FHL microfilms beginning with #1,728,001. Undertakers' records have been covered elsewhere in this guide (pp. 11-15).

The Labor Archives and Research Center, housed in the same building as Sutro Library, holds business and labor records, manuscripts, photographs and personal papers dating to the mid-1880s. Holdings are indexed at the Online Archive of California website, *http://www.oac.cdlib.org*.

The California State Archives in Sacramento holds biographical data relating to a number of professions, including dental examiners (beginning in 1885), medical examiners (from 1902) and the Pharmacy Board (from 1894). The American Medical Association allowed their numerous biographical files on deceased American physicians (1864-1970) to be filmed by the Family History Library. These records can be accessed by entering the first film number, #1,992,926 into the FHL online catalog. In 1993, prior to this filming, the American Medical Association published two volumes containing brief biographical sketches drawn from the Deceased Physician Masterfile. Titled *Directory of Deceased American Physicians 1804 – 1929* (Arthur W. Hafner, ed.; Chicago: American Medical Association, 1993), this publication is available at CGS.

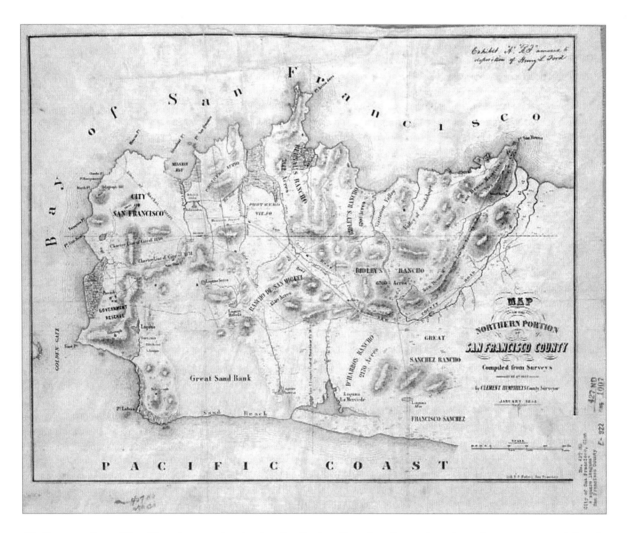

Northern portion of San Francisco peninsula showing the location of early ranchos, based upon a survey taken in 1852. North is to the left (courtesy of the Bancroft Library, University of California, Berkeley).

PRE-STATEHOOD SPANISH AND
MEXICAN RECORDS

*T*he San Francisco earthquake and fire of 1906 destroyed the Spanish Archives of California. Its holdings consisted of almost 300,000 documents that comprised most of the records of California under Spanish and Mexican rule, including journals, diaries, court proceedings, military records and mission reports. Land titles, secure in a safe, survived, and some alcalde records did as well. Duplicates existed for some records, archived abroad or in other parts of California or Washington, D.C.

From these scattered records and from publications written before 1906 and based upon the lost records, amateur historian Zoeth Skinner Eldredge compiled and published his comprehensive work, *The Beginnings of San Francisco from the Expedition of Anza, 1774 to the City Charter of April 15, 1850, with Biographical and Other Notes* (San Francisco, 1912, 2 vols.). This book can be found in its entirety online at *www.sfgenealogy.com*; SFPL has a copy; CGS has volume 2. Eldredge's original papers are in the Bancroft Library, University of California, Berkeley, with copies at the state library in Sacramento.

Eldredge and others extracted or pieced together from sources such as mission records and lists of soldiers at the Presidio early census enumerations called "padrones." Transcriptions of several padrones can be found at *www.sfgenealogy.com*, along with complete lists of sources. The earliest of these also includes biographies of and supplementary information for those in the Anza Expedition, which established the Presidio in 1776. Also online are a Presidio census for 1782, the combined Presidio/Mission census of 1790, and a census for 1842. Sources include, besides Eldredge:

- A transcription of the 1790 census in *Historical Society of Southern California Quarterly*, vol. 41, p. 386 (also on FHL film #1,036,747, item 6);
- William M. Mason, *The Census of 1790: A Demographic History of Colonial California* (Menlo Park, California: Ballena Press, 1998—copy at SFPL);

- Dorothy Gittinger Mutnick, *Some Alta California Pioneers and Descendants, 1776-1852*, 5 vols. (Lafayette, California: PastTime Publ., 1982—copies at Sutro, CGS and SFPL);
- Marie Northrop, *Spanish-Mexican Families of Early California: 1769-1850*, 3 vols. (vols. 1, New Orleans: Polyanthos, 1976; vols. 2 and 3, Burbank: Southern California Genealogical Society, 1984 and 2004)—all vols. at CGS, vols. 1 and 2 at SFPL, vol. 1 at Sutro);
- Thomas W. Temple, *Mission Abstracts* (on a CD-ROM publ. by Los Californianos; Mission Dolores only is on FHL film #944,282, item 3); and
- John W. Dwinelle, *The Colonial History of the City of San Francisco* (San Francisco: Towne & Bacon, 1867, addendum 25—at SFPL and CGS).

The 1782 Presidio census data includes name, rank, age, birth country and race. In 1790, name, age and origin are given; in some instances birth or death dates and women's maiden names that were found in supplementary sources are included. The 1842 compilation contains name, age, birthplace and occupation. Eldredge's population estimates for 1776 totaled sixty-two at the Presidio and the mission. Just prior to American occupation, the San Francisco population was still under 250.

Records of Spanish families can be found scattered in the works of Hubert Howe Bancroft, particularly in his seven-volume set titled *History of California* (San Francisco: The History Co., 1884-90), available in various editions at SFPL, Sutro and CGS. *The Annals of San Francisco, Containing a Summary of the History of California, and a Complete History of Its Great City: to Which Are Added, Biographical Memoirs of Some Prominent Citizens* by Frank Soule, John H. Gihon and James Nisbet (New York: D. Appleton, 1895; reprinted in 1966, by L. Osborne, Palo Alto) is available at SFPL, Sutro, the FHL and at *www.sfgenealogy.com*. Another good source is *Spanish-Mexican Families of Early California, 1769-1850*, by Marie Northrop, cited above.

Los Californianos, a heritage organization formed to preserve the heritage of early Hispanic Californians, maintains a website currently located at *www.loscalifornianos.org*. Genealogical information on many early families is available there and by writing.[30]

Records from Mission Dolores, including births, marriages and deaths, are described on p. 21, and surviving early land records under Spanish and Mexican occupation have been covered on pp. 64-66.

---

[30] Mailing address is PO Box 600522, San Diego, CA 92160-0522.

Diaries and First-Hand Accounts

*D*iaries and first–hand accounts, the genealogical gold we would like to find, may be squirreled away in attics or may have been given to an archive or library. People understandably find it difficult to part with such family treasures, and in some instances we can locate them only by identifying and contacting living members of descendant lines. Given their value in building a family history, the possibility of finding such accounts justifies efforts spent in their pursuit. The following suggests ways in which one might be able to locate original material that has made its way into library and archive collections.

NUCMC, WorldCat, Archive Finder and ArchiveGrid

From 1959 until 1986, manuscripts in an archive or collection that had been inventoried by the Library of Congress were cataloged in the printed volumes of the National Union Catalog of Manuscript Collections (NUCMC), found at large libraries. Until 1993, the catalog was produced annually in printed format, with indexes in each volume and periodic cumulative indexes. New entries created from 1986 to 1993 were made available both in printed form and online via RLIN (Research Libraries Information Network), the Research Library Group's electronic union catalog. Since 1993, free electronic access has been available at the NUCMC portion of the Library of Congress website, at *http://www.loc.gov/ coll/nucmc/*, via both RLIN (until 2007, when it ceased to exist) and via the Online Computer Library Center (OCLC) .

Only some listings in the two linked catalogs replicate pre-1986 NUCMC entries, so a thorough search must include the pre-1986 NUCMC paper editions if they can be found. Alternatively, two *subscription-based* cataloging programs that may be found at university and college libraries search all NUCMC entries and archival material submitted to other programs: ArchivesUSA (now renamed Archive *Finder*) and ArchiveGrid.

A no-charge, online NUCMC search (1986-present, via OCLC World Cat) is not particularly easy, but directions are included. Read them fully and carefully and include searches of both the RLG catalog and OCLC.

In 1988 Chadwyck-Healey published a two-volume set: *Index to Personal Names in the National Union Catalog of Manuscript Collections, 1959-1984*. In 1994 the company published in three volumes, *Index to Subjects and Corporate Names in the National Union Catalog of Manuscript Collections, 1959-1984*. The personal names volumes index not only personal names in collections, but also the names of those who donated them. They are available at both Bancroft and Doe libraries on the University of California at Berkeley campus and at the state library in Sacramento, but not in San Francisco.

LOCATING LOCAL REPOSITORIES WITH ARCHIVAL COLLECTIONS

The Archives of the City and County of San Francisco, accessed through the History Room at SFPL, receives pre-earthquake material on an ongoing basis. Many local libraries also hold archived material, including CGS. Check the *California Information File* (p. 143), special-category searches at Google and the Online Archive of California (OAC), accessible at *http://www.oac.cdlib.org*. The OAC site consists of descriptive summaries of holdings that have been cataloged at such institutions as the California State Archives, the California State Library, the California Historical Society, Bancroft Library, Stanford University, the Huntington Library, the Society of California Pioneers, and the Graduate Theological Union in Berkeley. A comprehensive search engine searches the site as a whole or the holdings of single institutions, covering not only the descriptive summaries, but also the names of the donors of each collection.

The "American Memory" collection of the Library of Congress, located at *http://memory.loc.gov/ammem/cbhtml/cbhome.html*, features "California as I Saw It, First-person Narratives of California's Early Years, 1849-1900." More than five hundred accounts written by pioneers, some of whom settled in San Francisco, are cited in J. S. Holliday's *The World Rushed In: The California Gold Rush Experience* (New York: Simon and Schuster, 1981). A smaller list of overland diaries is posted at the USGenWeb site for California, *http://www.cagenweb.com*.

The "Pioneer Index File" at the state library contains information supplied by "pioneers" (defined as those arriving before 1860) and their descendants. Descriptive cards to these files have recently become available online at *Ancestry.com*; fcomplete files are available for a fee from the state library.

Do not overlook the possibility that relevant information on an early San Francisco resident may lie in a distant library or archive. NARA, for example, catalogs archived material in the Archival Research Catalog (ARC), at *http://www.archives.gov/research/arc/*. Search for relevant biographical compilations and material left by family members residing in other counties or even other states.

ETHNIC RECORDS AND RESOURCES

*F*ew cities in the world have claimed as many differing nationalities amongst their populations for as long a time period as has San Francisco. According to government census figures covering the years 1850-1890, the foreign-born population in San Francisco ranged between 53.4 percent (1852) and 42.4 percent (1890). These are extraordinary numbers, for they do not reflect children born after their parents' arrival in this country. In 1880 the percentage of foreign-born San Franciscans was the highest of the ten largest cities in the country, surpassing even New York City. Many came to this country shortly before 1850 to escape political turmoil, epidemics or crop failures and, having had little time to form new roots, decided a better future was waiting in California, whether because of the Gold Rush or westward expansion in general.

The nativities of San Francisco school children in 1857 were reported in *Hutchings' California Magazine* (January 1858). Those numbers reveal that of the foreign-born students (16.7 percent of the school population), one-fourth were born in continental Europe and thus would be expected to have come from families where English was not the preferred language. The number born in Atlantic-bordering countries about equaled the number born in Pacific-bordering nations, particularly Australia, the birthplace of the greatest number. The large number of Australian-born children is perhaps attributable to the large mining industry in that country. Irish-born children, possibly children of parents who fled the potato-famine, constituted 7.45 percent of the school population in 1857, only half that of English-born children, but far greater when the relative populations of the two countries are taken into account. The Irish continued to come long after the Gold Rush, making up almost one-third of the city's population by the 1880s.

San Francisco's Black population was small, estimated to have been about two percent of the total population in the earliest years. Some Blacks had come as free men in California's Spanish and Mexican colonial days. California's status as a "free" state and, prior to that, a "free" acquisition did not necessarily confer equal rights upon these residents. Some indeed came as slaves during the Gold Rush and earlier; others arrived after escaping their owners in the South, seeking the freedom they felt would be available to them, and still others came west as free men, prepared to seek their fortunes alongside others in the gold fields. Nonetheless, the property rights of out-of-state slave owners were, from 1852 to 1855, respected in the courts, and arrested runaway slaves were returned to their owners. Free Blacks could not take advantage of free land, as homestead laws restricted those rights to white citizens having reached twenty-one, heading a household and never having borne arms against the United States. This remained the case until the turn of the century. Until 1863 Blacks and mulattos, along with Chinese, Mongolians and Indians, were not allowed to testify in criminal and civil cases involving white persons. In 1863 the restrictions against only Blacks and mulattos were lifted, and in 1870 citizenship rights were finally granted to those "of African descent." Other small, non-white minorities fared less well.

California eventually entered the union as a free state, but until that point, the rights of slave owners were respected. Occasionally manumissions took place. The 1849 manumission shown in part here was found in the records of the alcalde at San Francisco. Public Library.

The early history of Native Americans is tightly bound to the history and records of Mission Dolores, founded by the Franciscan fathers to bring Christianity to the natives. The missions were broken up in 1834 and the natives dispersed. Those who later remained in or came to live in Yerba Buena/San Francisco evidently were not sufficiently numerous or concentrated to form a visible and therefore effective minority. Affected by the same restrictions as those imposed upon Blacks, Native Americans were denied citizenship and the accompanying rights until 1924.

The Chinese, initially small in number, constituted an ever-growing presence. From 1860 through 1880 the Chinese population in San Francisco grew from a little under four percent to slightly over nine percent. This was a very important group in the history of the city, posing unique problems in and opportunities for genealogical research. The Chinese are separately discussed on pp. 132-134.

One of the best discussions of the various ethnic groups that comprised early California was written by Doris Marion Wright, "The Making of Cosmopolitan California: An Analysis of Immigration, 1848-1870," published in two parts in the *California Historical Quarterly* in December 1940 (vol. 19: 323-343) and March 1941 (vol. 20: 65-79)." Of the many statistics included is the rather startling change in the number of foreign-born over the decade 1850-1860. The 1850 census indicates that about 24% of Californians were not born in the United States, while in 1860, the percentage of foreign-born had grown to 61%.

CHURCH RECORDS

The non-English-speaking foreign-born, as might be expected, tended to settle in ethnic enclaves, where they established foreign-language-speaking churches. Churches with records documenting their births, marriages and deaths, if those records survived, probably were located close to the areas in which their congregations resided. Sadly, many immigrants settled just south of Market Street, a part of the city devastated by the earthquake and fire. Chinatown was another ethnic area with almost complete record loss--totally destroyed.

Among the Catholic churches with surviving records are St. Mary's (founded 1854, with many Chinese in its congregation), St. Boniface's (founded 1860--German), St. Peter's and St. Paul's (established 1884—Italian), Notre Dame (founded 1856--French), St. Anthony's (founded in 1893—German), and Nativity (established in 1902—Slavic).

Immigrants from Scandinavian countries and from what later became Germany usually attended Lutheran or Methodist churches, with the exception of Jewish immigrants. Surviving early synagogue records are discussed on p. 40. The earliest German-speaking church was First German Lutheran, which in 1866 became St. Mark's Evangelical Lutheran. St. Mark's exists today and retains records, although somewhat spotty, dating to 1860. St. Paulus Lutheran Church, also German-speaking, exists today. Most of its records were destroyed in a recent fire, but one register dating to 1867-1872 survived. Norwegian-speaking Lutherans founded Our Savior Lutheran in 1870 and Bethlehem Lutheran in 1901. The Evangelical Lutheran Church of America has filmed many of these records and the records of churches into which they merged (p. 34). Ebenezer (Swedish Evangelical Lutheran) was founded in 1882 by Swedish immigrants at 15th and Dolores; its records today are archived at the Swenson Swedish Immigration Research Center at Augustana College, Rock Island, Illinois (p. 34).

Records of most other foreign-language-speaking churches, as well as San Francisco's first African-American churches, Third Baptist (founded 1852) and A.M.E. Zion (African Methodist Episcopal, also founded in 1852), appear to have been lost. No church or temple records appear to have survived the complete destruction of Chinatown. Records of St. Nicholas (Greek Orthodox) Cathedral are known to have been destroyed in the earthquake and fire. Data on members of that church may possibly be found in the collections of the Center for Modern Greek Studies in the College of Humanities at San Francisco State University, where the long-term goal is to document the history of local Greek immigrants.

NEWSPAPERS

English-language newspapers were less widely read in ethnic communities, particularly among minority groups which had access to foreign-language newspapers (see also p. 45). Obituaries in foreign language newspapers, where they exist, can be rich in detail and may contain the deceased's town of birth. Most of these newspapers can be found in the Bancroft Library and Doe Memorial Library, at the University of California, Berkeley.

San Francisco's African-American community also had its own papers. The *Mirror of the Times* was published from 1857 to 1862, when it was succeeded by the weekly newspaper *The Pacific Appeal* (April 5, 1862 - June 12, 1880). This paper ceased publication for a period of two years midway into 1868, and not all issues from the other years survived. Issues of another weekly, *The Elevator*, have been filmed from April 7, 1865 through June 11, 1898. These films are held at SFPL, Doe Library, Bancroft Library and the California State Library in Sacramento. The Underground Railroad Digital Archives Project at the California State University at Sacramento has digitized films and other documents related to African-American life in early California.

CEMETERY RECORDS

Many ethnic groups had their own cemeteries, a number of which were encompassed within City Cemetery (also known as Golden Gate Cemetery). Some of these small enclosures represented Italian, German, French, Russian, Greco-Russian, Slavonic-Illyric, Japanese, Scandinavian and Chinese ethnic groups. Interments in the several Chinese cemeteries there constituted the greatest number of burials, although the burials were not necessarily permanent. In many instances the bones were later disinterred and returned to relatives in China.

There were a number of early Jewish cemeteries, the first of which was established in 1847. Remains from it were removed in 1861 to the twin cemeteries near Mission Dolores, Hills of Eternity and Home of Peace. Several smaller Jewish cemeteries were later formed as part of City Cemetery, including Beth Olam and Salem. Hills of Eternity and Home of Peace were moved to cemeteries of the same name in Colma in 1889, and removals from Salem Cemetery to "New" Salem Cemetery in Colma took place in 1891. Records for these cemeteries are discussed on p. 22. Yet another Jewish Cemetery, Eternal Home Cemetery, owned by Sinai Memorial Chapel Chevra Kadisha, was established in 1901 in Colma, but any records pre-dating the earthquake and fire have been lost.

Because many immigrant German residents belonged to the Independent Order of Odd Fellows (IOOF), they were frequently interred in that cemetery. The records are very detailed, but divided between CGS and Greenlawn Cemetery in Colma (pp. 24-5). Catholic burials other than those in City Cemetery generally took place in Calvary Cemetery near Lone Mountain. Most removals from Calvary went to Holy Cross Cemetery in Colma, where records are good (p. 24).

> *San Francisco's immigrant German residents, because many belonged to the IOOF, were often buried in Odd Fellows Cemetery. The original ledgers of this cemetery are split between Greenlawn Cemetery in Colma and CGS.*

ETHNIC COMPILATIONS

Occasionally members or descendants of San Francisco's early ethnic families have written large compilations, bringing together information from census enumerations, cemetery records, church records and family information. Ethnic social groups, such as Daughters of Norway or Dania, often published biographical material gathered from their membership. These compilations may not have been marketed broadly and are sometimes found only in the smaller libraries to which they were donated. Search for these in the online catalogs of SFPL and Sutro Library and catalogs of other local libraries. At SFPL many older books are located in the History Center stacks, so shelf browsing may not be productive.

Delilah L. Beasley's *The Negro Trail Blazers of California: A Compilation of Records from the California Archives in the Bancroft Library at the University of California* (Los Angeles: Times Mirror Printing and Binding House, 1919; reprinted in 1968 and 1997 by other publishers) contains photographs and biographies of many pioneer Black settlers and a comprehensive history of early legislation and court cases. A number of notable publications by Adam S. Enterovich contain burial and other genealogical information about Yugoslav

(Jugoslav) and Croatian immigrants. The Italian-American Association Archives comprise a specialized collection at SFPL. Carlos U. Lopez in *Chilenos in California* (San Francisco: R and E Research Associates, 1973) has extracted data for Chilean immigrants from the 1850, 1852 and 1860 census enumerations. This publication is particularly useful since the 1852 enumeration is difficult to read. CGS has in its collection Sophus Hartwick's hard-to-find Danish publication *Danske i California og California Historie*, 2 vols. (San Francisco: n.p., 1939), as well as most of the ethnic compilations mentioned above and some of the Spanish and Mexican sources mentioned on pp. 123-4.

ETHNIC MANUSCRIPTS AND ETHNIC STUDIES INSTITUTES

The Western Jewish History Collection at the Bancroft Library in Berkeley, in addition to archiving some original synagogue records, holds many letters, diaries and photographs of early San Francisco Jewish families. The Center for Modern Greek Studies at San Francisco State University has also been previously mentioned. Other institutes with ethnic collections that may include San Franciscans are the Balch Institute for Ethnic Studies, now part of the Historical Society of Pennsylvania in Philadelphia, and the Immigration History Research Center at the University of Minnesota in St. Paul. Locally, the Asian American Studies Collection at the University of California in Berkeley is outstanding. The Chinese Historical Society of America (965 Clay Street, San Francisco) holds manuscripts and personal papers, as well as oral history tapes. The African-American Historical and Cultural Society Library at 762 Fulton Street in San Francisco holds some manuscripts. As mentioned previously, the Underground Railroad Digital Archives Project at the California State University, Sacramento, has digitized documents relating to events in the African-American population in early California. Original manuscripts can also be located using the Online Archive of California, located at *http://www.oac.cdlib.org*.

THE SPECIAL CASE OF CHINESE IMMIGRANTS

The Gold Rush brought increasing numbers of Chinese to the state. It is estimated that by 1852 some twenty-five thousand Chinese immigrants were in California, most in the gold fields but some forming a small but growing service community in San Francisco. When gold fervor abated, they, along with newly arrived immigrants, were hired as farm laborers in the expanding agricultural central valley and then a few years later by the Central Pacific Railroad to lay the bed and dig tunnels for the western half of the transcontinental railroad.

Chinese laborers were willing to work hard and for lower wages than their American and European counterparts, which was not well received except by their employers. Discriminatory laws were passed and discriminatory taxes enforced, but Chinese laborers still could earn more in this country than in

China, and they continued to arrive. Following completion of the railroad in 1869, thousands of them were left jobless, homeless and often financially unable to return to China. Existing laws denied them naturalization until 1943, although children born here were considered citizens starting in 1868. Laws prevented all Chinese from testifying in court. During the nationwide depression of the 1870s, job competition with American workers increased racial tensions to an ugly level.

These factors culminated in the passage in 1882 of the Chinese Exclusion Act, barring Chinese laborers from entering the country over the next ten years. Exceptions were made for merchants, teachers, students and government officials. Nonetheless, in 1884 only 279 Chinese aliens were admitted, and in 1885, only twenty-two. The act had been tightened in 1884 and was tightened again in 1888, with the result that laborers already in this country were denied re-entry if they left. In 1892 the Exclusion Act was replaced by the Geary Act, which extended the ban, but which provided for residence certificates making re-entry possible for some. Resident laborers were allowed to travel abroad and return provided they had previously created a government file establishing their identity. Restrictions on entry and naturalization were not eased until 1943.

Enforcement of the act was initially turned over to the Customs Service and then in 1903 to the Bureau of Immigration. Many hopeful immigrants were driven to using fake papers, employing "paper" names of legitimate residents, both alive and deceased, in order to gain entry. The problem of identification was exacerbated by the destruction in 1906 of San Francisco birth and naturalization records. Prospective immigrants were relentlessly interrogated about minute details of their family relationships and history. The information that was collected in an effort to separate the "desirables" from the excluded resulted in an unparalleled accumulation of genealogical data for any immigrant ethnic group. Investigative case files were created not only for Chinese attempting to enter the country, but also for other Asian nationalities and even for American-born Chinese attempting to re-enter the country after traveling abroad.

Records created to implement the exclusion laws are in the custody of the National Archives; those relating to Asians arriving at or departing from San Francisco are at the NARA facility in San Bruno. Because they originated in three agencies, the documents for a given person are not centralized, but they are often cross-referenced. Most, but not all, of the record series are filmed. The formerly unnumbered holding, "Chinese Mortuary Records, 1870-1933," now is NARA microfilm #A4040. It consists of detailed Chinese decedent information extracted from city and state death records. An example is shown on p. 9. The project was ongoing before the earthquake and therefore also covers deaths in those periods up to 1905 for which records were lost. Compiled by the Department of Immigration, the ledgers created were consulted in order to help uncover identity theft. They have since become an important source for descendants researching their Chinese ancestry.

The NARA passenger list indexes and films (p. 90) can serve as an indicator as to whether a file might exist for a particular person. Searching was made easier with the creation of the "Early Arrivals Records Search" database (EARS). Created at the Haas School of Business at the University of California at Berkeley, EARS is available online at *http://casefiles.berkeley.edu*. It provides a case file number and location that should lead to the original textual records at NARA in San Bruno. The original records may include name, date and place of birth, occupation, residence, physical appearance, names and relationships of other family members, records of proceedings and references to file numbers of related cases. Case files may occasionally run over fifty pages in length. Be aware that the name and history presented in these documents may document instead the name and history belonging to an entirely different person used to gain illegal entry. A more complete description of various record types and search techniques can be found at several NARA websites. Search on the terms "Chinese Exclusion" together with "National Archives" or "EARS."

Some information on Chinese residents who arrived before implementation of the Exclusion Act may come from the files if residents later traveled abroad or brought in family members. Most information on early residents, however, will be found in sources described elsewhere in this guide.

Immigrants during the pre-earthquake years frequently retained ethnic naming patterns, which can complicate the search for a particular individual. All Chinese had a surname ("family name") which usually came first, followed by a given name. However, some documents reverse the order in order to conform to English usage. Women usually took a third name upon marriage, provided they used a given name before marriage. The use of nicknames can further confuse the situation. Many facets of Chinese research are discussed in *China Connection: Finding Ancestral Roots for Chinese in America* by Jeanie W. Chooey Low (first published in 1993 in San Francisco by JWC Low Co. with several subsequent revisions). This guide can be found at SFPL, Sutro and CGS.

Determining Immigrant Origins

Determining ethnic origins generally entails locating as many documents left by an immigrant as possible. The Odd Fellows Cemetery records are particularly useful in untangling German origins. Another set of documents created toward the end of World War I also may be of use. Non-naturalized residents over fourteen who were natives or former citizens of the German Empire were required to register as "alien enemies." SFPL holds those forms for San Francisco residents who registered, but it is evident that compliance was not complete. Each registration affidavit consists of four pages of detail, including names and birthplaces of parents, children and siblings and naturalization information. Additional sources are discussed on pp. 183-185.

UNITED STATES OF AMERICA

Department of Justice

REGISTRATION AFFIDAVIT OF ALIEN ENEMY

The registration affidavit must be filled in and sworn to in triplicate and accompanied by four unmounted photographs of the registrant, not larger than 3 by 3 inches in size, on thin paper with light background. All four photographs should be signed by registrant across the face of the photograph so as not to obscure the face, if registrant is able to write. If registrant is unable to write, he must make his mark in the signature space and affix his left thumb print in the space indicated for the same opposite the signature space.

The affidavit need not be filled out before, but must be signed and sworn to before, a registration officer, who will fill in the description and take the finger prints of the registrant. All registration officers are authorized to administer the oath hereto to persons registering as alien enemies.

I, _David Deubler_ hereby register as an alien enemy

(Here insert name of registrant.)

at _Police District No. San Francisco California_ and make the following statements

(Place where affidavit signed and oath administered.)

and answers under oath:

1. Name _David Deubler_ All other names at any time used _____

(Here insert any other names used by registrant.)

2. Present residence _63 Moss Street City_

(Street and number, city, town, county, State, and, if apartment house or tenement, the number of apartment or tenement.)

3. Length of residence at the foregoing place _since about 10 Dezember 1914_

(Here state date on which applicant began living at his present residence.)

4. All other places of residence since January 1, 1914 _____

(Here give particulars as to each of such places of residence.)

5. Born in _Langenau (Württemberg) Germany_ on _4 Mai 1883_

(Give city or town, province, and country of birth.)   (Give date of birth.)

6. Since January 1, 1914, employed by:

Name of place.	Date.	Occupation.	Name of employer.
North Alaska Salmon Co.	Mai to Sept 1915	Laborer	North Alaska Salmon Co.
Peerless Motor Dray Co	Dez 1915 - Jan 1917	Laborer	Peerless Motor Dray Co.
Scott & Bowne	1917	Laborer	Scott & Bowne
Natoma Warehouse Co	1918	Laborer	Natoma Warehouse Co.

7. I arrived in the United States _6. Dezember 1914_ at the port of _San Franzisko_

(Date.)   (State port.)

on ship _Phöbus_ and applied for entry under the name of _David Deubler_

(State name.)   (State name under which entry was made.)

8. (a) Name of father _David Deubler_ Living _jes_

(Answer "Yes" or "No.")

Residence of father, if living _Langenau (Württemberg) Germany_

(b) Name of mother _Barbara Deubler_ Living _No_

(Answer "Yes" or "No.")

Residence of mother, if living _____

(right margin, vertical text:) Surname **Deubler** (To be filled in by registration officer.) Given names **David** Card issued? Yes. G

Page from typical 1918 alien registration document. Note details such as place of birth and immigration data (San Francisco Public Library archives).

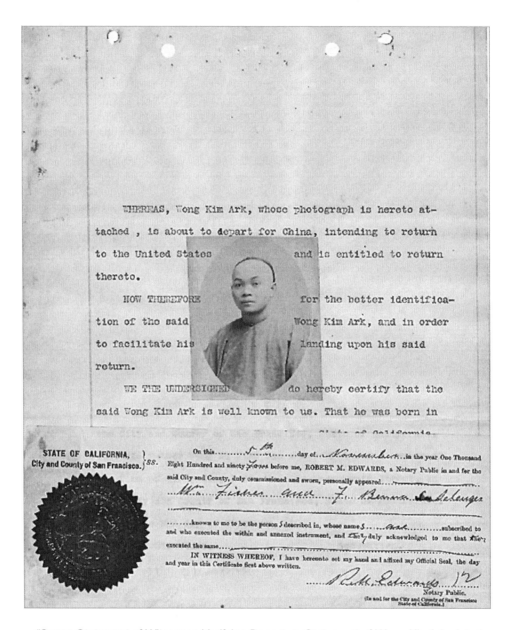

WHEREAS, Wong Kim Ark, whose photograph is hereto attached , is about to depart for China, intending to return to the United States   and is entitled to return thereto.

NOW THEREFORE   for the better identification of the said   Wong Kim Ark, and in order to facilitate his   landing upon his said return.

WE THE UNDERSIGNED   do hereby certify that the said Wong Kim Ark is well known to us. That he was born in

STATE OF CALIFORNIA,
City and County of San Francisco. } ss.

On this ....5th......... day of ....November.. in the year One Thousand Eight Hundred and ninety ....four.. before me, ROBERT M. EDWARDS, a Notary Public in and for the said City and County, duly commissioned and sworn, personally appeared...........

...........known to me to be the person s described in, whose name s .... subscribed to and who executed the within and annexed instrument, and .... duly acknowledged to me that ..... executed the same....

IN WITNESS WHEREOF, I have hereunto set my hand and affixed my Official Seal, the day and year in this Certificate first above written.

Notary Public.
(In and for the City and County of San Francisco State of California.)

"Sworn Statement of Witnesses Verifying Departure Statement of Wong Kip Ark, dated November 2, 1894"; File Number 12017/42223; Return Certificate Application Case Files of Chinese Departing ("12017 Series"), 1912-44; San Francisco District Office; Records of the Immigration and Naturalization Service, RG 85; National Archives– San Francisco (in San Bruno).

PART II

CONTINUING THE SEARCH: ADDITIONAL RESOURCES

"A reliable analysis cannot be made from partial evidence. Any pertinent record or collection or repository that goes unconsulted is a silent bomb waiting to explode our premature theories."

— Elizabeth Shown Mills
in *Evidence: Citation & Analysis for the Family Historian*

688   PIONEER REGISTER AND INDEX.

ii. 458. Agate, scientist attaché of the U. S. ex. exped. in '41. iv. 243. Agazini (Flaminio), '25, mr of the transport *Morelos*. iii. 148. Agnew (Hugh) 1847. Co. H, N. Y. Vol. (v. 499). Agredo, doubtful name of a school-boy at Mont. '15–20. ii. 429. Agricia (José), grantee of the Laureles rancho in '44. iv. 655. Aguado (Ignacio), Mex. lieut of the batallon fijo in '42–5. iv. 289. Aguiar (Francisco), soldier of 1769 et seq.; sergt at S. Diego in 1777. i. 314, 732.

Águila (José), Mex. settler at S. F. in 1791–1800. i. 716; munic. elector at S. F. in 1827. ii. 592. From '28 José Águila, or José M. Aguiiar (between which names there is evident confusion), was a somewhat prominent citizen of Mont. In '31–34 he was síndico; in '32–3 regidor and com. de policía. iii. 672–3; in '33 vocal of the diputacion. iii. 246; in '36 admin. at Soledad. iii. 690–1; in '38–9 clerk to admin. of S. Antonio. iii. 687–8; and in '44 grantee of the Cañada de Nogales rancho. iv. 634. In a Mont. padron of '36 José Águila is described as a painter, 50 years of age, native of Celaya, married to María Fran. García, a native of Mont., aged 37. Águila (Felipe), land near Mont. in' 35. iii. 678. A. (Joaquin), claimant for land at Sta Inés in '47. A. (Lugardo), resid. of S. Gabriel in '46. A. (Ramon), soldier of S. F. in '37–43. iv. 667. See list i. 732.

Aguilar (Blas), son of Rosario A., born at S. Diego about 1808. In '31 majordomo of S. D. mission, and in '34 at Temécula. Lived in '38–43 at the Palomares rancho, Los Ang. Co. In '41 got land at S. Juan Cap., where in '46 he was living at the age of 38 with his wife Antonia Gutierrez, aged 29. *Padron;* where he was alcalde in '48, and where he still lived in '76. See mention in ii. 443, 550; iii. 620; iv. 626; v. 624. An Aguilar is ment. as one of Bouchard's men in '18. ii. 232. A. (Antonio), soldier at S. F. '19–23; resid. of Los Ang. in '38, murdered in '42. iii. 564–5; iv. 632. A. (Casildo), trader at Los Ang., age 26, in '39; juez de aguas in '46. iv. 625; claimant for La Ciénega. A. (Cristóbal), resid. of Los Ang., age 24, from '38, when he was alcalde suplente; in '44–5, regidor. iii. 636; iv. 633.

Aguilar (Francisco Javier), soldier of the Loreto co., who served in the exped. of 1769 et seq. to S. Diego and Mont., but never came to live in Cal. A sergt from 1795; in command at C. S. Lúcas of a militia co. 1795–1800. A. (Gabino), at San Juan Cap. in '46, age 30, with his wife María Ant. Sesena and 6 children. *Padron.* A. (Ignacio), said to have fired the gun at Mervine's defeat '46. v. 319. A. (José M.), settler at Los Ang. fr. '14; regidor '21, '25–6; in trouble with Gov. Victoria in '31. In the padron of '39 he is noted as a bricklayer, age 54. ii. 349, 359, 559–60; iii. 196. (See also Águila, José.) A. (Macedonio), resid. of Los Ang. in '39, age 30; juez de campo in '43–5. iv. 632–4. A. (Martin), Span. com. of one of Vizcaino's explor. vessels in 1602–3. i. 98, 104, 242. A. (Ramon), killed by the Ind. in '46. v. 617.

Aguilar (Rosario), corporal of the escolta at S. Diego and S. Luis Rey missions from shortly after 1800. Lived at S. Diego fr. about '30, being majordomo of the mission in '38, and getting a grant of the Paguai rancho—which he is said to have refused—in '39. In '41 he was juez de paz at S. D., but obtained land at S. Juan Cap., where he was juez in '43–4, and where he died about '45. ii. 546; iii. 612, 619, 620–3, 626–7. His daughter married José Ant. Serrano. A. (Santiago), Mex. sergt, age 22, at Mont. in '36. In charge of the printing-office, and took part in the revolt against Alvarado, '37. iii. 470, 523–5. A. (Simon), executed at Mont. '31. iii. 190–1, 669, 673, 679.

Aguirre (José Antonio), 1834, Span. Basque, born about 1793; a wealthy trader at Guaymas, when in '33–4 he engaged in the Cal. trade, owning several vessels, and visiting Cal. frequently. From about '38 he made Sta B. his home, marrying María del Rosario, a daughter of José Ant. Estudillo, in '42. His second wife was a sister of the first. Grantee of the Tejon rancho in '43, and his wife of S. Jacinto Viejo y Nuevo in '46. On account of his great size he was sometimes nicknamed Aguirron; of fine presence, affable in manner, and well liked by all. An excellent type of the old-time Spanish merchant, keeping aloof for the most part from smuggling and politics, though often employed by the government. Still a resident of Sta B. after 1854. Ment. in iii. 620, 637, 659, 660, 727; iv. 12, 61, 100, 104, 332, 621, 635; v. 587,

Entries in Hubert Howe Bancroft's Pioneer Register and Index, *originally published at the end of volumes 2 and 3 of his series* History of California *(comprising volumes 19 and 20 of his collected works, 1885 and 1886).*

Biographical and Historical Publications

*A*n attempt should be made to verify information found in compilations such as local histories, family histories and biographical compendiums. These publication types often do not include citations, and errors are inevitable whenever information is copied and recopied from many sources. Biographical compendiums are rarely indexed for every name, if they are indexed at all, but online digitizations if they can be found, may be searched and names located, speeding up a once tedious task.

Biographical compilations can be located in many online library catalogs, most of which permit searching by subject or keyword. In those of SFPL, Sutro Library and CGS, for example, enter a surname in the search box under keyword, or "biographies, California" under subject matter. Alternatively, enter a particular profession or occupation under subject matter or possibly "pioneers" as a keyword. In the online FHL catalog perform a "place" search entering "San Francisco," and explore the topics under both "San Francisco" (the county) and "San Francisco, San Francisco" (the city). Manuscripts, such as family histories prepared from multiple sources, can be accessed in this catalog by performing a "surname" search. Some biographical compilations that are harder to find, such as directories of university graduates, contain useful information. The University of California, for example, published early directories of graduates in 1905, 1911 and 1916, containing matriculation information, post-graduation occupation and date of death. Unpublished or more obscure manuscripts such as family histories possibly can be located using the archival search engine Online Archive of California or Google, Google Scholar and Google Books.

Hubert Howe Bancroft included many capsule biographies as well as ancillary genealogical information in his seven-volume work *History of California*. Most volumes can be found at Sutro Library, SFPL, CGS and on FHL films #982,473 (items 1-5) and #1,321,070 (item 4). This monumental work was indexed by the Zamorano Club as *The Zamorano Index to the History of California by Hubert*

Howe Bancroft (Los Angeles: University of Southern California, 1985) available at both Sutro and SFPL. Over the years Bancroft collected names and genealogical information for pre-1800 California residents and intermittently published lists. *California Pioneer Register and Index, 1542-1848: Including Inhabitants of California, 1769-1800, and List of Pioneers* (Baltimore: Regional Publishing Co., 1964) is probably the most complete compilation. Copies can be found at SFPL, Sutro and CGS and online at *www.sfgenealogy.com* and at Nancy Melton's Rootsweb site, *http://freepages.genealogy.rootsweb.ancestry.com/~npmelton/state.html*. Bancroft's "List of Inhabitants" and "List of Pioneers" were compiled from volume 1 and consist primarily of males for whom name, occupation and time frame are provided. The portion titled "Pioneer Register and Index" was compiled from names appearing in volumes 2-5 and consists of name, year arrived, a very brief description and a reference to volume and page in *History of California*.

Another useful compilation of California pioneer arrivals, *Argonauts of California, Being the Reminiscences of Scenes and Incidents That Occurred in California in Early Mining Days*, was published by Charles W. Haskins in 1890. The last 141 pages of his book consist of a compiled list of the "Names of Pioneers Who Came by Land and Sea to California in 1849." These pages contain data on 27,000 people who arrived in California by the end of 1849, arranged not as one, but in a series of alphabetized lists according to their general source—pioneer organizations, mining company membership lists, and names evidently extracted from passenger lists but without further documentation. Information is often fairly minimal. Many years later Libera Martina Spinazze, under the auspices of the Society of California Pioneers, prepared a comprehensive index to Haskins's publication, which was copied by DAR volunteers and published by Polyanthos in 1975. Both the original and the index are available on FHL films #1,033,667 (the book) and #928,163 (the index) and microfiche series #6051188 (book) and #6051192 (index). Many libraries have copies of the index. Copies of the original text (book or film of book) plus the index can be found at Sutro, SFPL and CGS. The original Haskins publication is online at *Ancestry.com* and at Nancy Melton's Rootsweb site (see above).

A card file at the state library known as "Pioneer Card Records" capsulizes the content of files holding information submitted by a large number of pioneers or their descendants. Files may include date and place of marriage, previous residences, parents' names and even maiden name of the mother. Digitizations of the card file have recently been placed online at *Ancestry.com*.

Biographical material about pioneers has appeared in various publications over the years. One of the more scholarly of these is the *California Historical Society Quarterly*. Indexes to material appearing over the years 1922-1978 were published by the society in two volumes (1965 and 1977). Both indexes, along with full runs of the periodical, can be found at SFPL and CGS. Articles also

appeared over the years in the magazine *The Grizzly Bear.* Many of the names
from early articles were indexed in 1917 by Lois B. Benton. Her index is at the
Bancroft Library. Referenced issues can be found at SFPL.

Many early immigrants stayed only briefly in San Francisco before moving
on to settle more outlying areas. Information possibly can be found in local,
county and regional histories, many of which have been indexed as part of the
California Pioneer Project hosted by the California portion of USGenweb (*http://
cagenweb.com*). This project covers pioneers who arrived before 1880 and provides
citations to secondary sources where additional information can be found, as
well as contacts for those who have been researching some of the names. A
similar project indexing sources where information on pioneers can be found
was begun in 1987 by Richard Nelson, later joined by Diana Whitworth. It now
consists of twelve volumes, all titled *Goin' West, 1830-1880: A Record of Some Who
Went West.* All are available on fiche or films from the FHL (access by entering
fiche #6126183 or film #1,698,278 in the FHL online catalog). Sutro Library has
volumes 1-8 and 12. How many entries represent San Francisco residents is not
known.

The following indexed sources contain biographies of San Francisco
residents, generally successful businessmen or people otherwise socially
prominent: *History of the San Francisco Bay Region* by Bailey Millard (three
volumes plus a supplement, published by the American Historical Society,
Chicago, 1924, separate index prepared in 1999 by Wayne Hasemeier, Modesto
Genealogical Society); *The Bay of San Francisco: The Metropolis of the Pacific Coast
and Its Suburban Cities: A History,* 2 vols. (Chicago: Lewis Publishing Co., 1892);
*The Builders of a Great City: San Francisco's Representative Men, the City, Its History
and Commerce,* 2 vols. (San Francisco: Journal of Commerce Publishing Co., 1891);
and *The History of San Francisco,* 3 vols. by Lewis Francis Byington (San Francisco:
S. J. Clarke, Publ., 1931). All are available at SFPL and on FHL microfilm; several
are available at Sutro and CGS and as digitizations online.

In the case of stubborn lineage problems, success may come from casting
a wider net and following descendant lines of collateral relatives and even the
lines of friends, neighbors and business associates. Two publications index
biographies in histories of other California counties: J. Carlyle Parker, *An Index to
the Biographies in 19th Century California County Histories* (Detroit: Gale Research,
1979) and Barbara Ross Close, *California Surname Index: Biographies from Selected
Histories* (Oakland: California Genealogical Society, 2000). Both publications may
be found at SFPL, CGS and Sutro.

> *In the case of
> resistant lineage
> problems, the
> researcher
> may need to
> cast a wider
> net, collecting
> the records of
> descendant
> lines of collateral
> relatives and
> relatives by
> marriage, and
> even those of the
> descendants of
> friends, neighbors
> and business
> associates.*

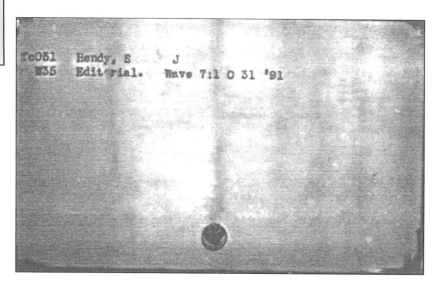

THE ∴ WAVE

Vol. VII. No. 26.   San Francisco, October 31, 1891.   10 Cents

The Wave

A SOCIETY, LITERARY AND POLITICAL JOURNAL,

Is published every Saturday by the proprietors at 26 and 28 O'Farrell street, San Francisco.

Subscription, $4 per year, $2 six months, $1 three months. Foreign subscriptions (countries in postal union) $5 per year. Sample copies free on application. The trade is supplied by the SAN FRANCISCO NEWS CO., 210 Post street; East of the Rocky Mountains by the AMERICAN NEWS CO., New York. Eastern applications for advertising rates should be made direct to the New York manager, MR. E. KATZ, 230 Temple Court, New York City.

THE WAVE is kept on file at THE AMERICAN EXCHANGE, 15 King William street, London, and 17 Avenue de'l Opera, Paris; BRENTANO'S, 5 Union Square, New York, and 206 Wabash avenue, Chicago.

For advertising rates and all other matters pertaining to the business of the paper, address Nos. 26 and 28 O'Farrell street, San Francisco.

J. F. BOURKE, Business Manager.

Entered at the Francisco Post Office as second-class matter, by COSGRAVE & HUME.

SAN FRANCISCO, OCTOBER 31, 1891.

"THE WAVE'S" PORTRAIT ALBUM.

Timothy Hopkins, whose rather handsome face

all occurred came out in the Courts, but it's a long-tangled tale, not worth repeating. However, Steen shed, the luck seemed to turn for Hendy. The firm began to make money. Some of the mining schemes panned out. Hendy prospered. Steen, on the contrary, lost ground. Then he brought suit against his former partner, claiming that large sums were taken out of the business, that in the dissolution he had not fared fairly. The legal contest lasted five or six years, and the verdict was for the plaintiff. Mr. Hendy appealed the case, and a final decision is now awaited.

* * *

If the tribunal of last resort considers the findings of the lower Court correct, there will have to be paid to E. F. Steen a sum of money so large that the contemplation of the possibility, it is said among iron men, hastened the dissolution of S. J. Hendy. Between the two there existed the bitterest antagonism. The legal contest was fiercely fought. Time and again Steen swore he would never let up on his old partner until he had driven him to his grave. Now Mr. Hendy is dead.

* * *

The fortune of the late Judge O. C. Pratt is variously estimated. He was a man of unusual financial ability and considerable penetration, and his life has been devoted to amassing dollars. The most conspicuous over a million dollars. After his retirement from the bench he traveled all over Europe, spending quite a long time abroad. For years he lived on the corner of Sutter and Jones Streets, in a handsome mansion which is now being converted into a boarding-house. Among his most recent acquirements was the residence on California Street, where he died. Judge Pratt was married three times. His first wife died. His second matrimonial venture was a failure, that is, he obtained a divorce, and married Mrs. Jones, adopting her two daughters, who are now Mrs. Dr. Keeney and Mrs. Harding. A daughter by his second marriage is Mrs. Goodspeed.

* * *

THE LOCAL DEMOCRACY is saved. That will be startling information to a number of people who looked anxiously for a fight over the payment of the bills of the Eastern statesmen who came hither a few weeks ago to organize clubs and put the party of principle on its feet in California. The expenses of the fine gentlemen, who did little but cause dissention in the ranks, amounted to nearly $1000 for *two* days. Of course the altitude of that figure was not reached by personal expenditure; halls were rented, eloquence was bought, and carriages were engaged, but I must do the Easterners the justice of saying that they knew the difference between terrapin and crab.

fc051   Hendy, S   J
W35   Editorial.   Wave 7:1 O 31 '91

Card from California Information File *(bottom) and the referenced article (top) in the holdings of the state library.*

The *California Information File*

*T*he *California Information File* is an enormous card file prepared by State Library librarians and researchers that indexes names and information dating from the 1840s, gleaned from early California newspapers, periodicals, biographies, histories, manuscript collections and pioneer records, all of which are available at the California State Library. The file as it existed in 1986 was microfiched; entries since that time have been entered in an electronic file formerly available only at the state library in Sacramento. In 2010 the electronic index was made available at the library website, *http://www.library.ca.gov/calhist/ calinfofilell.html*. The fiche collection, representing over 721,000 cards and about 1.4 million citations, must still be examined separately. It is available at Sutro, SFPL, CGS and many city, county and university libraries. There is also a set at the FHL, but it does not circulate to individual Family History Centers. It is up to the individual researcher to locate and obtain copies of the indexed material. More than half the entries are personal names, but one should search the subject categories creatively. Examples of subject categories are "Divorce," "Mining" and "Artists."

This periodical was published from January 1854 through December 1855. Copies are available at SFPL. Original depositions (usually in Spanish) are available on FHL microfilm, with copies at SFPL.

Before Commissioner ROBERT A. THOMPSON.

"My name is Henry L. Ford; my age, thirty years; and residence, Colusi County, California; I have resided in California since the 11th of September, 1842. In 1843, I knew nearly all the persons who resided in San Francisco at that time. In March, 1844, I was riding from San Francisco to the Mission Dolores, in company with Capt. Hinckley, at that time Alcalde of San Francisco, and in the course of the conversation he stated to me, that the pueblo line commenced at a point of rocks in the west, beyond the Presidio, and ran over in a direct line, crossing Mission Creek near its mouth, to a point of rocks or boulders, at a place known, at that time, as the 'Potrero.' Capt. Hinckley died in 1846; he was regarded as a very intelligent man; I supposed him to be about forty years of age. I had a conversation with Francisco Guerrero, who died in June or July, 1851. A short time before his death, he was showing me a piece of land on the north side of Missouri Creek, which he stated had been granted him by the Alcalde of the pueblo of San Francisco; he was standing on the south side of the creek at the time, and he stated, that the land on that side belonged to the Mission, and on the other to San Francisco; he also pointed out to me the way the line ran between the Mission and the pueblo, and where it would strike the bay which was very near the point formerly shown me by Hinckley; the place pointed out to me by Capt. Hinckley, was just below the juncture of the main creek with another, coming in on the south side.

Question.—Look on the map, marked A, and with the initials, R T, herewith filed, purporting to be a map of the northern portion of the county of San Francisco, and state, if you can identify on said map the point described in your last answer.

Answer.—I would cross near where the letter R occurs in the words, 'Mission Creek,' which is identified by a small cross on said map; this place was called 'Yerba Buena,' when I knew it, from 1842 to 1846; it was generally called 'San Francisco,' by the Americans and English; the people of the country generally called it 'Yerba Buena;' the Mission was called the 'Mission Dolores.' I believe Francisco Guerrero was Alcalde or Justice of the Peace of this jurisdiction before I came here; during the time that I knew him, he resided part of the time at the Mission and part of the time at his ranch on the coast; the piece of ground which Guerrero pointed out to me in 1851 as having been granted to him by an Alcalde of San Francisco, he stated to me, was four hundred varas; I think I could point the land out if I was at the Mission; Mr. Hinckley lived in this place; the precise spot, as near as I can recollect, would be between Clay and Sacramento streets, and between Montgomery and Kearny; Jack Fuller lived between Sacramento and California streets, and between Montgomery and Kearny; in 1845, a Frenchman built a house in what is now known as 'Happy Valley'; I do not know whether he owned the land; I know of no other this side of the Mission.   HENRY L. FORD."

Translation of original depositions taken in connection with court cases appealing for recognition of pre-statehood alcalde land grants (from Pioneer Monthly Magazine, *April 1854, p. 199).*

Records of Pioneer and Other Lineage Societies

*T*o gain membership in a lineage society, one must submit documentation showing descent from a qualifying ancestor appropriate to that particular society. If a San Francisco ancestor belonged to such an organization, there are or once existed application papers bearing the required documentation. The lineage, however, may or may not be the line of interest to the researcher. Step one is to determine if the person being researched or a relative might have belonged to a lineage-based organization. Clues to this may come from an obituary, from a membership pin among family memorabilia or from publications that occasionally can be found in libraries. Obituaries are particularly useful; once a death date has been determined, every newspaper that may have carried an obituary should be examined.

For many societies, membership directories containing brief lineages without citations are available at local libraries or on film through the FHL. Some of these include the 1917 register of California Mayflower descendants (FHL film #1,321,004); a 1902 book roster (at SFPL) and a filmed 1916 roster (FHL film #824,082, item 14) of California members of Sons of the American Revolution; lineage books of members of the California Society of the Order of Founders and Patriots of America (at both Sutro and CGS); lineage books of members of the California branch of the National Society of Colonial Dames and of the California State Society of the Daughters of 1812 (both at Sutro); and DAR publications, which are discussed in a separate section below. Most of these organizations will provide copies of application papers. One particularly interesting but little known source, the original enrollment ledger of the Territorial Pioneers of California, is at the state library in Sacramento and is discussed on pp. 148-149. Entries in this ledger, transcribed by Jim Faulkinbury, are available at CGS.

Once membership has been determined, the next step should be to determine if membership applications have been retained by the organization and will be made available to researchers. Several sources can provide a national address to contact: the *Hereditary Society Blue Book* (1992 and 1994 editions at Sutro Library), *The Source: A Guidebook of American Genealogy* (by Loretto Szucs and Sandra Luebking, available in most genealogical collections; 2006 edition at CGS) and, of course, the Internet. Documentation accompanying membership applications may or may not have been returned to the applicant. Information about the most recent generations, which are the ones of immediate interest here, is generally more reliable than information about earlier parts of a lineage.

California No. 95   General No. 8587

BETHUEL MERRITT NEWCOMB
Berkeley, California

STEPHEN HOPKINS, died Plymouth, Mass., between 6 June and 17 July, 1644.

GYLES HOPKINS, died Eastham, Mass., before 16 April, 1690; married 9 October, 1639, to CATHERINE WHELDON, died after 5 March, 1688-9.

DEBORAH HOPKINS, married Eastham, Mass., 27 July, 1668, to JOSIAH COOK.

ELIZABETH COOK, born Eastham, Mass., June, 1674; married October, 1698, to THOMAS NEWCOMB, died after 1722.

THOMAS NEWCOMB, born Eastham, Mass., 13 August, 1697, died after 1761; married (1) HEPZIBAH ————, died before 31 May, 1732.

SILAS NEWCOMB, born Provincetown, Mass., 19 April, 1725; married 5 August, 1748, to SUSANNAH KILBOURNE.

SILAS NEWCOMB, born Provincetown, Mass., 16 December, 1761, died Hingham, Mass., 13 May, 1848; married, about 1782, to AZUBAH CROWELL.

WILLIAM NEWCOMB, died Burnham, Maine, 25 August, 1850; married Warren, Maine, 10 April, 1815, to ELIZABETH SIDENS-PARKER, born Thomaston, Maine, 25 August, 1798, died Milford, Maine, 18 September, 1866.

JEDIDIAH NEWCOMB, born Thomaston, Maine, 30 January, 1820, died Yankee Jim, California, 2 July, 1852; married Burnham, Maine, 1 March, 1846, to DEBORAH CHARLOTTE SHAW, born Franklin County, Maine, 26 February, 1826, died Oat Hill, California, 6 September, 1906.

BETHUEL MERRITT NEWCOMB, born Burnham, Maine; married Belfast, Maine, to ANNIE SARAH HARKNESS, born Belfast, Maine.

Capsule ancestral line in Register of the Society of Mayflower Descendants in the State of California, *vol. 1, 1917 (California Genealogical Society Library).*

DAUGHTERS (OR SONS) OF THE AMERICAN REVOLUTION

Member applications documenting lineage are retained at the national headquarters of these two organizations. There is a charge for copies of a file. An application form for the papers of a present or deceased member can be downloaded at the DAR website, where instructions can be found (see more following), but the process with the SAR is not easily fathomed. Summaries of lineages were published periodically over the years and can be found at large libraries; *Ancestry.com* has made DAR lineages available online to subscribers.

California DAR members over the years have submitted information on ancestors who were California pioneers, many of whom resided in San Francisco. These submissions were published in several series starting in 1928 and eventually totaled twenty-eight volumes. Usually titled *Unpublished Records of the Families of California Pioneers* or something very similar, volumes 1-19 and volume 28 are at Sutro; all twenty-eight volumes are available at the California State Library in Sacramento. The series is also available on FHL microfilm beginning with film #844,436. An index to records in volumes 1-27 is in volume 28; another index published by Robert L. Davignon is available on FHL film #1,421,606 (item 7), and yet another, published in 1988 by the Solano County Genealogical Society, is shelved at Sutro Library.

The DAR extraction and abstraction program has been very comprehensive over many years. Many of their publications available locally have been mentioned elsewhere in this guide, but the numerous Bible records that have been collected from members have not. Whereas formerly, locating a Bible record, cemetery or other type of record was more or less a hit and (usually) miss operation, now the many, many records of the Genealogical Records Collection (GRC) have been electronically indexed and placed on the DAR Library website. The master page of this website is located at *http://www.dar.org/library/*. Clicking on "Online Research" will bring up a number of options. Many of the volumes have been renumbered. Thus, a reference appearing in the index often does not correspond to a volume number of a publication that may have been purchased years ago or filmed by the FHL. Copies, however, may be ordered online for a reasonable fee. A search on a name will turn up any type of record that has been published that contains the name. With respect to Bible records in particular, do not limit the search geographically to California when entering information in the GRC search box. One never knows who may have inherited the family Bible.

The National Society of the Sons of the American Revolution also maintains a library, located at its national headquarters in Louisville, Kentucky. NSSAR does not have a similar records collection program but does allow its members and prospective members to request application files of previous members or files linked to a particular Revolutionary War participant, although the process is not made clear at the SAR Internet site, *http://www.sar.org*. The SAR publishes the *SAR Patriot Index* on a CD that lists proven patriot ancestors and lineages. Sutro holds the 1999 earlier version; no local libraries hold the newer 2002 publication.

PIONEER LINEAGE SOCIETIES

A number of defunct organizations have left behind membership lists. The California GenWeb project has made available on its website a list of those who were members of the Association of Territorial Pioneers of California, a male lineage organization based upon arrival before statehood, September 9, 1850, and has asked descendants to provide contact information. No information is available on the site except names and arrival dates, obtained from the society's first (and perhaps only) annual, published in 1877. This book is shelved at SFPL and at the state library in Sacramento.

These records at the California State Library have recently been abstracted for the California Genealogical Society by Jim Faulkinbury.

The original enrollment ledgers and records of this organization are archived at the state library. They were abstracted for CGS by Jim Faulkinbury and are part of the CGS lookup service. In the first ledger, each member entered his place and date of birth, place and mode of arrival, and additional remarks if desired. There may or may not be a date of death and a reference to a memorial or obituary entered into the minutes in ledger number two.

The several surviving pioneer organizations most relevant to San Francisco ancestry that make their files available are described on the following page.

Example of entry (above and facing page) in original enrollment register of Association of Territorial Pioneers of California (photographed at the California State Library for CGS member Grace Frontin).

SOCIETY OF CALIFORNIA PIONEERS

The library associated with this society holds biographical books, diaries, manuscripts, journals and other donated materials about the lives of pioneers.[31] Membership is predicated upon descent from a person who arrived before January 1, 1850. Biographical files submitted by members are available, as well as eight volumes of pioneer reminiscences, letters and journals and over ten thousand books, periodicals, ledgers and pamphlets dating to pioneer days. Those with pioneers ancestor should go beyond the roster to seek these records.

NATIVE DAUGHTERS OF THE GOLDEN WEST

Membership in this organization is based upon descent from someone who arrived in California or was born in California before January 1, 1870. The organization maintains a research library where one can find information on over thirty thousand pioneers, generally those whose descendants joined the organization.[32] Available information may include date and place of birth, previous residence(s), method and date of arrival, education and occupation and even parents' names, but information more often is minimal. In 1985 the Native Daughters of the Golden West published *Index to Roster of California Pioneers*, which indexes name, volume and page where informational summaries can be found. It is available at Sutro Library, SFPL and CGS. Films of the summaries that were indexed at that time are also at CGS. Applications since 1985 are indexed online with summaries available through Native Daughters.

The corresponding men's organization, Native Sons of the Golden West, requires only that a member be California-born and does not offer similar research facilities.

LOS CALIFORNIANOS

Member-submitted lineages of Hispanic Californians who arrived in the state before 1850 are available through the organization. Contact information is available on p. 124.

---

[31] Alice Phelan Sullivan Library and Archives, 300 – 4th Street, San Francisco, CA 94107. Phone 415-957-1849 for hours.

[32] Native Daughters of the Golden West Library, 555 Baker Street, San Francisco, CA 94117. Phone 415-921-2664 for hours.

*O*ver the past ten years, the Internet has profoundly changed how we approach and carry out research—in most ways for better, in a few ways for worse. It is an increasingly powerful resource with almost unlimited potential, but only one of many resources and needs to be kept in proper perspective. The convenience it provides is immeasurable. The burden of evaluating the reliability of available genealogical information, however, has reached new levels.

Many guides have been and will be written on the use of the Internet in genealogical research. Most will be out-of-date soon after they reach the bookstore. Times change, locations change, sites disappear, and new, useful sites come into being. There seems to be little point, therefore, in providing a long list of the most helpful websites. Those that are extremely useful are described here and mentioned elsewhere in this guide. Where attention has been called to a particular site, either a host's or a provider's name or the name of the site has been provided so that, if the address should change, the new location can be found. One of the primary objectives here is to provide guidance and perspective so that the reader can better evaluate reliability and act accordingly.

THE UPSIDE AND THE DOWNSIDE

The convenience that the Internet provides immeasurably shortens the time needed to accomplish a research goal. What genealogists five years ago only dreamed might be accomplished is now happening. The potential for the future is stunning to contemplate. We can now access electronic digitizations of census records, newspapers and ship manifests; view library catalogs and archive finding aids; download maps; and examine many genealogical indexes. Dedicated volunteers and employees of archives and libraries have transcribed or scanned and placed online countless abstracts and indexes and, in some instances, even the original material from which they were prepared. A number of ongoing projects involve digitizing and placing online books and newspapers that once were available only at libraries and archives. In the instance of San Francisco, increased newspaper digitization is perhaps the most exciting event that has come along.

This is but a short summary of the upside. The downside is that by far the larger part of the genealogical content available on the Internet has been placed there by well-meaning enthusiasts who lack the genealogical skills needed to verify the content and who do not provide accompanying documentation that will allow others to verify it. Incorrect or non-verifiable postings spread throughout the genealogical community at a speed and breadth never before possible, bringing to the eyes of the uninitiated, undeserved authenticity.

The Challenges

The burden of evaluating the reliability of genealogical information found on the Internet necessarily falls upon the researcher. How does one decide whether or not to pursue what appears to be a lead, knowing that weeks, months and even years can be wasted following leads generated by incorrect material? Should one simply ignore sites where no documenting information is provided? Should one ignore information on sites where no personal and/or identifiable contact is provided? The answers to these questions depend first upon how much time one is willing to invest and ultimately upon the insight and intuition that develops after time is repeatedly wasted following questionable, unsourced leads.

On the other hand, is electronic misinformation really any different from the misinformation generated in the past by printed material? In some ways no, in others, yes. Misinformation is not new, but it is arriving from more directions and in new clothing. While digitized census enumeration sheets may be reliable, the associated indexes that allow us to access them have in many cases been produced by paid transcribers with little or no experience in assessing the meaning of abbreviations or without the skill to interpret correctly unusual or poorly formed names. The Optical Character Recognition (OCR) process that converts the content of scanned books and newspapers to a format that can be recognized by search engines presents problems as well. Indistinct printed type is often misinterpreted, with the result that the researcher may miss entirely the name or word that was the object of the search. Entering a common surname such as "Richards" into a search engine accessing scanned material may turn up many instances of "Richards," but the one entry you want may be accessible only by entering the similarly appearing word "Kichands." In many instances it seems we have invested much faith in new technologies but at the same time have become somewhat blind to the problems they engender.

The numerous problems encountered over the years with published printed material apply just as much to content on the Internet. We need to remind ourselves that even the most careful transcribers omit or misinterpret material. Original sources may have been faded or unreadable. Proofreading may have been faulty or never have taken place at all. We must remember that every extraction project begins with a decision as to what to extract and what to leave behind and, unless we seek out the original sources, we do not know what was omitted. Some pages or years of coverage may have been missing from an original source and perhaps described as such in an introduction to a printed compilation; the compilation may then have been abstracted or transcribed and placed on the Internet without the introductory, qualifying material. We are usually not in a position to judge the genealogical experience of those who post information, but it shouldn't be a surprise that less experienced or careless researchers reach unsound conclusions.

A SAMPLING OF THE BEST

That all said, how can we find the most useful and reliable Internet sites that can directly help in researching early San Francisco ancestry? Among the most helpful are online library catalogs and archival finding aids that allow us to locate and evaluate available sources. An entire section in this guide is devoted to utilizing the Family History Library in Salt Lake City. Its online catalog can guide one to films and fiche of countless original sources that, over the decade to come, will gradually be placed online in digital form. SFPL and CGS have searchable catalogs, as does the state library system, which includes Sutro Library. Smaller libraries, both public and private, are putting their catalogs online. *Melvyl* searches holdings of University of California branches, the state library and Sutro branch, and several private libraries and archives, including the California Historical Society. The Online Archive of California searches holdings of the state archives and a number of other libraries and archives, including the Bancroft Library.

Some websites are fee-based and also meet the criteria of usefulness and reliability; many excellent sites are free. Throughout this guide the comprehensive site devoted entirely to San Francisco research has been referred to by its address, *www.sfgenealogy.com*. It presents a large body of extracted material and links to extracted material, including a number of unique compilations, databases and digitized material. The California Names Index at *http://www.CaliforniaAncestors.org* indexes over 350,000 names in various sources. The California USGenWeb site, *http://www.cagenweb.com*, is not as useful for San Francisco research, although it does contain a database of pioneer diaries and their locations. This database is discussed in the section on diaries and manuscripts, where larger online catalog sites are also described.

Software writer Stephen P. Morse has performed a wonderful service in placing online (at *http://www.stevemorse.org*) software that simplifies and improves the search of immigrant databases. By automatically searching surname variations, his software also facilitates searches of databases about nineteenth-century New York City, from where many San Francisco immigrants came. At a more basic level, the use of his databases provides those researching foreign surnames a useful list of possible spelling variations.

Projects that make available scanned books and manuscripts, such as those currently offered or under development by a growing number of universities, are often free and of immeasurable value. The firm Internet Archive (*www.archive.org*) is currently scanning material at San Francisco Public Library, and links will be instituted between the SFPL website and catalog to these images. Large fee-based or partially fee-based scanning projects are underway by ProQuest, Readex, NewsBank and Google. One scanning project of prime interest to San Francisco searchers is the California Newspaper Digitization Project, with a website currently at *http://cdnc.ucr.edu/cdnc/*. This project, largely funded by the National Endowment for the Humanities, shares scanned images of the *San Francisco Call* with the Library of Congress offering "Chronicling America," 1900-1912. At its own site it also gives access to digitizations of the *Daily Alta* over almost all years of publication, the *California Star* and several Sacramento papers.

As publications emerge from copyright protection, many are scanned and placed online by large subscription organizations such as Ancestry, Footnote and ProQuest, all of which also offer digitized census enumerations. Large institutions, libraries and genealogical societies, in subscribing to these projects, make them available to many users. Both Ancestry and Footnote, recently purchased by Ancestry, offer digitized passport applications and countless federal military documents through a digitization partnership with NARA.

One series of free databases of considerable value, although very different, are the summaries of selected California State appellate cases dating back to the 1850s. Some of this offering can be accessed from remote computers, while the larger part must be accessed at the San Francisco County Law Library (p. 82).

Other online databases useful in early San Francisco research include the free indexes to the fee-based services offered by Jim Faulkinbury, a certified genealogist (CG) who researches at the state library. One of his many projects is an extraction of vital records published in the *San Francisco Call* newspaper over the years 1875 to 1900; another consists of abstracts made from the *California Great* [voting] *Register of 1872,* which includes naturalization data of foreign-born voters. His site can be found at *http://www.jwfgenresearch.com*. The information in most of the databases at the website of the California Genealogical Society (*www. CaliforniaAncestors.org*) must be purchased, but the index to them, the *California Names Index,* is free.

FAMILY HISTORY LIBRARY RESOURCES

*T*he Family History Library in Salt Lake City, Utah, took root in 1894 with the founding of the Genealogical Society of Utah, the purpose of which was to assist members of The Church of Jesus Christ of Latter-day Saints (referred to by many as simply "LDS") with their genealogical research. In conjunction with the society, a library was established, and an extensive microfilming program was begun. Name changes and alterations in function occurred over the years. In 1944 the society became a corporation called the Genealogical *Society* of The Church of Jesus Christ of Latter-day Saints. In 1975 the Genealogical *Department* of The Church of Jesus Christ of Latter-day Saints was created. It assumed most of the functions of the Genealogical Society of Utah, including operation of the library, while the society continued to operate as a record collection and preservation organization. In 1987 the Genealogical Department was renamed the Family History Department and the library renamed the Family History Library, and in 2000 the Church's Historical Department combined with the Family History Department to create the Family and Church History Department.

The Family History Library, located at 35 North West Temple Street in Salt Lake City, houses an enormous collection consisting of about 2.5 million rolls of film, 742,000 microfiche, more than 310,000 books and over 4,500 periodicals, much of which is currently undergoing digitization. This record collection, the largest in the world, is available not only in Salt Lake City, but also via some four thousand Family History Centers throughout the world. At these centers, most filmed records may be borrowed from Salt Lake and used onsite, and photocopies of selected pages of non-circulating books in Salt Lake may be requested. Much of the material will eventually be made available online (see following page). The catalog of the FHL book and microfilm collection can be viewed at *http://www.familysearch.org*. Larger (regional) centers tend to hold more films onsite and allow access to more databases and subscription sites. Hours and locations of centers are available at the website. A nominal fee is charged for those films that must be obtained from Salt Lake City.

FHL Catalog

The library catalog can be searched by title, author, place, keyword, subject, surname, book call number and by film or fiche number. Unfilmed books do not circulate to local centers. Unless the title or author is known, either a keyword or place search is generally the best way to proceed. The keyword search retrieves all works with the user-submitted word or words present in the title, the descriptive summaries or the author. Place searches can be conducted using either broad or specific location parameters. A broad parameter such as "California" generally brings up items that cover California as a whole, such as state-held military records or biographies of California residents. Since San Francisco is both a city and a county with identical boundaries, there will be some confusion about whether to search by the city or the county. Although the general rule is that records found in county offices are cataloged by county and records held in city offices are cataloged by city, there is a great deal of overlap, particularly in instances where the holding repository, such as a library, is neither city- nor county-owned. Researchers should search for items of interest at all three levels. As more films and fiche become available as scanned images, this will be noted by a small camera icon. Until links are created, locate digitizations by selecting the "Browse by location" option.

Digitizations, Including Historical Record Collections

In 2005, the Church began an imaging program, recording new records electronically and converting existing film and fiche holdings to electronic format. This effort is projected to be completed by 2020. Images have been and are being indexed by volunteers, both LDS and non-LDS, from all over the world. Once indexed, they can be accessed from the main search box. To view unindexed digitizations, start by clicking on "All Record Collections" at the main web page. Previously indexed censuses and record extractions, formerly available in a separate section of the website, are now largely accessible from the main search box. The longterm goal is to make all records, with the exception of those for which permission cannot be obtained, available as indexed, scanned images. A large proportion of these records represent original material such as vital, town, land, probate and court records, making this resource of inestimable value to researchers everywhere.

Electronic Databases, Including Family Trees

The FHL formerly made available a number of electronic databases, including the International Genealogical Index® (IGI), a database indexing birth, christening, marriage and a few death dates, with which researchers have long been familiar. It served an important function for church members, who submitted much of the data, but has not been necessarily reliable since no proof was required for submitted information. Some of the entries, however, came from comprehensive extraction programs. Extracted information, along with many submissions that have been deemed verifiable can now be accessed from the main search page.

Other electronic databases included the Ancestral File, a compilation of submitted, linked lineages that were merged, unfortunately, causing many errors. Another, more recent lineage database called the Pedigree Resource File included submissions that were not merged. As of this writing, these two databases remain available; it is not clear whether or not error-filled information will be sorted out and removed. These records, as with all submitted information, should be used with caution and the information contained taken only as clues.

Prior to online census imaging projects, LDS members extracted key information from the 1880 U.S. census and have since begun to index the remaining censuses. The plan is to link them to digitizations. The census indexes, as is the case with all FHL name-accessed information, standardize surname spelling automatically to include spelling variants, making multiple trials of wildcard combinations unnecessary. Given the large number of immigrants in early San Francisco, these census indexes and the 1880 database can serve as a useful check when searching for a foreign name that may have been misspelled by the enumerator or misinterpreted by the indexer of the digitization.

OTHER WEBSITE FEATURES

The FamilySearch website also offers useful research aids. The tab marked "Learn" links to *https://learning.familysearch.org/* where there is a search box for the "Research Wiki," a collection of over forty thousand research articles that, like the website in general, is changing from day to day. The section that is destined to contain information on San Francisco research is at present rather minimal, but like any wiki is open to additions.

At the time of this writing, the entire website is evolving. There is, however, a link on the main page to a pdf pamphlet that explains how the website is organized and how to use it. Clicking on "What's New" provides updates. Longtime users as well as new users should read this frequently until the new website becomes more stable.

The National Archives San Francisco: The Pacific area regional branch, located in San Bruno, holds copies of most NARA films of interest to genealogists, in addition to many items of local interest, such as court records and Chinese Exclusion Act documents.

Researching pre-earthquake San Francisco residents will be slower from outside the Bay Area, but when time is not a factor, those who live elsewhere can accomplish almost as much by utilizing a variety of resources. Family History Library films are available on loan through local Family History Centers throughout the country and at some point in the next decade will be available on the Internet. All holdings at the regional branch of the National Archives in San Bruno, except for the unique items described on the following page, are available at other regional branches or in Washington, D.C. Many of the most-used NARA publications are available on FHL film and have been made accessible to subscribers to Footnote and Ancestry. Films of older newspapers can be obtained through interlibrary loan, and scanned images of a number of publications are available online through the California Newspaper Digitization Project (p. 48) or remotely to cardholders of public libraries subscribing to ProQuest. Many books with a San Francisco focus are available online at *www.Archive.org* or other digitized book sites; those that are not can often be borrowed on interlibrary loan. One Internet site in particular, *www.sfgenealogy. com*, offers a large variety of useful, San Francisco-related databases. Other Internet databases are available by subscription, privately or through society and library memberships; the *San Francisco Call* abstract and photocopying services offered by Jim Faulkinbury (p. 46) are reasonably priced and widely used.

The list on the following pages was created for those who do not live in the greater Bay Area and are unfamiliar with the most-used facilities, but who may find themselves able to spend a week or so researching here. Additional libraries, museums and archives with a more narrow focus have been mentioned where appropriate throughout this guide. Descriptions of or links to descriptions of their holdings and those of other collections with limited utility for genealogists, along with addresses and hours, can be found on the "California Cultural Directory" page of the website of the California Historical Society and also at *www.sfgenealogy.com*.

San Francisco Public Library (SFPL), Main Branch, Civic Center, 100 Larkin Street, San Francisco, CA 94102; (415) 557-4567. SFPL is currently open every day, but check for hours. The History Center on the sixth floor can provide access to archived holdings that are described throughout this guide. Access the library website at *www.sfpl.org*, the San Francisco History Room at *www.sfpl.org/sfhistory*. The Newspaper/Periodical Center holds an excellent collection of the most-used San Francisco newspapers; a smaller collection of historical newspapers and periodicals is kept in the History Center. A description of holdings is available at *www.sfgenealogy.com*, and the library catalog is available online. Items of historical interest are currently being digitized and placed online at *Archive.org*.

California Genealogical Society (CGS), 2201 Broadway, Suite LL2, Oakland, CA 94612-3031; (510) 663-1358. Open Thursday and Friday, 9–4, Saturdays, 10–4 and at other times by arrangement. A fee is charged non-members. The San Francisco and California collections are large and continually growing. Copies of the most helpful FHL films are available, including the following: all surviving vital records; DAR cemetery, Bible and newspaper extractions; all extant San Francisco deeds and grantor/grantee indexes; all newspaper indexes; and several state-held military compilations. The collection also includes the DAR extracts of the 1852 state census, most San Francisco city directories, digitized indexes to post–1906 probates (known as Registers of Actions) and original IOOF records. Users have computer access to a number of society–created databases and many subscription Internet sites. The society's website, *http://www. CaliforniaAncestors.org*, includes a link to its searchable library catalog.

Sutro Library, 480 Winston Drive, San Francisco, CA 94132; (415) 731-4477. Check for current hours. This branch of the state library has one of the largest genealogical collections west of Salt Lake City. The San Francisco and California collections are less comprehensive than at the state library in Sacramento. Holdings can be viewed online on the catalog of the California State Library, *http://catalog.library.ca.gov/F?RN=902597453*, and on the comprehensive catalog of all state libraries, *Melvyl* (*http://www.melvyl.cdlib.org*).

National Archives San Francisco, 1000 Commodore Drive, San Bruno, 94066-2350; (650) 238-3501; email contact: sanbruno.archives@nara.gov. Open Monday–Friday, 7:30 a.m.–4 p.m. with extended hours on Wednesday. Most holdings are typical of regional branches throughout the country and thus include all censuses and the most widely used filmed military indexes and records. Unique holdings include the 1852 California Census, San Francisco Passenger lists beginning in 1893, United States Circuit Court and United States District Court naturalizations and Chinese Immigration and Custom records and Exclusion Act documents.

U.C. Berkeley: Bancroft Library, Berkeley, CA 94720; (510) 642-3781. The
Bancroft Library is open Monday–Friday, 10 a.m.–5 p.m., except during holidays
and college breaks. The library holds a superb collection of manuscripts
and books focusing on the West and catalogs a number of foreign–language
newspapers. Newspaper films may be found at Doe (below); bound copies are
at the Bancroft. Holdings of both libraries are cataloged in *Melvyl* (*http://www.
melvyl.cdlib.org*) and in *OskiCat,* the online catalog that is specific for Berkeley
(*http://oskicat.berkeley.edu/*). The Bancroft's website is located at *http://bancroft.
berkeley.edu;* holdings are also cataloged at the Online Archive of California
website, *http://www.oac.cdlib.org.*

U.C. Berkeley: Newspaper Room, Doe Memorial Library, Berkeley, CA 94720;
(510) 642-6657. Doe Memorial Library is open daily except during college breaks
and holidays. Holdings include all San Francisco newspaper films found at San
Francisco Public Library and more, many foreign–language newspaper films and
films of business- or occupational-focused periodicals.

*Doe Library (center) at the University of California in Berkeley. Bancroft Library
adjoins it at the left, and the landmark Campanile can be seen in the background
(photograph by Jeremy Frankel).*

Oakland Public Library, Main Branch, 125 14th Street, Oakland, CA 94612; (510) 273-3134. Open daily, closed some mornings. Call first or check the library Internet page for current hours as well as for holdings. The History Room (closed Sunday and Monday) has a good California collection, and the film collection in the newspaper room includes early issues of the *Sacramento Bee*. This paper also covered San Francisco events and is not held by SFPL. There is a link to the main branch catalog at its website, *http://www.oaklandlibrary.org/Seasonal/Sections/mainhrs.html*.

California Historical Society, 678 Mission Street, San Francisco, CA 94105; (415) 357-1848. Library hours are 10-5, Wednesday through Friday and by appointment. Founded in 1871, the collection contains 500,000 photographs, 150,000 manuscripts, thousands of books, periodicals, prints and paintings, gold rush diaries and so forth, with a focus more on history than on genealogy. There is a charge, and the library does not have open stacks. Some holdings are cataloged on the CHS website, *http://www.californiahistoricalsociety.org*, others on the Online Archive of California website, *http://www.oac.cdlib.org*.

Society of California Pioneers, 300 Fourth Street, San Francisco, CA 94107; (415) 957-1849. Library hours are 10-5, Wednesday through Friday and by arrangement. Although the collection focuses upon information about Californians who arrived before 1850, holdings also include material that has been donated over the years, including scrapbooks, photographs, diaries, business materials and ledgers that cannot be found elsewhere. Among the archived materials are the original ledgers of Lone Mountain and Laurel Hill cemeteries, dating from 1854 through the final removals in 1936. The website is located at *http://www.californiapioneers.org* but does not yet offer a library catalog.

California State Library, 900 N Street, Sacramento, CA 95809; (916) 445-4149. Check for current hours. The California History Room (Room 200) contains materials that support research about the history of all of California. The portion that deals with San Francisco is not extraordinarily large, but does include the complete California DAR collection and a unique finding aid to it; pioneer (pre–1850) records not found elsewhere; the complete *California Information File* and the computerized addendum to it; the 1852 census in book format; and the original enrollment ledgers of the Association of Territorial Pioneers of California. Holdings are cataloged online both in the California State Library Main Catalog (*http://catalog.library.ca.gov*)and in *Melvyl* (*http://www.melvyl.cdlib.org*).

*T*his guide has been directed primarily towards a researcher with some genealogical experience but is nevertheless unfamiliar with the availability of pre-earthquake San Francisco records and resources. Nonetheless, there is certainly no reason why a novice in search of family history cannot understand and use it. Indeed, those first starting out are often so competent in Internet research that the techniques the rest of us have had to acquire in recent years are already second nature. Whether experienced or inexperienced, every researcher may eventually reach a point in his or her research where outside help is required.

Professional or experienced researchers living at a distance from the Bay Area, particularly after reading this guide, may feel they know precisely what records they wish examined and thus want to engage a professional researcher with access to Bay Area facilities. While the Family History Library at Salt Lake City and the California State Library at Sacramento have much to offer, there are some resources that are unique to San Francisco or nearby repositories and require onsite visits. Professionals can be found on the Internet by selecting the focal area "San Francisco" (or less so, "Sacramento") on the website of the Association of Professional Genealogists, *http://www.apgen.org*. The initials "CG" following a name represent national board certification in research, a process that requires submission and evaluation of work samples and resubmission every five years. Expect to pay such a researcher from $35 to $50 per hour or more. Most researchers require payment or at least a retainer in advance.

When one is faced with a pre-1906 research problem and is not certain exactly what records should be accessed or what is available, the California Genealogical Society in Oakland offers an excellent research service with fees going to support and expand the CGS library. An extensive number of lookup categories at fixed fees is offered, in addition to a non-structured, reasonably priced research service. Experienced volunteers conduct the research, using resources available not only at the CGS library, but also at facilities and repositories throughout the Bay Area. The library has extensive local holdings and also a large collection of military sources and books, films and fiche that make it possible to trace a San Francisco resident or family back to previous abodes, particularly in New England, New York and Pennsylvania. When a problem requires information from more distant repositories, referrals are usually provided. Details on contacting the society and the sources available to be searched are described on its website, *http://www.CaliforniaAncestors.org*, which is linked to the library catalog. Payment may be made conveniently online if preferred. Otherwise, direct information and payments to the California Genealogical Society, 2201 Broadway, Suite LL2, Oakland, CA 94612-3031 (Attn: Research Director).

In hiring any professional or organization, be prepared to describe the problem or objective in detail, and provide a summary of what is already known, as well as a list of sources already consulted in order to obtain this information. Not to do so sacrifices valuable research hours to client-researcher communication and also opens up the possibility that work already completed will be repeated. What may seem irrelevant to the client or peripheral to the problem at hand may suggest to the experienced researcher sources and avenues of research that may not have occurred to the client.

PART III

RESEARCH TECHNIQUES FOR SOLVING GENEALOGICAL PROBLEMS

"The ability to ask the right question is more than half the battle of finding the answer."

—Thomas J. Watson, Sr.

AMBROSE McSWEENEY

In the field of public service Ambrose McSweeney has done important and valuable work as tax collector for San Mateo county, an office which he has filled for sixteen years, and his activities as a realtor have been equally beneficial. He was born December 20, 1870, in San Francisco, California, and was graduated from the Lincoln grammar school in that city. He was employed as a clerk in the San Francisco post office and in 1896 came to South San Francisco as a federal inspector of the department of animal industry, holding the position for nine years after which he entered the political arena. He was elected justice of the peace of the first township and acted in that capacity for four years. He was made city recorder of South San Francisco and for eight years was a member of its board of school trustees. He champions every project for civic growth and betterment and belongs to the Chambers of Commerce of South San Francisco and Redwood City. Mr. McSweeney is a stanch republican and since January, 1911, has been tax collector for San Mateo county. He gives to the office the service of an expert and his long retention in the position proves conclusively that his worth is appreciated. At first he had one assistant during the busy season and now requires twelve deputies. Introducing new and improved methods, Mr. McSweeney has wrought a marked transformation in this department and in one year there was a gain of twenty per cent in tax collections.

Mr. McSweeney is a sagacious, farsighted business man and receives substantial returns from his investments. He has laid out a number of subdivisions, figuring conspicuously in development projects throughout the county, and is also a director of the Bank of South San Francisco. He joined the Order of Yeomen at San Bruno and is also a member of San Mateo Lodge, No. 1112, of the Benevolent Protective Order of Elks. During the World war he acted as vice chairman of

Typical biography from the published history of an adjacent county. Note that this man was born in and was for some years employed in San Francisco (from volume 2 of History of San Mateo County California *[Chicago: S. J. Clarke Publishing Co., 1928]).*

Assembling and Assessing the Evidence

As a consequence of either the earthquake and fire or the removal and destruction of San Francisco's cemeteries, large numbers of sources that could help us with family research are gone. The Hall of Records and the County Courthouse were destroyed. Most of the business district was lost, and many churches burned. This resulted in the loss of all but a few vital and coroners' records, many undertakers' records, all probate records and about two–thirds of the county land records. Compounding this loss, several years earlier legislation had been passed ordering burials in the city to cease and San Francisco's cemeteries to be removed to locations outside the county. During the years over which removals occurred, many original records were not retained, and countless tombstones were broken up and used to construct breakwaters or simply dumped into ocean and bay waters.

With the absence of so much definitive material, careful genealogists must build a case by assembling a much wider body of evidence than would have been required if original sources were available. Much, if not most of the relevant evidence, moreover, will necessarily be less reliable derivative material, material that repeats something already written or spoken and, more often than not, material several layers removed from its original source. This type of research is frequently very time–consuming, and it is not surprising that many researchers simply give up. On the other hand, the expanded search that may be necessary can result in a much richer picture of a person or family in San Francisco than would otherwise be obtained from a conventional assemblage of vital and probate records.

To be meaningful, evidence needs to be drawn from a variety of independently created sources. A derivative source based in part or wholly upon another does not constitute independent evidence, even if it points in the same direction. When conflicting evidence is encountered, each piece must be weighed for credibility and all contradictions resolved. In order to assess reliability, one

> *To be meaningful, evidence needs to be drawn from a variety of independently created sources. A derivative source based in part or wholly upon another source does not constitute independent evidence.*

needs to ask how many steps a piece of evidence is removed from the original, for the likelihood of transcription errors increases with each layer of processing. How many people recorded, copied and recopied a piece of data before it reached us? Timeliness—data first recorded near the time of an event—generally adds to the credibility of a source. The importance of the accuracy of the information to the person who recorded it must also be weighed. Some evidence will be direct, such as the appearance of a name in a newspaper obituary; other evidence will be indirect, such as the notation "widow" in a city directory. Searching for derivative sources that are credible and unrelated to each other and for as wide a body of evidence as is necessary to build a case requires time, care, persistence and a good measure of creativity. The search will not necessarily be straightforward.

Onsite searching in San Francisco is ideal. Searching from a distance will be less productive once Internet sources have been exhausted and films that can be obtained through or at large libraries, regional archives and the Family History Library have been viewed. It may be necessary at some point to hire a researcher, since few newspaper indexes or other useful sources found locally, such as the *Annual Municipal Report,* have been filmed to date. Nonetheless, there is much that can be accomplished from a distance. The amount of material that has been placed on the Internet is already substantial and will only increase, particularly as digitization of pre-existing films and old newspapers proceeds. Be aware that many electronic postings that are not scanned images but are transcriptions or abstracts contain errors. They often fail to include otherwise useful information that appeared in the source from which they were taken, if that source was mentioned at all. The careful researcher, upon finding something in an electronic posting, should always regard it with healthy skepticism and track down and examine the parent source, which may well have been more complete or which may contain slightly different information. By the same token, when nothing of relevance is found in an electronic database, one should not necessarily conclude that no relevant information existed in the parent source.

This part of the guide deals with and attempts to prioritize research strategies to pursue when definitive evidence cannot be found in easily located sources. It also includes research tips where they are appropriate and points out pitfalls that have often been found to block success. Your search may entail considerable time and energy, or you may, on the other hand, be fortunate enough to find your answer in short order among surviving original records. There is no way to know until you start.

THE BASICS: THE CENSUS AND CITY DIRECTORIES

Census enumerations and city directories go hand in hand. Listings in city directories often help us to locate a household somehow missed or mis-entered in a census index. The census, despite its many inaccuracies, constitutes a starting point and is often underused. Admittedly one needs to assess a household entry with flexibility. Its accuracy was dependent upon the knowledge and memory of the informant, sometimes an older child, a maid, a grandparent or even a neighbor. Recorded ages of persons often seem to stray beyond what might be expected from enumerations gathered in other years. A full, given name might have been reported in one census, while a middle name, nickname or just an initial was recorded in another. Enumerators were often hurried and made many errors; some failed to follow directions, in particular not adhering to the date as of which ages and other information was to be based. These "as of" dates were the first of June for 1860 through 1900, the 15th of April in 1910, the first of January in 1920 and the first of April in 1930. In accord with this rule, a child born after June 1, 1860 *should not* have been recorded. Similarly, those who died after June 1 *should* have been recorded on the form as though they were living. This often did not happen. Enumerators had to deal with foreign accents, foreign names and names that could be spelled in multiple ways. They often made errors in transcription when they copied their original record onto additional forms, as happened in the 1850, 1860 and 1870 enumerations. In some instances the enumerator in recopying may have failed to notice a slippage in column alignment.

Despite these many sources of inaccuracy, census records remain vitally important. They should be sought for every family member, no matter how distantly related, in every census year. The 1910, 1920 and occasionally 1930 enumerations are just as relevant to a search as the pre-earthquake enumerations. Although this guide is directed towards the pre-1906 years, following descendants, collateral relatives and relatives by marriage, friends, neighbors and even business associates down through the years can provide clues to a migrant group's trail before reaching San Francisco or to an immigrant's birthplace.

Census records should be sought for every family member, no matter how distantly related, in every census year.

The 1850 federal census enumerations for San Francisco and nearby Contra Costa and Santa Clara counties were lost, destroyed or possibly never taken. In 1852, however, a state census was taken that recorded name, age, sex, race, occupation, place of birth and previous place of residence for everyone in a household. The 1852 census was indexed and transcribed by the DAR. This version is often used first because the film of the original census for San Francisco County is very difficult to read. Many of the names evidently were undecipherable, and transcribers appear not to have recorded entries for Chinese and Native Americans. The digitizations that *Ancestry.com* recently brought online are clearer than the film. The Southern California Genealogical Society has prepared and markets a CD that indexes both the DAR transcript and the original census. CGS has this CD.

In 1860 several new questions were asked: the value of real estate and personal property owned (only asked in 1860 and 1870), whether one had been married in the previous year (asked 1860 through 1880 only, with specific month asked in 1870), whether each member could read and write (possibly a clue to a new immigrant) and whether a resident was a pauper or a convict (1860 only). In 1870 a question regarding citizenship for males over 21 was added (eligible to vote?, to be answered yes or no), along with questions about whether one's father and mother were foreign–born and whether a child had been born within the previous year (asked in 1870 and 1880 only). The important new questions on citizenship and foreign–born parents did not return until 1900, at which time they became more detailed. The 1870 enumeration was later refilmed by NARA because one of the two facing pages that had been taken together was out of focus. The second filming, taken one page at a time, is clearer but at times fainter because of copy deterioration before the second filming. In 1880 city street addresses were recorded for the first time, and marital status and the relationship of each person to the head of household were indicated. Finally, in 1900 and continuing thereafter, the enumerator asked the length of time an immigrant had been in the United States and whether he was naturalized; the year of naturalization was asked in 1920. The numbers of children born and living were asked of women in 1900 and 1910 only, and questions regarding home ownership and literacy reappeared. In 1920, "mother tongue" was recorded, yet another clue to origins. In 1910 only, it was asked whether a person was a Civil War veteran or the widow of one. The trend since 1920 has been to include less information of genealogical value.

Enumerators were provided with lengthy, detailed instructions. These instructions have been posted on the Internet by the University of Minnesota program called Integrated Public Use Microdata Series (IPUMS). They could be extremely useful in interpreting the exact meaning of the various columns on a census form if enumerators had only followed them. For example, "the name of every person whose usual place of abode . . . was in this family" was intended to include as family those members away on a trip or at school. In 1870 the question of citizenship was directed to males twenty–one and older. They were to respond "yes" only if they qualified according to the 14th Amendment to the Constitution, or were the sons of fathers who were citizens at the time of their birth, or if naturalized, had completed final papers. During the 1800s, many territories became states or new states were formed from old states. In 1870 and 1880 it would appear from the enumerator instructions that birthplace must have referred to the name of the birth state or territory at the time the person was born. Then in 1900, 1910 and 1920, the enumerator was instructed to record for those born in what had become Oklahoma, North Dakota, South Dakota and West Virginia, the present name of the state and not the former name. There were no instructions given at any time for what to call the birthplace of those born in territories that belonged to Mexico at the time of birth. This, of course, included California.

Written descriptions of voting wards were published in city directories. They often help to narrow the search in a census for a person who, for whatever reason, was misindexed. Misindexing is not uncommon, but searching the census of a big city page by page can be a bit of an undertaking, even when the ward is known. For that reason every available census index, printed or online, should be searched before a page by page search of the census is begun. FHL film #1,377,700 contains ward maps for the years 1853, 1856, 1867, 1877 and 1894. Some quite adequate, hand–drawn ward maps are available on subpages at *www. sfgenealogy.com* for the years 1852, 1860, 1870 and 1880. The maps contained in this guide should also help, and the History Center of the San Francisco Public Library has many more maps starting with the earliest years of settlement. Be aware that the 1870 *printed* index for California does not include San Francisco. The 1870 San Francisco printed index was a separate publication.

While digitized online enumerations are convenient, the indexes to them were often not well done. Many entries were misindexed for reasons ranging from illegibility or spelling errors to carelessness. Electronic indexes to digitized census enumerations permit one to search on fields other than surname, and the subscription–based Ancestry index permits the use of wildcards in entering names. A carefully chosen array of fields with no surname entered may lead to the misindexed family. Ancestry has prepared every–name indexes to all census digitizations, which, although the indexing is sometimes poor, can help when only the name of a child is known. The search options offered by the FHL database of the 1880 census are also useful.

Persistence in the use of multiple indexes—filmed, paper and electronic—supplemented by creative spelling and the use of other strategies usually brings success. Stephen P. Morse has written software programs to provide enumeration district numbers when name indexes fail (p. 154).

Neighbors of a person in the census are important for many reasons. Make it a habit to copy the two pages before and after the page on which the person in question is found. This usually picks up most neighbors, although there is no certainty that the census taker followed a direct route or that the household in question was not located on the outer edge of the area to which an enumerator was assigned. Adjacent pages often contain enumerations of family members, of other members of an immigrant group or even of the household in which a future spouse resided. In the instance where all strategies fail, locating the enumeration of a neighbor from a previous census, or a more recent neighbor if you are fortunate enough to identify one, can lead to the missing enumeration. Block books (bound ledgers of city blocks with owners' names printed on each lot) are available for many years. Although they do not include the names of those who were renters, they can provide the name of a property owner living near an already known address of a misindexed family and thus lead directly to the correct part of a census much faster than page–by–page searching of a ward.

In starting a search, begin with known descendants and collateral family members in the most recent federal census and work backwards to the census preceding the earliest family member to arrive. Following this, work forward again, collecting records of those on any newly found collateral lines. At the same time, use the city directories (available at SFPL, CGS and as digitizations at *http:// www.archive.org*) to bracket the presence and recorded addresses of all family members. This makes it possible to establish whether there was another San Francisco householder with the same name. With this information one can then move on to search for additional evidence from sources such as those described in the first part of this guide.

Digitized city directories are becoming increasingly available online. The directories at SFPL were scanned by *Archive.org*. An up-to-date list with convenient links to these digitizations can be found at *www.sfgenealogy.com* under "databases." Most of the directories at SFPL from the first two decades are on film and fiche, while later ones are in paper format. The CGS collection includes 1850 and then skips to 1868. The years before 1868 are also on long-term film and fiche loan at the Oakland Family History Center. Searching usually is faster in paper format, but we can expect these copies to become less and less available due to wear and the need for shelf space and ultimately to be de-accessioned.

A Quick Survey
of the Most-Used Sources

*A*fter censuses and directories, the sources outlined on this and the following page often produce answers to research problems that the few surviving civil (vital) records do not solve. These sources include newspaper indexes; filmed and digitized newspapers; voter registers; cemetery and mortuary records; some printed sources available in local repositories; and, of course, military records, often generated long before a person reached San Francisco. The order in which these records are accessed will differ according to the problem at hand; there is no universal roadmap that will fit all situations. Genealogical research is most definitely an art, not a science.

One of the early steps should be to search for newspaper evidence. In the case of San Francisco research, this is without question one of the most productive sources. Even when one has gone in another direction and found something, the trail always seems to suggest a search of newspapers for additional information. For the years 1846 through the earthquake, the scanned images offered by the California Newspaper Digitization Project (p. 48) are indispensible. From 1869 through 1899, check the online index to the fee–based newspaper extraction service offered by Jim Faulkinbury (p. 46). Coverage in indexes on film and fiche at SFPL and CGS begins in 1894. For years before 1869, help may come from the several collections of newspaper indexes and extractions (pp. 46-48) or from the *California Information File* (p. 143).

Newspaper accounts, although not necessarily accurate, were created close to the time of the event in question and often provide detail not found in abstracts and indexes. Besides providing obituaries, birth, marriage and engagement information, notable court proceedings and legal notices, newspapers furnish historical context and insight into contemporary life. Once an article is found, be sure to search every likely newspaper over the same range of dates. What may have been deemed routine and not particularly newsworthy by one city editor may have been appropriate (or useful as a space–filler) to another. A more than adequate collection of San Francisco newspapers is held at SFPL; there are sizeable collections also at Doe and Bancroft libraries on the University of California campus in Berkeley, at Sutro Library and at the California State Library in Sacramento. Bancroft and Doe libraries, in particular, hold films of ethnic newspapers in which the death of an immigrant may have been covered in more detail. Films are located in the Newspaper Room at Doe, while bound holdings must usually be obtained at the Bancroft.

Voter registers (pp. 85–88) are another source that should be searched at an early stage. For a male citizen age twenty–one or more living in nineteenth–century California, they serve as a supplement to the census and are available over years when the census was not taken. Because they contain naturalization information through 1898, they are particularly useful in the instance of foreign–born voters, who comprised a very large portion of the adult citizenry of early San Francisco.

> *Voter registers, in the years they contained naturalization information, are particularly useful in researching foreign-born residents.*

Cemetery inscription and record searches, which we usually rely upon, may or may not be productive since much did not survive. Abstracts made from early records are better than might have been expected, but the majority of tombstones were destroyed during the mandatory relocation of remains, and associated records often were not preserved. Records of burials (as opposed to reinterments) that took place after 1900 are generally good. The Book of the Dead, a compilation of abstracted early mortuary records supplemented with several other sources, is discussed on pp. 12–13; it should always be searched for deaths dating to the years 1849–1863 and can lead to more information in the original mortuary ledgers archived at SFPL.

Pioneer lists and records and "argonaut" lists are among the helpful printed sources. Biographies, histories and the *California Information File* are generally more applicable to prominent citizens, who seem to have comprised a rather small percentage of San Francisco citizenry.

Military records (pp. 97–112) often contain marriage or birth information not found in other sources. They may be based upon service performed before or after arrival in California. The California Civil War enlistment ledgers (example on pp. 104-05) record not only the state or country of birth, but frequently the name of the town (even foreign) in which a man was born. Locating records for those who enlisted in other states is more problematic since previous residence is often exactly the answer one is looking for.

Finally, consider poring over issues of the *San Francisco Annual Municipal Report* (p. 59). These publications consist of annual reports from a number of city agencies, including the Coroner's Office, the Public Administrator and the Health Department. Information found here often suggests a combing of newspapers for articles that may not have been indexed.

A Less-Used Source: Religious Records

Religious records are not among the most used sources, but they should be. For that reason, an attempt has been made to include in this guide the location of pre–earthquake records that are available, even for churches no longer in existence. Religious records once constituted the only original source for vital records, and even after the advent of town, county and state record–keeping, they should be pursued since they often provide detail that civil records lack. First, locate the church or synagogue a family likely attended and then determine where the records might be today. This often entails following a congregation through mergers and changes in name. For foreign-language churches, see pp. 129-130.

While the fire that followed the earthquake destroyed many of San Francisco's churches, church records were considered sufficiently precious by ministers that more than a few were rescued in the face of approaching flames. They vary greatly in content and scope according to the record–keeping practices and conventions of the various denominations. One cannot expect to find, for example, infant baptismal (and thus, birth) records in denominations that practiced only adult baptism. The genealogical information available in marriage records varies from a recording of a date and two names to the inclusion also of age, residence, birthplace and parental names. Similarly, death records range from including only name and date of burial to a listing of date of death, birthplace and occasionally parental names. Confirmation records in those denominations in which confirmation was practiced also vary greatly, from simple lists of names to unexpectedly detailed information, including in some instances not only parental names, but even where and when a child was baptized. In general, detailed records were (and are) kept by Catholic, Lutheran, Episcopal, Congregational and Presbyterian churches, by Eastern Orthodox churches and by Jewish synagogues.

Locating the right church or synagogue may involve a bit of detective work. Clues to attendance may come from a number of different sources, including obituaries and newspaper accounts of weddings, or from known ethnicity or

*Baptism of John Fay, 7 December 1873, born 24 November, child of Thomas Fahey
of (County) Clare, Ireland, and Catharina Davern of Galway, Ireland
(from baptismal register of Mission Dolores, courtesy of Vernon Deubler).*

from fraternal organization membership. If this information cannot be found for the person in question, perhaps it can be found for siblings, children or relatives and friends. People usually attended churches near to where they resided. Check the city directories for family addresses over time and look for the addresses of churches in the same directories, noting locations on city maps. City directories also list the names of associated clergymen, a clue perhaps already found on a marriage record or in a newspaper announcement.

The next step, once a church or a denomination is identified, is to determine where the records might be today if they survived. Many Congregational and Methodist ledgers have been lost. Mergers and changes in name over the years often complicate the situation. Lutheran churches, in particular, seemed to undergo more mergers and schisms than other denominations. Some Congregational churches may have become Congregational Christian, which eventually merged with the Evangelical and Reformed Church to become the United Church of Christ. Lutheran churches may have affiliated with one of the many synods, the largest of which is Missouri Synod, or with the Lutheran Church in America (LCA) or the American Lutheran Church (ALC), which in 1988 merged to form the Evangelical Lutheran Church of America (ELCA). Today's affiliation of such wandering denominations often determines the archives in which earlier records can be found for churches that no longer exist.

The section on religious records (pp. 29–41) deals primarily with baptismal, marriage and death or burial records and lists the names and locations of denominational archives where records possibly can be found. When a family is found, search for the records of all siblings and children, their children and their in–laws. Make a note of baptismal sponsors if any are mentioned. Records other than the standard ministerial records (which would include confirmation records) may also help in rounding out an extended family. Some denominations keep detailed admission and dismissal records; ministers' minutes and communicant lists may also provide clues. The information generated by less closely related family members may help to unravel a resistant problem or break through a genealogical roadblock.

In a few cases, church records may have been the only place in which a marriage was ever recorded. Starting in 1877 and lasting until the late 1900s, the California Civil Code provided that a couple who lived together out of wedlock as man and wife and were not minors could be married by a clergyman without having to obtain a marriage license. A record of this marriage had to be placed in the church register, but there would have been no record in the newspaper. This was the forerunner of the provision for Confidential Marriage, which is part of the Family Code today. Many of these certificates were found among the pages of a surviving ledger from the First Congregational Church in San Francisco, several reflecting cohabitation of only one day.

Marriage without a license, from the ledgers of the First Congregational Church. Civil Code section 79, enacted in 1877-78, provided that unmarried persons, not minors, living together as man and wife, could without a license be married by any clergyman as long as it was recorded in the records of the church.

LOCATION, LOCATION, LOCATION

"Where did they come from?" is perhaps the most common question posed by those in search of their San Francisco ancestors. While many early San Franciscans did come from eastern states, a large number were born abroad. Whatever their origins, they may not have come to San Francisco directly. If they stopped somewhere en route, they may have left records there of value. What was their route? Many other research problems revolve around location detail—problems, for example, such as distinguishing various residents with the same name from one another. We may need to locate a street that is no longer in existence in order to find a family in a census; at other times we puzzle if two people with the same name living at different addresses on the same street in different years represent one person or two. In narrowing the list of churches a family may have attended, we need to know what churches were located nearby. At the time of the earthquake, we may need to define the area of destruction in order to assess the likelihood that a person who subsequently disappeared from city directories survived.

RESIDENT MOBILITY AND (OCCASIONALLY) IMMOBILITY

City directories, as mentioned previously, are important resources. Most of them are available at SFPL, CGS or the FHL (pp. 55-57). Digitizations are posted at *http://www.archive.org* with links to them at *sfgenealogy.com*. Nineteenth–century San Francisco was a big city and city residents often tended to be transient. Many newcomers never put down roots and left before generating many, if any, surviving records. On the other hand, if a newcomer stayed a year, chances are you can find his or her head of household listed in a directory.

City dwellers tended to be mobile. They usually did not own their residences and moving, for many, appears to have been a frequent event. Moving, moreover, may have entailed a change in church affiliation. Search over as long a period as it takes to establish an approximate period of residency as well as a chain of residences for all potential family members. A complete record of addresses may also help in identifying residents with the same name from one another. Unfortunately, reverse directories, which are based upon address and thus help to identify family or immigrant groupings, were not published until well into the 1900s.

Do not assume that a man who disappears from the city directory and leaves no further record has died. Look elsewhere, first in nearby counties, then possibly even out of state. Older residents may have gone to live with an out–of–town or out–of–state child. Miners, in particular, were migratory. Unsuccessful in

This map can be viewed at SFPL. An 1873 map has been placed online and can be enlarged to show striking detail via a link at sfgenealogy. com.

Map of San Francisco, California, 1853
(Library of Congress, Geography and Map Division).

California, a miner may have gone to Nevada, Montana, Colorado, Idaho, Mexico or perhaps even to Alaska.

Consider that newcomers may have had no reason to stay in the first place and may have had other final destinations in mind. "He [or she] went to San Francisco" does not necessarily mean that a person settled there at all. "San Francisco," moreover, may mean anywhere in the entire Bay Area, just as "New York City" may mean eastern New Jersey, Long Island or southernmost Connecticut. If you are convinced that a man or a single woman "went to San Francisco" yet cannot find evidence of residence in a city directory, broaden the search to include surrounding and nearby counties.

A very few residents who seem to have disappeared from San Francisco in the early years may never have moved at all. San Francisco County was formed when statehood was achieved, February 18, 1850. The county then included all of what today constitutes San Mateo County. County government was established April 1, 1850, and the city of San Francisco (then geographically distinct) was incorporated two weeks later. In April 1856, as a result of the Consolidation Act, the southernmost part of San Francisco, consisting of a little over thirty–two hundred residents, was broken off to form San Mateo County. Effective July 1, 1856, the part of San Francisco County that remained, consisting of about thirty thousand residents, was consolidated into "the City and County of San Francisco."

This geographical unification remains today. Except for the passing back and forth of Angel Island and the transfer of some water acreage, this is the only boundary change San Francisco has undergone since 1856. While San Francisco records were for the most part destroyed in the earthquake and fire, San Mateo County vital records start in 1865, and the first county newspaper, the *San Mateo County Gazette*, dates to April 9, 1859. With very early "San Francisco" ancestry, you may be surprised to find your family in this county just to the south, never having moved at all.

Finally, those in search of turn–of–the–century residents need to be aware that the greatest out–migration in the history of the city occurred following the earthquake and fire. While the real death toll far exceeded the "official" number of 478 (in fact, it is now known to have exceeded 3,400 by a very large number), some 226,000 residents fled the city, never to return. The majority of city residents, as mentioned above, were not bound to their addresses by real property ownership. Deprived of both housing and possessions, those who could find employment elsewhere left, usually to surrounding counties, but sometimes to other states. Look for death records and perhaps related birth and marriage records among the unburned records of surrounding counties before assuming an earthquake-related death.

DEFINING THE AREAS OF DEVASTATION

The earthquake itself turned to rubble large areas of the city that had been built upon fill. Much of what wasn't flattened during the initial shocks was destroyed or rendered unlivable during the three days of fire that followed the shaking. Homes, businesses and churches that were located south of Market Street were the first to be destroyed by fire. In the areas north of Market, business owners and ministers had time to rescue valuable records before the inferno reached them. Two small islands of buildings were left untouched: the summits of Russian Hill and Telegraph Hill and the blocks bounded by Washington, Battery, Jackson and Montgomery streets. Altogether, the destruction area included 490 city blocks and portions of thirty–two more, including an estimated twenty–eight thousand buildings or nearly one–third of the taxable property in California.

*The A. P.
Hotaling whiskey
warehouse
on Jackson
Street next to
the Appraisers
Building was
miraculously
untouched by
fire. This led
Charles K. Field
to compose the
following bit
of well-quoted
doggerel:*

*"If, as some say,
God spanked the
town for being
over frisky,
Why did He burn
the churches
down and save
Hotaling's
whiskey?"*

It is important to pinpoint geographically exactly where a resident lived. The researcher can use a combination of city directories and the official map of fire destruction shown below to determine whether a home or place of business was very likely destroyed. Assume that the church a family may have attended was not distant from their residence. City directories, which list church addresses in a separate section, if used in conjunction with a detailed map, not only suggest what church a family may have attended, but also whether it lay within the burned area.

Sanborn Fire Insurance Maps covering the years 1886–1893, 1899–1900 and 1905, and block books for the years 1868, 1890, 1894, 1901 and 1906 are available at SFPL and also at the Bancroft Library. Maps and block books from SFPL have been digitized and will soon be available as links from the catalog. These may be useful in adding details and color to one's family history, but probably won't be required in order to determine whether a residence or church lay within the burned area. It is interesting that federal buildings, such as the main branch of the post office and the federal court offices above it, the U.S. Mint and the Appraiser's Building and Custom House in the Montgomery Block survived the fire. This is attributable in part to the fact that city officials did not have the authority to demolish federal structures in order to create firebreaks against the encroaching inferno. City structures, businesses and residences, on the other hand, if they were not destroyed naturally, were in many cases dynamited, sometimes recklessly, to slow the approaching fire.

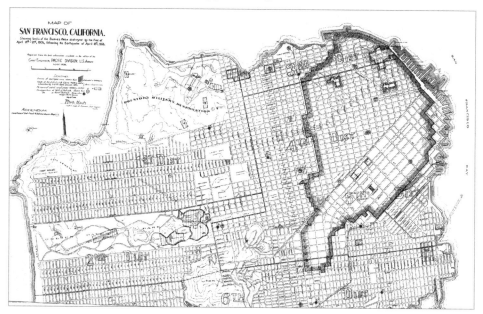

1906 U. S. Army Map of San Francisco *outlining the area destroyed by fire (Earth Sciences Library, University of California at Berkeley).*

Defunct Street Names

Streets that disappeared during post–earthquake rebuilding or were renamed at various times can confuse your search. "Montgomery Avenue," for example, once originated at Montgomery Street and extended through North Beach. It later was renamed Columbus Avenue. Dupont Street became Grant Avenue after the earthquake and fire. Gladys Hansen, in her book *San Francisco Almanac*, lists street name changes on pages 143–148. This book can be found at Sutro, SFPL and CGS. A number of early street maps are available at SFPL, and an excellent one for 1873 that can be enlarged to show detail, is available online at *www.sfgenealogy.com*.

Tracing a Pre–San Francisco Residence

Determining where a San Francisco resident lived before arrival, along with determining if a person who "disappeared" from another area can be found in San Francisco records, are the two research questions CGS most frequently deals with. Newcomers continually arrived not only from other states, but from all over the world. Thus, without evidence of previous residence, unless the surname being researched is unusually uncommon, a connection cannot be established with much certainty. If the person in question was in San Francisco in 1852, his or her previous general residence (state or country) was recorded in the 1852 census. Later census enumerations of families with children may suggest a migration trail if the children were born elsewhere. Still, except in unusual cases, only the name of the state or country of birth can be learned. Newspaper obituaries, even obituaries of relatives, friends and neighbors, may provide clues, and it is even possible that the death record of one of these relatives, friends or neighbors was one that survived. The records of some churches, particularly Catholic churches, and the original ledgers of N. Gray & Co. mortuary often provide more detailed information regarding birthplace or previous residence. Compiled Civil War army recruitment ledgers also may contain the name of the town where a man reported he was born, even a man of foreign birth.

It is imperative to follow a family and collateral members down through every census. Even when a person died before the 1860 federal census or lived in San Francisco only during the years between two enumerations, other family members and friends likely survived, and their data may provide clues to a migration trail and possibly the birthplace of the deceased. If a migrant group can be established—perhaps from city directories, the census or church records, or by noting witnesses to surviving documents—the number of possible research strategies will be multiplied.

Given the loss of so many naturalization records and the lack of detailed information in those that did survive, the origins of the foreign–born pose the greatest research problem. The discovery of gold brought men from all corners of the globe. Successful or unsuccessful, many stayed. Even as late as 1872, the foreign–born comprised about fifty–five percent of San Francisco's registered voters. Until a few years before 1900, voter registers (p. 85) included place of birth and naturalization information, including the location of the court where final papers were obtained. Many immigrants sought citizenship by volunteering in the Civil War. Their Civil War enlistment records (pp. 104–5) often contain wanted detail. Those who returned for visits to their homeland often wished to insure re-entry by obtaining passports. Passport applications, if they were made, usually bear exact place of birth and occasionally father's immigration details and place of birth (pp. 94-5).

Pre–1893 government–recorded passenger lists for non–Asian San Francisco arrivals, if they were ever kept, were lost. This loss is unfortunate when tracing those immigrants for whom San Francisco was the first port of entry. On the other hand, records for Asian immigrants, most of whom were Chinese, date to 1882. All pre–earthquake arrival records are available on NARA microfilm publications (p. 90). Many foreign–born immigrants, however, first reached U.S. shores at other ports for which immigration information is more available. Various NARA publications, such as *Guide to Genealogical Research in the National Archives of the United States*, describe surviving government–generated immigration and passenger lists. Be aware that Customs Passenger Lists indicate country of birth only, but Immigration Passenger Lists, which first began to be kept in 1882, were to include last legal residence.

Immigration through New York City between the beginning of 1847 and June 1897 has for a long time been a stumbling block, given the lack of indexing and the non–survival of some records. The majority of immigrants, moreover, came through this port. New York Customs Passenger Lists 1820 through June 17, 1897 and the indexes to them for the years 1820 through 1846 are available on National Archives publications, FHL films and now at several Internet subscription sites. Immigration Passenger Lists and indexes extend from June 1897 onwards and have also been made available on the Internet. NARA established digitization partnerships with both Ancestry and Footnote and keeps a running list, currently located at *http://www.archives.gov/digitization/digitized-by-partners.html*. Both Ancestry and Footnote may be accessed at Family History Centers and often through institutional subscriptions held by local libraries and genealogical societies.

The Ellis Island online database and the (earlier) Castle Garden online database provide abstractions of immigrant imformation. The website of Stephen P. Morse, located at *http://www.stevemorse.org*, is particularly useful not only in providing links to both free and subscription information, but also because searches are not limited to the spelling of a surname, but are automatically extended to other surnames that sound similar. Another summary of and links to available immigrant information, including NARA and FHL publication and film numbers, has been posted online by Joe Beine, currently located at *www. germanroots.com/passengers.html*.

Brigham Young University is undertaking a project to create databases from existing *emigration* records. More information is available at *http://immigrants.byu. edu/*, where a detailed discussion of various source types can be found. A number of existing compilations abstract both immigration and emigration information of designated ethnic groups. In the instance where family groups are recognizable or the surname is very rare, they offer good leads to original records. The largest of these are the following:

- *Germans to America, Lists of Passengers Arriving at U.S. Ports, 1850–1897*, ed. by Ira A. Glazier and P. William Filby, 67 vols. (Wilmington, Delaware: Scholarly Resources, 1988–2002)
- *Germans to America, Series II: Lists of Passengers Arriving at U.S. Ports in the 1840s*, ed. by Ira A. Glazier, 6 vols. (Wilmington, Delaware: Scholarly Resources, 2002)
- *The Wuerttemberg Emigration Index*, ed. by Trudy Schenck, Ruth Froelke and Inge Bork, 8 vols. currently covering 1808–1890 (Salt Lake City: Ancestry, 1986–ongoing?)
- *Italians to America: Lists of Passengers Arriving at U.S. Ports, 1880–1901*, ed. by Ira A. Glazier and P. William Filby, 16 vols. (Wilmington, Delaware: Scholarly Resources, 1992–2002)
- *Migration from the Russian Empire: Lists of Passengers Arriving at the Port of New York*, ed. by Ira A. Glazier, 6 vols. (Baltimore: Genealogical Publishing Co., 1995–ongoing?).

Serious errors and omissions have been found in the *Germans to America* series, but the books are nevertheless extremely useful, particularly for the years over which official lists have not been indexed. If any immigrating family member or close friend survived to 1918, researchers should most definitely check, among other records, the Alien Enemy files discussed on pp. 134-135.

While Scandinavian immigrants comprised a slightly smaller proportion of the early San Francisco population, emigration records from these countries are both excellent and available. For Danish records see the Danish Emigration Archives website *www.emiarch.dk*. Norwegian descendants will find many useful links at the Norway Heritage website *www.norwayheritage.com/norwegian-emigration-records.htm*. A database of 1.3 million Swedish emigrants may be purchased on a CD ROM at *www.goteborgs-emigranten.com*.

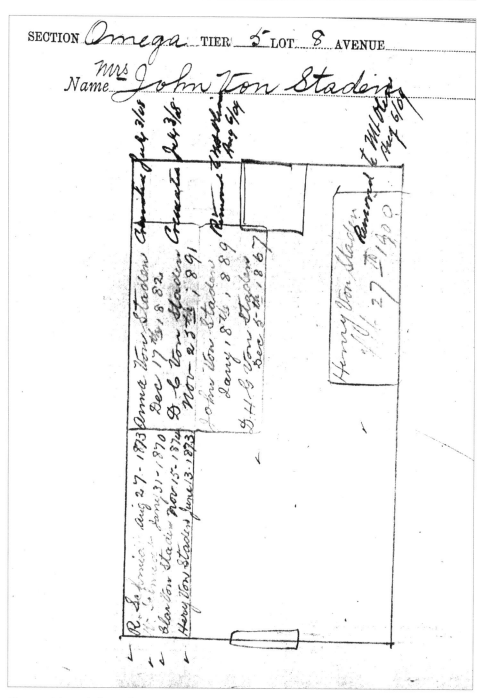

Researching relatives often untangles puzzles, and cemetery lot books may provide useful information. The lot books of the old Odd Fellows Cemetery, as well as those of several other old cemeteries, somehow survived the 1906 fire. In the example shown here, not only were death dates recorded, but removal details of most remains were noted.

Expanding Your Search: Wider and Later

*A*t some point it may become necessary to cast a wider net—to find and examine records of those who touched the life of the person being researched, even in the slightest way. These would include not only relatives or relatives by marriage and their descendants, but also friends, neighbors and business associates. To do this you likely will need to access records created after April 1906.

The Importance of Records of Descendants, Collaterals, Friends, Neighbors and Associates

Some researchers become so narrowly focused on their target that they forget the information they are seeking may reside in the records left by a descendant, a collateral relation, a relative by marriage, a friend or fellow immigrant, a neighbor or even a business associate. While we do not have access to pre-earthquake civil marriage records, probate records and many deeds, all of which might have revealed relationships or provided useful names, we do have access to directories, the census, some church records, newspaper accounts and burial information. In addition, we have countless records made after the earthquake and fire, records that point back to written information that was lost. The time involved in working out a family tree down to every living descendant may pay off not only in information, but in old photographs, family Bibles, stories and memorabilia.

Clues useful in establishing a complete descendancy or in locating close friends may come from unexpected sources. Coroners' abstracts, for example, list the name of the person to whom personal effects were given (pp. 59–60). Newspaper articles occasionally list the names of those present at social functions. The names of cemetery lot owners and plot "neighbors" may be significant. Follow, if necessary, everybody connected with the target of your search, even into surrounding counties or other states. The sought–for answer may lie where you least expect to find it.

SOURCES NECESSARY FOR CASTING A WIDER NET

A detailed description of post–earthquake sources, necessary in order to locate information generated by descendants, lies outside the intended scope of this publication. However, the search is not particularly complicated. There have been very few record losses, although some records have been intentionally destroyed. The website *www.sfgenealogy.com* provides locations and fees for Bay Area county records. On these pages only brief descriptions of the most common sources for San Francisco have been included.

Birth, Marriage, Death and Divorce Indexes and Records

CGS and SFPL hold statewide birth indexes beginning July 1, 1905 and running through 1995, as well as death indexes from July 1, 1905 through 1997. The birth index is also available at *sfgenealogy.com*, where both wildcard and soundex options exist. Many dates of birth can be found online in U.S. Army enlistment records; extractions of California births from this database are posted at *sfgenealogy.com*. Dates of both birth and death are part of the Social Security Death Index (SSDI), the various versions of of which occasionally differ from one another. Death indexes through the year 2000 (three additional years) are available at *http://www.vitalsearch-ca.com*, where 1930-39 is by subscription only; for deaths occurring 1989-2000, subscribers can access more detailed information. Copies of San Francisco birth and death records are available with same-day service at the Department of Health, but the indexes are not available for public searching.

The statewide marriage indexes available at CGS, SFPL and by subscription at *Ancestry.com* cover 1960 through 1985 or 1986, depending upon the source. Indexes for 1949 through 1959 are at the San Francisco Hall of Records in book format and at *http://www.vitalsearch-ca.com* by subscription. Both CGS and Vitalsearch offer filmed bride and groom indexes covering 1913-1915, and CGS holds films of the accompanying marriage affidavits. Pre-1949 statewide indexes are no longer available; one must contact the county where the marriage took place. San Francisco marriage indexes can be searched at the San Francisco Hall of Records (Assessor-Recorder's Office), where copies of records can be obtained the same day. Some of the early indexes, however, are almost unreadable.

Divorce indexes covering 1966-84 are available to individual subscribers to Ancestry. Earlier indexes are on film at Superior Court. Complete San Francisco divorce files (and other non-criminal files except for probate) dating to before 1950 were destroyed; only final judgments and Registers of Actions were retained. Newspaper indexes and digitizations thus become the best sources for pre-1950 divorce information. Military pension files for widows from a serviceman's second marriage will also provide prior divorce information.

An example of the curious case of marriages that took place without a license and were not civily recorded, but otherwise were entirely legal, is pictured on p. 178. Section 79 of the California Civil Code, enacted in 1877-78, provided that unmarried persons living together as man and wife, with the exception of minors, could be legally married by any clergyman, as long as the minister provided the couple with a certificate and recorded the proceedings in the church register. The requirement that the person performing the ceremony need be a clergyman was later broadened to include other designated functionaries, and that section of the code was renumbered several times. This provision lives on today as "Confidental Marriage," with the only substantial change being that a blood test is now required.

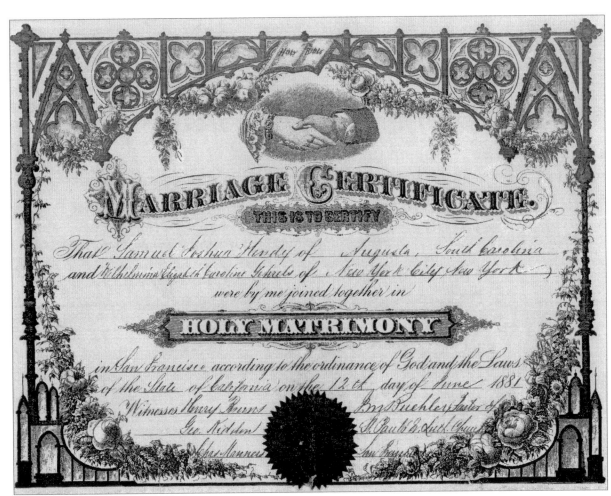

Casting a wider net: the marriage of this San Francisco immigrant couple was eventually located in records of the Cross family in Massachusetts (contributed by Ann Cross Cobb of Conifer, Colorado) .

Since 1900 most burials of San Franciscans have taken place in the cemeteries in Colma, San Mateo County, or at Mt. View Cemetery in Oakland. Records for these cemeteries tend to be fairly complete. Burials in other nearby counties are available in many genealogical society publications, while the number of transcriptions and abstracts available on the Internet continues to grow.

Detailed coroners' records from 1950 are available at the San Francisco Medical Examiner's office. Those dating to before 1950 are archived at SFPL. Between the years 1905 and 1915, deaths that resulted in a coroner's inquest often appear not to have generated a death certificate and may not appear in the state death index. While the coroner may have been called to the scene of a death, not all such occurrances resulted in an inquest. These records include death registers, necropsy reports and personal descriptions of unknown and unidentified bodies.

Most pre-1920 records that were held by mortuaries that merged over the years to become Halsted N. Gray - Carew & English were transferred to San Francisco Public Library (p. 14), along with records for Petersen & Co. (1906-16) and Gantner Bros. (1906-21). Continuing records for those mortuaries, and for Martin & Brown (1911-74), Gantner-Maison-Domergue (1916-75), and Gantner-Felder-Kenny (1922-75) were acquired by an arm of *sfgenealogy.com* known as Researchity and can be ordered online at that website.

Land Records

Grantor and grantee deed indexes and land transfer indexes arranged by block and parcel may be searched at the Hall of Records. The former are only roughly alphabetized and tedious to search; thus, the block and parcel route is often preferred. Copies are available the same day. Water tap records indicate when water service to a property was established. Although they must be accessed by address, they are useful in approximating the time period over which post-earthquake property (to 1937) may have been purchased or restored. These are available at SFPL and are discussed further at *sfgenealogy.com*.

Probate Records

Indexes to San Francisco probate files are available on film in the viewing room at the courthouse. Only recent probate files can be accessed the same day. For probates initiated from April 1906 through March 1942, or reopened or continued after the earthquake and fire, the process can be shortened by requesting a copy of the digitized Register of Actions held by CGS. These are available as part of the CGS lookup service, and if a personal visit to the courthouse is not possible, arrangements can be made to have the individual files examined and copies made (see p. 163). The CGS two-volume publication, *San Francisco Probates, 1906-1942: Register of Actions* (Oakland, California: California Genealogical Society, 2010), indexes the Registers of Action by surname; the same index is part of the California Names Index at *http://www.CaliforniaAncestors.org*.

The FHL filmed seventeen years of wills starting with 1906 on FHL film #1,276,339, but not the packets. Occasionally copies or full descriptions of wills are not in the packets and must be requested separately.

Suhr Mortuary record from ledgers archived at SFPL. Note the additional detail compared to earlier funeral home records, here, for example, the maiden name of child's mother.

Post-earthquake Newspapers

Both CGS and SFPL hold indexes covering 1904-1980. The State Library holds films of selected newspapers from across the state. Doe Memorial Library at the University of California has a very large collection of films of greater Bay Area newspapers and of some publications from other areas. SFPL holds films of almost all surviving San Francisco papers (see Appendix) as well as the *Los Angeles Times*. The California Newspaper Digitization Project (p. 48) includes the *San Francisco Call*, 1890-1913, plus post-earthquake years for several other non-San Francisco papers. ProQuest has digitized the *San Francisco Chronicle* over the years 1880-1922. If non-California papers are needed, consider the "Chronicling America" project of the Library of Congress (*http://chroniclingamerica.loc.gov*); several websites (e.g., *http://sites.google.com/site/onlinenewspapersite/Home*) track the availability of online digitizations, both free and by subscription.

Immigration, Naturalization and Voter Records

Since 1906, most naturalizations have taken place in the U.S. Circuit Court and District Court. Some also were processed at San Francisco Superior Court into the 1960s. The NARA regional facility in San Bruno holds records through 1989 created in the two federal courts and will provide copies for a small fee. For Superior Court records, contact the Clerk of the Court. The United States Citizenship and Immigration Services (USCIS), formerly the Immigration and Naturalization Service, has received copies of naturalization applications since September 27, 1906. USCIS holdings also include immigration files, irrespective of whether or not an immigrant chose to become a citizen. Instructions for initiating a search can be found at the USCIS website, *www.uscis.gov*.

During the World War I, nearly 3200 non-citizen soldiers stationed at Camp Fremont (now Menlo Park) were naturalized in a shortened process. An index to these records is available as *Camp Fremont Naturalization Index, 1918-1919*, Cath Madden Trindle, ed. (San Mateo County Genealogical Society, 1999); copies are available at CGS, SFPL and Sutro. Only brief records are held locally; full records are archived at the USCIS.

Also toward the end of World War I, non-naturalized residents over fourteen who were natives or former citizens of the German Empire were required to register as "alien enemies." SFPL holds forms for those San Francisco residents who registered, but it is evident that compliance was not complete. Each registration affidavit consists of four pages of detail, including names and birthplaces of parents, children and siblings and naturalization information. (An example is on p. 135.) Similar registration was required from August 1940 through March 1944. Those forms are at the USCIS.

Women were given the right to vote in California in 1911. Their names first appear in the 1912 *Great Register of Voters* (see pp. 85 ff.), but naturalization information was not included in that era.

*O*f all the obstacles that stand in the way of successful big–city research, a misspelled or mistaken surname is perhaps the most common. This problem is hardly unique to San Francisco research, but a review of the many reasons why we are led astray is useful.

FOREIGN NAMES

San Francisco was a magnet that attracted settlers from all over the world. They arrived with names difficult to pronounce or, at the least, a challenge for a record–keeper to spell. Realizing this, an immigrant may have simplified the spelling or possibly changed completely his or her surname or given name. Occasionally immigrants did this in order to appear "more American" and/ or to become more employable. Karl Jansson shortly after stepping off the boat became Charles Johnson; Ludwig Schwarzfeldt may have chosen to become Louis Blackfield.

Toward the end of the 1800s, the patronymic naming systems that had been in use in Scandinavian countries for untold generations were abandoned in favor of surnames that would remain stable across generations. There were, however, so many Olesons and Petersens and Jonssons by that point that immigrants often decided to take as their surnames the name of the village or farm where they lived or had lived, or perhaps one that reflected their occupation. If not everyone in an extended family made the same choice—and occasionally that was the case—the researcher may miss identifying family members whose records could have otherwise led to an ancestral origin. It certainly was not the immigrant's intention to befuddle descendants, but that may be exactly what has happened.

Shifts in spelling, whether intentional or unintentional, make research difficult. When your imagination runs dry, there is a technique that can help develop a list of possible alternate spellings that is particularly useful with eastern or southern European names. This involves using either the Ellis Island website or the website developed by Dr. Stephen Morse (*www.stevemorse.org*), where one can enter a surname and receive a list of spelling variations and similar sounding names. Read the instructions carefully and try this when all else fails.

ETHNIC CONVENTIONS

German families, in particular, had naming customs that can confuse the researcher who has not encountered them before. At the time of baptism, a child, particularly a Catholic child, was accorded the given name of one or more baptismal sponsors. This resulted in multiple names, all of which may have been legal, but only one of which may have been commonly used. In northern Germany, each son and each daughter may have been given the same first name, followed by the child's unique name, which might be the only name they went by. In the same family, for example, there may be Anna Marie, Anna Adelheid, Anna Sophie and Anna Elena. The Anna in one census may be one and the same as the Sophie in another census and not a child of a different family.

Old–country Spanish families, of which San Francisco had a good number, had very elaborate naming customs. Complex names may or may not have been retained in their entirety after immigration. In a two–part surname such as Garcia y Gonzales, the Garcia portion came from the father's surname and Gonzales was the mother's pre–marriage (maiden) name. Men upon marriage tended to drop their mother's maiden name. Women, on the other hand, may have retained their hyphenated surname after marriage and have added their husband's name as an attachment following "de." If Maria Garcia y Gonzales married Jose Sanchez, in the old country she would have been Maria Garcia y Gonzales de Sanchez. If Maria as a widow later immigrated to this country with her children, she might have called herself Maria Sanchez, but she certainly would have had a few other options open.

The Chinese had unique naming customs; some of the names one encounters in surviving records may not have been the person's name at all. A good discussion of Chinese naming customs appears in *China Connection: Finding Ancestral Roots for Chinese in America* by Jeanie W. Chooey Low (San Francisco: the author, 1993–1996, multiple revisions), which can be found at SFPL, Sutro and CGS.

COMMON SURNAMES

There is something to be said in favor of a foreign surname. The person you are searching for in a city directory or census might have been named John Brown instead! This is not so much a problem in rural research, but in a city with a population approaching a half million, the number of Millers, Greens, Joneses and Whites can be overwhelming. Common surnames such as these wave a warning flag over the accuracy of presented evidence. It is almost impossible to lay out a strategy for those who are searching for John Brown. You will need to collect information for every man with this or a similar name, including those Browns identified by initials only, and then hope you can eliminate certain data that does not fit on the basis of the names of wives or children, or on the basis of age, address, previous residence or other factors.

Nickname Confusion

Experienced researchers should not need to be reminded of the stumbling blocks that the use of nicknames and favored middle names sometimes cause. With very few legal documents to work from, those researching San Francisco ancestry will run into multiple–naming confusion far more often than they would under normal circumstances. People who were recorded under a legal name in one instance might be recorded under a nickname in another. In order to save time, a clerk may have used a man's initials instead of his given and middle name. Everyone knows that any number of girls will answer to "Elizabeth:" Liz, Beth, Betty, Elsie, Elissa, Liza and Libby. If you are researching a man named Will, moreover, are you certain he was legally William? Might he not have been Willard or George Wilton or G. W.? Were the Martha Jones and Patti Jones mentioned in newspaper articles the same woman? Was the Harry Smith you are looking for the same man as Harold Smith, or was he Henry Smith? Was Fred really Frederick, or was he Myron Alfred?

Unexpected Rearrangements and Indexing

Occasionally, indexing accidents or misentries can mislead even the most experienced researcher, but then this happens in all genealogical research when we work with indexes and censuses. Could Douglas Alexander have been misentered as Alexander Douglas? Was the O', Mc, Mac, San, D', De, Della or Van inadvertently dropped from a surname? Did an entire chunk of the alphabet disappear only to pop up somewhere else, far out of alphabetical order?

Thinking beyond San Francisco: not all San Francisco residents married there
(from Marin County, California, marriage licenses; FHL film #981,525).

Thinking Beyond San Francisco

*I*n considering record types that survived the earthquake and fire, it is important not to overlook those that were archived outside the city—a prime example, perhaps, being military records. Participation in the Mexican War brought many early settlers to California. Not only the Civil War, in which many San Franciscans participated, but also the Spanish American War and the Philippine Insurrection took place before the 1906 earthquake and fire. Consider also federal and state supreme court records, immigration records and published compilations that had been distributed, such as the *Annual Municipal Report*. Occasionally, copies of church records were sent to church archives located elsewhere, and there are other record categories for which this may have been true. San Francisco residents may have owned real property in other counties, where records survived. They may even have been married in or had a child baptized in another county and, of course, occasionally a San Francisco resident died in a nearby county.

Burials starting in 1900 necessarily took place outside the city, usually in Colma, which lies just over the border in San Mateo County. After running out of space, some ethnic cemeteries were established there well before 1900. Short of buildable land within the city boundaries, San Francisco city officials in 1900 passed legislation forcing the eventual relocation of all cemeteries except the military cemetery at the Presidio, the cemetery adjoining historic Mission Dolores and the columbarium on the grounds of the old Odd Fellows Cemetery. Remains from all but one of the other cemeteries were eventually removed and reinterred. Most remains in City Cemetery (also called Golden Gate Cemetery) were never removed. Grave markers from it and unclaimed markers from relocated cemeteries were destroyed, pushed into the bay or ocean, or used in constructing breakwaters. Some detailed initial interment records followed the reinterments, but in many cases the information that traveled to new locations was minimal. Depending upon the particular cemetery, a search of Colma cemetery records may be worth the time spent.

> *It is important not to overlook records that were archived outside San Francisco. Examples include military records, federal and state Supreme Court records, immigration records and published compilations such as the* Annual Municipal Report.

A good example of a publication distributed beyond the burned area is the page shown below taken from published records of the First Congregational Church, the originals of which were all lost in 1906. Baptismal records do not necessarily follow closely upon births, but nothing more definitive may have survived.

FIRST CONGREGATIONAL CHURCH.   **87**

LIST OF CHILDREN BAPTIZED.

Names.	When Baptized.
Allen, Geo. W	March, 1859.
Allen, Edward O	May, 1877.
Andrews, James M	April, 1875.
Andrews, Robt. S	April, 1877.
Atkinson, Clara E	March, 1859.
Ayres, Clara H	June, 1856.
Ayres, Kate M	November, 1861.
Bacon, Alice S	January, 1864.
Bacon, Ellen T	November, 1857.
Baker, Chas. H	June, 1882.
Baker, Louis Eugene	June, 1882.
Baker, Walter R	June, 1882.
Barker, Albert D	March, 1864.
Barker, Carrie L	September, 1866.
Bartlett, Henry	July, 1851.
Barnes, Wm. S	February, 1865.
Batturs, Lizzie W	March, 1857.
Baxter, Arabella	September, 1857.
Baxter, Wm. S	September, 1857.
Benchley, Edward K	January, 1858.
Benchley, Gertrude C	March, 1854.
Benchley, Helen K	May, 1862.
Benchley, Wm. F	July, 1868.
Blake, Theodore G	April, 1882.
Blakeslee, Herbert S	March, 1854.
Blakeslee, Helen S	November, 1855.
Bliss, Lucia M	March, 1859.
Bokee, Robert O	January, 1864.
Boardman, Sam'l. H	November, 1866.
Bowers, Frank T	June, 1870.
Bowers, Carrie P	June, 1870.
Bowers, Letta T	May, 1872.
Box, Isabella R	March, 1864.
Box, Jane Ann	September, 1867.
Box, John R	March, 1869.
Box, Arthur	May, 1873.
Braman, Mary L	June, 1873.

List of baptisms of the First Congregational Church of San Francisco as published in Manual of the First Congregational Church, San Francisco, Cal., with List of Members, 1884.

SOURCE SUMMARIES: WHERE TO FIND WHAT

Substitutes for missing vital records are spread throughout this guide. Not everyone will read these pages from cover to cover, however. Thus, in focusing upon a particular topic, the reader may miss entirely the description of a helpful source. Those needing the date or place of a birth, marriage or death may find the following summaries convenient in that they bring together in one place potentially useful sources scattered throughout this book. Page numbers, not importance, for the most part determine the order in which items are presented. The sources listed refer to pre-1906 research only and not to post-earthquake sources, which are discussed on pages 188-192.

The identity of parents is not considered here as a separate objective but is included in the summary of birth information. Once an exact birthdate is known, check newspapers following the birth for vital or social coverage where parental names might be included. However, normally only "son of" or "daughter of," and not the child's first name was published. Parentage can also come from death abstracts starting in 1940 (p. 188). They bear the maiden name of females and the maiden name of the mother if listed on the certificate. If an approximate marriage date is determined, one can also occasionally glean parentage by searching for coverage of the event in the society section of newspapers. Parental names can also come from census records, immigration records, passport applications of children of immigrants, newspaper articles, tombstone inscriptions and occasionally land records. Search for parental names of all identified siblings, employing the same resources.

Other common research objectives not treated separately here are the determination of previous residence and date of arrival. Previous residence may occasionally be found in birth, marriage or death records, particularly those of children. Thus, don't ignore the records of siblings. Because it is such a common research objective, it is discussed in some depth on pp. 183-5. Look for clues to date of arrival in immigration, naturalization and lineage or pioneer society records, in passport applications, county histories and biographical compendiums, and in digitized newspapers.

WHERE TO LOOK FOR BIRTH INFORMATION			
SOURCE	INFORMATION PROVIDED		
	Date?	Place?	Parents?
Surviving death ledgers (pp. 4-5)	age in y/m/d	no	no
Mortuary records (p. 11 ff.)	varies	state/country	rarely
IOOF ledgers (pp. 16, 24-25)	age in y/m/d	state/country	no
Other burial records (pp. 19-28)	often	occ.	occ.
Church records (pp. 29-41)	yes	usually	yes
First Congreg. Church extracts (p. 36)	yes	usually	usually
Newspaper marriage record (p. 44)	age occ. given	rarely	occ.
SF Call extracts 1869-1900 (p. 46)	yes	SF only	usually
SF newspaper indexes 1894-1949 (p. 46)	yes	occ.	usually
Sacramento Bee index (p. 46)	yes	Bay Area	usually
DAR newspaper extracts 1854-1906 (p. 46)	yes	Bay Area	usually
Sacramento Union extracts 1859-86 (pp. 47-48)	yes	Bay Area	usually
DAR Stockton newspaper extracts (p. 48)	yes	Bay Area	usually
Newspaper articles and digitizations (pp. 48-49)	yes	usually	usually
1860 census (p. 52)	probable year	state/country	no
1870 & 1880 censuses (p. 52)	mo. if prev. year	state/country	1880 only
1900 census (p. 52)	month/year	state/country	yes
Passport applications (pp. 94-95)	yes	yes	no
Military records (pp. 97-112)	often	occ. detailed	no
Calif. Civil War enlistment records (pp. 104-106)	age in years	oft. town/city	no
Institutional records (pp. 117-121)	probable year	no	occ.
Diaries (pp. 125-126)	occasionally	occ.	occ.
Biographies (pp. 139-141)	usually	usually	usually.
Lineage/pioneer society records (pp. 145-150)	usually	usually	varies

The amount of information that can be obtained from military pension records is impressive. In the example below, note that on one sheet of the file, not only are exact birthdates given for both children, but the death date of the soldier and date of remarriage of the widow are also provided--all pre-earthquake.

Minors' Declaration form from Louise Gordon Ruhland Fifield widow's pension application no. 709330, based upon service of George P. Ruhland (Corporal, First Reg't., California Cavalry), Case Files of Approved Pension Applications, 1861-1934, RG 15, National Archives (courtesy of Shirley Brook).

WHERE TO LOOK FOR MARRIAGE INFORMATION

SOURCE	INFORMATION PROVIDED	
	Date?	Place?
Refs. to marriage records in 1850-58 land indexes (p. 4)	date posted	San Francisco
Surviving 1904-06 marriage license index (p. 5)	date of filing??	license filed in San Francisco
Church records (pp. 29-41)	yes	yes
First Congregational Church extracts (p. 36)	yes	San Francisco
SF Call newspaper extracts 1869-99 (p. 46)	yes	yes
Sacramento Bee newspaper index (p. 46)	yes	yes
SF newspaper indexes 1894 - 1949 (p. 46)	yes	yes
Alsworth newspaper extracts 1846-51 (p. 47)	yes	yes
Sacramento Union newspaper extracts (p. 47)	usually	usually
DAR Stockton newspaper extracts (p. 48)	yes	yes
Newspaper digitizations on the Internet (pp. 48-49)	probably	probably
1850-1880 censuses (p. 52) (1870 indicates month married during prev. yr)	married during previous yr??	no
1900 and 1910 censuses (p. 52) (1910 also gives whether previously married)	number of yrs married	no
1930 census (p. 52)	age at first marriage	no
Military widows' pension records (pp. 100-103)	yes	yes
Diaries (pp. 125-126)	often	often
Biographies (pp. 139-141)	usually	usually
California Information File (p. 143)	occasionally	occasionally
Lineage society records (pp. 145-147)	yes	usually
Pioneer society records (pp. 148-150)	sometimes	sometimes
Post-earthquake divorce records (p. 188)	sometimes	rarely
Marriage records from adjacent counties (pp. 196-197)	yes	yes

A widow applying for a military pension based upon her husband's service must be able to document the marriage. When no official record can be found, several witnesses must attest to the marriage. Records such as the one shown below may be the only record that exists to document an early marriage.

Widow Subdivision M.B.A.B.
W.O. 1695006
William Burd
F 6th N.Y. Cav.

State of California) ss
County of Alameda)

On this 27th day of August, 1931, before me SILES S. BROWNING A Notary Public, in and for the County of Alameda, State of California, personally appeared BESSIE SEDGWICK DARGIE of San Mateo, California, who having first been duly sworn according to law deposes and says:

"That she was present on the occasion of the marriage, in the City of San Francisco, California, on August 26th, 1875, of Mary ?. Davis and the late William Burd. That she has continued her acquaintance with both of the parties to the said marriage until the death of the said William Burd on May 16th, 1931. That the said Mary M. Davis, now known as Mary D. Burd and William Burd lived together in the same places of residence before the year 1900 and in fact from August 26th, 1875 to May 16th, 1931 as husband and wife. Deponent further states that for many years she has heard references to the fact that the said William Burd was a soldier in the Civil War and that he served for a period of about four years. Deponent is of the firm opinion and belief that the said William Burd is the identical person who drew a pension as such soldier under pension certificate 221345. Deponent further states that the said Mary M. Davis, now known as Mary D. Burd is the identical person referred to in that certain family record of the Davis family, a copy of which was certified to by Chas. C. Dawson, Notary Public in and for the County of Contra Costa, State of California, on August 24th, 1931.

Further the Deponent sayeth not:

Bessie Sedgwick Dargie

Sworn to and subscribed in my presence this 26th day of August, 1931

Syles S. Browning
NOTARY PUBLIC
IN AND FOR THE COUNTY OF ALAMEDA STATE OF CALIFORNIA

I certify that I am in no way interested in this case, nor am I concerned in its prosecution; and that the said affiant is personally known to me and that she (Bessie Sedgwick Dargie) is a creditable person and so reputed to be in the Community in which she resides.

Syles S. Browning
NOTARY PUBLIC
IN AND FOR THE COUNTY OF ALAMEDA STATE OF CALIFORNIA

My Commission expires July 21, 1934
This affidavit and certificate consists of one page.

Deposition from Mary D. Burd widow's pension file, no. w. o. 1695006, for service of William Burd (Private, Co. F, 6th Reg't. New York Cavalry), Case Files of Approved Pension Applications, RG 15, National Archives (courtesy of Michael Burd).

WHERE TO LOOK FOR DEATH AND BURIAL INFORMATION

SOURCE	INFORMATION DETAILS/COMMENTS
San Francisco Deaths 1865 - 1905 (p. 3)	Indexes all surviving death ledgers/certificates; entries are also in the California Names Index
Surviving death ledgers (p. 4)	Date, place, cause of death, disposition of remains
Mortuary records at SFPL and CGS, with digitizations at www.FamilySearch.org (pp. 11-14). See also the Book of the Dead card file or manuscript (p. 12)	Info. varies; ledgers incl. Halsted & Co. (1883-1906), N. Gray (1850-96), Carew & English (1890-1906), Godeau (1894-1906), Clark & Booth (1896-1906) and Suhr (1901-06); O'Connor records 1882-1920 (films)
Cemetery record extracts (pp. 12-13 and 22-23)	Info. varies. Yerba Buena and Lone Mountain cems. are in the Book of the Dead manuscript/card file; Masonic headstones are at the end of the card file.
Bunker & Lunt transcriptions 1903-06 (p. 13)	Information is unusually detailed, including date and place of birth and parents' names
Coroners' repts in SF Municipal Reports (p. 17)	Incl. date of death and dispostion of personal effects
Original cemetery ledgers (pp. 21-27)	Ledgers for Mission Dolores, Old Hebrew, Hills of Eternity, Lone Mountain, Laurel Hill, Calvary, IOOF and San Francisco National. Some removals from North Beach and Yerba Buena appear in the Book of the Dead. IOOF removals are in original ledgers. Masonic and Laurel Hill are in filmed publications. Jewish removals are at the joint cem. office in Colma.
Colma burials (p. 27)	Pre- and post-1900 records at most, but not all Colma cemeteries are good and important to check.
Religious records (pp. 29-41)	Among surviving records, death and burial data is less common than birth and marriage data

Newspaper resources (pp. 46-49)
    SF Call extracts 1869-99
    Sacramento Bee index
    SF newspaper indexes 1894 - 1949
    Alsworth *Alta* extracts 1846-51
    Sacramento Union extracts
    Newspaper digitizations
	Online digitized newspapers will play an increasing role in the future. At present, many years of the *Daily Alta* (1800s) and *SF Call* (through 1912) are available without subscription. Subscription-based digitization services are often available at public and university libraries.

Probate records (pp. 76-79)	
Military records of all types (pp. 97-112)	
Hospital records (p. 120)	
Biographies (pp. 139-141)	
Lineage and pioneer society records (pp. 145-150)	

Death information is the most available among all pre-earthquake vital records. The time-frame to be searched will suggest what source will most likely produce an answer. Check first to see if the death may have been covered in any of the surviving registers (p. 4). Names that appeared in the surviving registers or certificates appear coded as "Early Deaths" in the California Names Index database at the CGS website, *www.californiaancestors.org*.

For deaths thought to have occurred 1850-1863, check for mention in the Book of the Dead card file or manuscript and, if found, follow through by examining digitizations of the original records (pp. 11-12). A check of entries in the N. Gray Mortuary records, or the Book of the Dead transcriptions has shown that very few deaths in the earliest years were ever published in the *Daily Alta*. Nonetheless, you should not neglect to search the digitized newspaper collection of the California Newspaper Project (pp. 48-49), particularly if the death occurred somewhat later when N. Gray was not the only mortician or, alternatively, before N. Gray opened for business, July 1, 1850. The Newspaper Project digitizations continue through the 1906 earthquake and may be searched at *http://cdnc.ucr.edu/cdnc*. Since digitizations are not always clear enough to be found by electronic searches, try also Jim Faulkinbury's hand-indexed listings in the *San Francisco Morning Call* found at *http://www.jwfgenresearch.com/* (p. 46). This newspaper was also hand-indexed by the state library over the years 1894-1903 (p. 46).

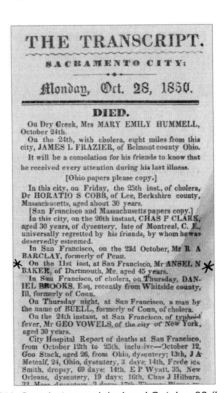

Of the many deaths recorded in the records of N. Gray between July 4 and October 23 (left), only the death of Ansel P. Baker was found by searching digitized Northern California papers (right: from search of California Digital Newspaper Collection) .

Putting It All Together

Assembling and analyzing evidence in order to solve a pre–earthquake genealogical problem will in many instances tax your genealogical skills. The difficulties encountered as a consequence of record loss in the 1906 fire, however, are not that different from the roadblocks created by other disasters. The plan of attack is basically the same. First determine the precise extent of the record loss. Then go about gathering evidence from (1) information that was sent to other places prior to the disaster, (2) from records generated in other places, (3) from records that were reconstructed following the disaster, and (4) from records and recollections created long after the disaster.

Analysis and evaluation of the evidence you have gathered demands both skill and care. Does the evidence all point in the same direction? Does it point in the same direction because the assembled clues are in a large part derived from each other or from the same non–surviving piece of evidence? One way to analyze the evidence you have gathered is to lay all the pieces out in tabular form, summarizing what each piece says, noting as best you can the *immediate* source from which each was derived, and finally including a personal assessment of its credibility, based upon independence, chronological closeness of the document from which it was derived to the original event, and other factors such as knowledgeability of the author.

Thomas J. Watson, the former president and CEO of IBM once said, "The ability to ask the right question is more than half the battle of finding the answer." This statement particularly applies to approaching tough genealogical problems. Because each problem is unique it is impossible to provide a roadmap that even begins to apply to all situations. Instead, perhaps the best advice we can offer is to ask the most pointed questions and then devise an appropriate research plan based upon the answers. The first question to ask is, of course, "Is the evidence I have that suggests that this family (or person) was ever in San Francisco for any length of time reliable?" It would be a complete waste of valuable time to search for records of a family or person who merely touched down briefly in San Francisco before settling in a nearby county.

> The plan of attack for circumventing record loss is fairly standard. Determine first the exact extent of the loss, then gather evidence from sources sent elsewhere before the loss, from records initially generated elsewhere, from reconstructed records and from relevant records created many years later.

If reliable evidence suggests a family or person really did reside in San Francisco long enough to have left records, if every known living descendant has searched for old family records and if the census, city directories and the most easily accessed records and databases have been examined and no progress has been made, then questions to be asked might include:

- Could this person have moved somewhere else before "disappearing?"
- Did I fully explore the lives of and footprints left by every sibling and descendant?
- Might there be records elsewhere for children born before the family reached San Francisco?
- Have I located and contacted living descendants of collateral relations?
- Did a collateral relative or friend leave clues either in San Francisco or in the place where he or she lived before?
- Did some collateral relation move from San Francisco to another county where he or she may have left relevant information?
- Might the person of interest or a known relative have served in the military before or after arrival in San Francisco?
- Have I explored all name variations and spellings?
- Are there clues that might lead me to the family church or synagogue?
- Did this person own property and, if so, might deeds yield clues?
- Have I checked for every significant event in all existing indexes, abstracts and digitizations of newspapers then published?

Rather than assuming a mindset that you have checked everything, be open to alternative sources and ideas. Be patient. Important records that were previously thought lost or were privately held continue to become available. Volunteers continue to abstract and index less common records that will at least add color to family histories and possibly suggest new approaches. Unindexed sources continue to be digitized. Electronic searching of scanned images is a blossoming field that will undoubtedly help to solve countless genealogical problems in the years to come.

There is, on the other hand, an upside to difficult early San Francisco research. Rather than amassing a collection of "begats," we develop robust families. In collecting many times the usual amount of evidence, we probably form a much richer picture of our ancestors and the city they lived in.

APPENDIX

Pre-Earthquake Newspaper Collections:
Titles, Local Sources and
Dates of Coverage

Supplementary List of Pre-Earthquake Newspapers				
	Period Published	**California State Library**	**SF Public Library**	**UC Libraries (Doe and Bancroft)**
General Newspapers				
*Californian & California Star**	1/9/1847 to 12/23/1848	1/9/1847 to 12/23/1848	1/9/1847 to 12/23/1848	1/9/1847 - 12/23/1848
*continued by *Alta California*	1/4/1849 to 6/18/1891	1/4/1849 - 6/2/1891	1/4/1849 - 6/2/1891	1852 - 6/1891
Daily Dramatic Chronicle/Daily Morning Chronicle/ S.F. Chronicle	1/16/1865 - present	1/16/1865 - present	1/16/1865 - present	1/16/1865 - present
Daily (Evening) Bulletin/ S.F. Bulletin	1855 to 8/28/1929	10/8/1855 to 8/29/1929	10/1/1855 - 8/1/1929	1855 - 1929
(Daily) Examiner; later *(The) S.F. Examiner*	1/16/1865 - present	6/12/1865 - present	6/1/1865 - present	Jan. 1865 - present
(Daily) Morning Call and S.F. Call	12/1856 to 12/6/1913	12/8/1863 to 12/6/1913	12/8/1863 - 3/1/1914	1856 - 1913
S.F. Herald & Daily Herald & Mirror	6/1850 - 7/14/1863	1852 to 12/1862 (bound)	1858 - 1861 (broken run)	1850 - 1863
Specialized Newspapers				
(The) Argonaut	1877 - 1958	3/25/1877 - 7/3/1880	3/25/1877 - Sep 1958	3/25/1877 through earthquake; some issues missing
(Daily) California Chronicle	11/21/1853 to 5/12/1858	11/21/1853 - June 1855; Jan. - June 1856; Nov. 1856 to May 1857	—	11/1853 - 5/1858
California Chronik; Sonntagsblatt des California Demokrat	1852 - 1944	—	1866 only	1866; 1863 - 1964 (misc. issues)
California Farmer & Journal of Useful Sciences	1854 - 1889	1854 to 4/1/1880 (bound)	1854 - 1855	1854 - 1889 (broken issues)

	Period Published	California State Library	SF Public Library	UC Libraries (Doe and Bancroft)
California Journal und Sonntags-Gast	1872 to 1879	1878 only	—	1872 to 1878
California Mail Bag	6/1871 to 1879?	6/1871 to 8/1874; 8/1875; 7/1877; 9/1877; 1/1878	6/1871 to 2/1872; 5&6/1877	6/1871 to 2/1872; incomplete 1872 to 9/1879
California Police Gazette	1859 to 1873?	4/10/1859; 10/17/1868	—	1859 to 1869
California Spirit of the Times and Underwriter's Journal	1870 to 1893	1875 to 7/1882; 10/1882 to 93	1879 only	full run
California Staats-Zeitung; California Demokrat	7/7/1852 to 1918; 1853 to 1944	1868, 1874; 4/1878 to 6/1878	—	1863 to ???
Chung Sai Yat Po	2/16/1900 to 1953?	2/23/04	—	2/1900 to 7/1905
Commercial Advocate	11/17/1876 to 12/21/1878	Feb., March, Sept. 1877	—	1876 to 1878
Commercial Herald & Market Review	7/10/1867 to 1911	1/11/1868 to 1/14/1869; 1/7/1870 to 1/14/1875	1868 to 1879; some of 1882	1867 to 1882
Courrier de San Francisco; Le Franco Californien	1852 to 1885; 1886 to 12/31/1926	—	—	1867 to 1882
Daily American Flag	4/18/1864 to 9/7/1867	4/18/1864 to 12/18/1866; 4/18 to 9/7/1867	—	1864 to 1867
Daily California Courier	7/1/1850 to 1856	12/24/1853; 1/7 to 28/1854	—	1850 to 1851
Daily Evening Journal; S.F. Evening Journal	5/25/1852 to ?	12/6, 12/22/1852: 2/11/1853; 12/21/1854 to 5/31/1855	—	6/11/1861 and 8/21/1871
Daily Evening Picayune; and	8/3/1850 to 12/12/1853	9/16/1851 to 3/12/1852	9/16/1851 to 3/12/1852	many broken issues, Aug 1850 to May 1852
S.F. Daily Evening News and Picayune/True Californian	11/1853 to 5/20/1856	1853 -1855 (broken issues)	—	broken issues of *Daily Eve. News* Nov. 1853-May 1856
Daily Evening Post/ S.F. Weekly Post/ (The) Evening Post	1871 to 1885/ 1875 to 1886/ 1885 to 1909/	12/4/1871-9/2/1885; July-Aug./1875; 9/3/1885-6/29/1909;	1/3/1876 to 9/2/1885; — 9/3/1885 to 8/31/1905	12/4/1871 to 9/2/1885; broken issues 1876; 9/3/1885 to 6/29/1909

	Period Published	California State Library	SF Public Library	UC Libraries (Doe and Bancroft)
Daily Exchange	?	--	—	1/1876 to 1884
Daily Journal of Commerce; S.F. Journal of Commerce	1/25/1872 to 6/21/1924	6/3/1874 to 6/1874; 1880 to 1882	—	1880 to 1890
Daily Pacific News	8/25/1849 to 5/1851	various issues 1850	—	1849 to 1851
Daily True Californian	5/26/1856 to 5/31/1857	5/26/1856 to 4/3/1857	—	5/26/1856 to 12/8/1856 and 29 Jan 1847
Deutsche Vereins-Zeitung	1892 to 1907	4/14/1892	—	1902 to 1904
(The) Elevator (see also *Pacific Appeal*)	1865 to 1906?	4/7/1865 to 1904	8/13/1869 to 6/11/1898 (broken run)	1865 to 1898 (broken run); 1901to 1906
Figaro (theater)	1865 to ?	12/14/1868 to 12/5/1890 (bound)	1870 to 1904	12/1865 to 8/1895
Fireman's Journal and Military Gazette; California Spirit of the Times	4/7/1855 to 1893	10/6/1855 to 2/5/1857; 2/12/1859 to 3/22/1862	10/6/1855 to 2/5/1859	1855 to 1857; 1859 to 1892
Frank Leslie's Illustrated Newspaper	1855 to ?; then weekly to 1894	12/15/1855 to 11/28/1891	12/15/1855 to 10/12/1891	12/15/1855 to 11/28/1891
Golden Era; Vanity Fair & the Golden Era	12/19/1852 to 10/29/1881; 11/12/1881 to ?	Dec. 1852-Dec. 1854; July 1855-1882; April 1884-1886; March & Sep. 1893	12/11/1859 to 12/31/1871	12/1852 to 3/1893
Guide (aka *S.F. Shipping Guide*)	4/2/1865 to ?	some issues from 1872, 1876, 1877, 1886	1/1906 to 12/31/1966	1865 to 1917
The Hebrew	1863 to ?	1868, 1872, 1881, 1884	2/7/1868 to 11/26/1869	1867 to 1887
Hutching's (Illustrated) California Magazine	1856 to 1861	7/1/1856 to 6/5/1861	7/1/1856 to 4/1861	7/1/1856 to 6/5/1861
Illustrated (California) News	9/1/1850 to ?	7/29/1869 to 10/9/1869 (bound)	9/1/1850 to 12/1/1850	8/14/1869 to 9/11/1869
(The) Irish News	1860 to 1876	11/14/1868	—	1865 to 1872 (broken run)

	Period Published	California State Library	SF Public Library	UC Libraries (Doe and Bancroft)
La Voce del Popolo and **L'Italia and La Voce del Popolo**	*La Voce del Popolo 1867-1943; L'Italia and La Voce . . . 1886 to 1943*	single issues each in 1872 and 1893	1868 - 1905	both publications: broken issues 1868 - 1943
(The) Jewish Progress	1875 to 1900?	11/16/1894 to 9/2/1898	1/15/1897 to 11/18/1898	1875-1890 (broken run)
(The) Jewish Times and Observer	1879 - 1906	10/20/1882 to 11/6/1882; 11/14/1890	1/15/1892 to 1911 (broken run)	—
(The) Leader	May 1873 - ?; 1902-1957	5/1873	—	1902 - 1955
Mercantile Gazette & Shipping Register	6/19/1856 to ?	5/4/1859 - 7/26/1864	1/3/1857 - 4/28/1859	1857 - 1867 (var. issues)
(The) Monitor (and Guardian)	6/6/1858-?	12/14/1861-1/12/1878; 1/7/1893 to 1953	12/14/1861-2/20/1875 (broken run); 7/31/1875-1/12/1878; 1901 & 1904 (var. issues)	3/20/1858; 1867-1901 (broken run)
(The) Pacific Appeal (a weekly journal for people of color)	1862 - 1880	4/5/1862 to 1873	4/5/1862 to 6/12/1880 (broken run)	1862 - 1880 (irregular weekly)
Political Record	1882 - 1905	9/6/1884 - 12/24/1897 (bound)	—	1882 - 1905 (broken issues)
Public Opinion	12/4/1880 to 1901	1882, 1883, 1886, 1896, 1897, 1898 (various issues)	1890 - 1899 (broken run)	1880 - 1899
San Francisco Abend Post	1860 - 1904	12/8/1863 - 1/1864; Apr - May 1864 (bound)	—	1861 - 1903
S.F. China News	1874 - 1875	7/17/1875 only	—	July 1874 - Aug 1875
S.F. Commercial/ Advertiser; S.F. Daily Whig	5/31/1852 - 9/27/1854	1853; 1854 (various issues)	—	1852 - 1853

	Period Published	California State Library	SF Public Library	UC Libraries (Doe and Bancroft)
S.F. Daily Report (incl. *Daily Stock Report & Daily Report*)	1863 to 3/6/1899	12/1882 - 3/6/1899 (bound)	6/1893 - 6/1894	1872 - 1896
S.F. Journal of Commerce/ S.F. Journal of Commerce and (Weekly) Price Current (varying titles)	1872 - 1907	6/3/1874 - 6/1876; 1880 - 1882	—	1873 - 1892 (various issues)
S.F. (Daily) Law Journal/ Calif. Legal Record/ Pacific Coast Law Journal	Sep 1877 - Mar 1878/ Mar 1878 - Mar 1879/ Mar 1878 - Jan 1884	Sep 1877 - Mar 1878/ Mar 1878 - Mar 1879/ Mar 1878 - Jan 1884	—	Sep-Oct 1877 and 1880-85 — —
San Francisco News Letter and Advertiser	7/20/1856 - 8/25/1928	7/1/1871 - 6/27/1925	1/4/1868 - 6/30/1928	5/25/1867 to 1872
S.F. Tribune	11/12/1875 to 1883	9/30/1876	—	1876 - 1883
(The) San Francisco Vindicator	1874 - 1906	9/20/1884 - 10/27/1894	1874 only	1887 to 1889; 1894; 1896
(The) Spectator	3/5/1865 to ?	1/19/1867; 10/29/1868	—	1867 to 1871 (broken run)
(The) Weekly Star/ (The) Star	7/5/1884 - 1/1921	1890 through 1898 (specimens only)	—	—
Sun; Daily Sun	5/9/1853 - 9/5/1857	1853 - 1856 (various issues)	—	8/21/1856 - 12/31/1856 (various issues)
(The) Wasp	1/1/1876 - 8/25/1928	8/5/1876 - 8/25/1928	1/1/1881 - 8/14/1926 (various issues)	8/5/1876 - 8/25/1928
Weekly Gleaner	1857 to ?	—	1/16/1857 - 12/18/1857	—
Wide West	3/17/1854 - 7/4/1858	3/19/1854 - 7/4/1858	3/1854 - 5/1857	1854 - 1858

A

adoption records 84
African-American. *See ethnic records and resources*
Alien Enemy registrations 134, 192
archival collections 125–126

B

biographical sources
  compilations 139–140
  Spanish, Mexican and pioneer biographies 140–141
  university directories 139
birth records and indexes
  abstracts 7
  online indexes 5
  state-held 5
  work-arounds summary 200
Book of the Dead (card file and manuscript) 12, 23, 24, 174
boundary changes 181
business records 117, 121

C

California Genealogical Society
  location and holdings 160
  publications 3, 4, 16, 28, 47, 68, 78-79, 141
  research service 163
California Information File 47, 143
cemeteries and cemetery records
  Calvary Cemetery 20, 22, 24
  City Cemetery. *See Golden Gate Cemetery*
  Colma (San Mateo County) cemeteries 20, 27, 197

DAR abstracts 21, 23
Golden Gate Cemetery (City Cemetery) 19, 20, 22, 26
Hebrew Cemetery, old 21
history 19
Jewish cemeteries 21, 22, 26
Laurel Hill Cemetery 20, 22
Lone Mountain Cemetery 19, 20, 22
lot books 186
Masonic Cemetery 12, 20, 22, 24
miscellaneous early cemeteries 21, 22
Mission Dolores, cemetery at 19, 21
Odd Fellows (IOOF) Cemetery 20, 22, 24, 186
Presidio Cemetery, old 19
removals from San Francisco cemeteries 20, 22-24
San Francisco National Cemetery 26
Serbian Cemetery 22
U.S. Marine Hospital Cemetery 27
Yerba Buena Cemetery 19, 20, 22
census
  enumerator instructions 52, 170
  errors 169
  non-population schedules 53
  online digitizations and indexes 51, 171
  population schedules and indexes, sources 52
  population schedules, questions asked in 170
  population schedules, second copies 52
  state census, 1852 51, 170
  tips on using 169–172

using to fullest advantage 183
ward descriptions and maps 171
children's home records 84, 118-119
Chinese. *See ethnic records and resources*
church records. *See religious records*
columbariums
San Francisco 28
Bay Cities Cemetery Association 28
Cypress Abbey 28
records 25, 28
coroner's records
abstracts 17, 58-59
surviving 4, 16
court records and indexes
adoption records 84
appellate records 82
courts with surviving records 71
divorce records 79–81, 188
federal court records, researching 82
legal newspapers 84, 214
loss of records 71
naturalization 72–75
naturalization information in voter
records 74
naturalization, evidence of 72
post-earthquake records as clues to
earlier marriages 80
probate, post-earthquake 190
probate, reconstructed files 78
probate records, abstracts and indexes 76–78
probate records in reports of the
Public Administrator 60
probate Registers of Action 78, 190
state court records, researching 82
wills 78
crematory records, IOOF 16, 25

D

death records and indexes
abstracts 7
state-held 5
work-arounds summary 6, 204–205
diaries and manuscript collections
125–126
directories, city
information in and uses of 30, 55–57,
169, 179–180

locations 56, 172
street names 183

E

earthquake and fire
events xi
extent of destruction 181–182
list of those who perished 8
map of destruction 182
records destroyed xi, xii
sources xiii, xiv
statistics xi, 8, 181
ethnic records and resources
African-American history 127–128
cemeteries 130–131
Chinese immigration and Exclusion
Act records 133–134, 136
Chinese naming patterns 134
Chinese presence 129, 132–133
Chinese Mortuary Records 9, 14, 133
churches 129–130
compilations 131–132
demographics 127
legal restrictions 128
Los Californianos 124
naming customs 194
Native Americans 129
nativities of students, 1857 127
newspapers 130
record repositories 132
evidence, evaluating 167–168

F

Family History Library
databases 157
holdings 155–157
local Family History Centers 155
foreign-born, tracing the origins of
183–185
fraternal organizations and benevolent societies
Ancient Order of Hibernians 115
ethnic organizations and archives
113, 115
GAR 115–116
IOOF (Odd Fellows) 16, 24-25, 114
Knights of Columbus 115
Knights of Pythias 114

Masonic organizations 114
  society periodicals 116
funeral home records. *See mortuary
  records*

G

German immigrant records 134, 185
Great Registers. *See voter records*

H

historical publications 139-141
hospital records 111, 120

I

immigrant origins 134
immigration and emigration
  Argonauts 89, 94
  California Information File 94, 143
  early arrivals 89–90
  immigrant origins, locating 184–185
  immigration, post-earthquake 192
  Maritime Heritage Project 91
  naturalization, post-earthquake 192
  passport applications 94–95
  railroad passenger lists 93
  ship passenger and crew lists, NARA
    90, 184–185
  ship passenger lists, other sources
    91–92
  Stevenson's Regiment (New York
    Volunteers) 91–92
  wagon train lists 93
institutional records
  hospital records 120
  occupational records 121
  old age home and poorhouse records
    111, 120
  orphanage records 33, 118–119
  prison records 121
  professional records 121
  school records 119
Internet resources
  sampling of the best 153–154
  scope of the most useful and reliable
    resources 151–152
Irish. *See ethnic records and resources*
Italian. *See ethnic records and resources*

J

Jewish. *See ethnic records and resources*

L

land records
  bounty land records 108
  California Land Patents Database
    67
  liens, mortgages and other docu-
    ments 68
  maps (Sanborn) and block books
    69, 172, 182
  post-statehood land entries, deeds
    and indexes 67–68
  pre-statehood land grants and
    deeds 64, 66
  reconstructed records (McInerney
    Actions) 69
  Spanish and Mexican records and
    claims 63–64, 66
Lawndale 20
lineage societies
  DAR extractions (GRC records)
    146–147
  locating records 145–146
  pioneer 148-150
local libraries and archives
  California Genealogical Society 160
  California Historical Society 162
  California State Library (Sacramen-
    to) 162
  National Archives San Francisco
    (in San Bruno) 160
  Oakland Public Library 162
  other 33-41, 91, 132
  San Francisco Public Library 160
  Sutro Library 160
  UC Berkeley: Bancroft and Doe
    libraries 161

M

manuscript collections. *See archival
  collections*
maps
  block books 182
  fire destruction map, official 182
  Sanborn fire insurance maps 69,
    182
  voting ward maps 171
marriage records and indexes
  abstracts 7
  marriage license index, surviving 4

marriage source summary 202
marriage without a license 177–178,
     189
re-recorded marriages 4
state index 5
Mexican land records 64-66, 123
military records
   bounty land records 108
   cemetery and gravestone records
        110–111
   Civil War draft records 108–110
   Civil War enlistments 104-106, 174
   Coast Guard records 107
   enlistment records, regular army
        1798-1914 106
   holdings at NARA and NPRC 98–99
   Letterman Hospital records 111
   NARA records, how to request
        111–112
   NPRC records, how to request 107
   pension lists, indexes and abstracts
        101–105
   pension records, usefulness of 100
   Presidio history and records 97, 111
   retirement home records 26, 111
   service records, federal 103–107
   state and local records 107–108
   usefulness of 174
   Veterans' Home records 111
mortuary records
   Book of the Dead 12, 174
   Bunker & Lunt 13
   Chinese Mortuary Records 9, 14, 133
   J.C. O'Connor & Co. 13
   mortuaries in business before and
        after the fire 14-15
   N. Gray & Co. 11
   other surviving records 14
municipal records
   Annual Municipal Reports 59ff., 84
   arrest and prison records 61
   Public Administrators' reports 60
   tax ledgers 60

N

names
   naming complications 193
   common surnames 194
   ethnic and foreign 193-194

   indexing aberrations 195
   name changes 193
   nicknames 195
   spelling variations 194
Native Americans
   population, early 129
naturalization
   records 72–75
   naturalization, post-earthquake 192
newspapers
   abstracts 46–48
   African-American 44
   digitizations 48–50, 154, 173
   filmed at SFPL 44–45
   foreign language 45
   indexes 44, 46–48
   Jewish 45
   locations of collections 43
   newspapers, post-earthquake 192
   occupational and labor 46
   pre-earthquake 210-214
   specialty 46
   usefulness 173-174

O

obituaries. *See newspapers*
occupational records 117, 121
orphanage records 84, 118–119

P

pioneer records, sources and societies
   Argonauts 89, 140
   Association of Territorial Pioneers of
        California 148–149
   biographies and historical accounts
        139–141
   Los Californianos 124, 150
   member directories 145
   Native Daughters (and Sons) of the
        Golden West 150
   Society of California Pioneers 150,
        162
pre-statehood Spanish and Mexican
        records and accounts
   census records 123-124
   historical accounts 123-124
   Los Californianos 124
prison records 61, 121
probate. *See court records, probate*

R

railroad passenger lists. *See immigration and emigration*
railroad records 121
record repositories, Bay Area 159–162
records, post-earthquake
  death sources, other 190, 197
  divorce 188
  immigration 192
  importance 187
  land records 190
  naturalization 192
  newspapers 192
  probate records 190
  vital records 188–189
religious records. *See also, ethnic records and resources*
  archives 33, 34, 35, 37, 39
  Baptist 40
  Catholic 32, 33
  Congregational 36, 198
  Episcopal 36–37
  Evangelical 33–35
  German language churches 33–34
  Jewish 40
  LDS (Mormon) 40–41
  locating records 29–31, 175-178
  Lutheran 33–36
  mergers and name changes 30, 33, 36, 38, 177
  Methodist 38–39
  newspapers 41
  Presbyterian 37-38
  Scandinavian language churches 33, 34, 35, 40
  United Church of Christ (UCC) 34–36
  usefulness of 175–177
  WPA inventory 33, 36, 37, 40
research assistance 163–164

S

school records 119
Spanish land records 63-64, 66–67, 123–124
street name changes 183

V

vital (civil) records
  city death records 3–4
  city marriage records 4
  statewide birth, marriage and death records 5
  work-arounds 6, 199–205
voter records
  foreign-born voters, 1872 87, 174, 184
  Great Registers, history of 85
  Great Register films and abstracts 86–88
  naturalized voters, 1898 88
  use as supplement to census 174

W

wagon train lists. *See immigration and emigration*
wills. *See court records, probate*

California Genealogical Society library interior in Oakland, California (photograph by Judy Bodycote). The film and fiche collection of genealogically useful pre-earthquake San Francisco records is second only to SFPL. San Francisco records found here but not available at SFPL include original IOOF cemetery and crematory records, detailed films of Civil War enlistments and veteran records and probate Registers of Action ledger digitizations.

*T*he California Genealogical Society and its library are located at 2201 Broadway, Suite LL2, Oakland, California 94612, and may be reached at (510) 663-1358 or at *contact@californiaancestors.org*. Founded in 1898, the society maintains a large library collection, featuring more than 38,000 genealogical references, including 10,000 local and family histories, 2,500 reels of microfilm, a large selection of CDs, hundreds of reference books, periodicals, city directories, and perhaps the most complete array of San Francisco genealogical resources in the Bay Area, including films of all surviving deeds and deed indexes and the original IOOF Cemetery, Crematory and Columbarium ledgers. Library users have access to a number of online services, including *Ancestry. com* (Library Edition), *Footnote.com*, *NewEnglandAncestors.org*, *NewspaperArchive. com* and *VitalSearch.com*. The society's website, *CaliforniaAncestors.org*, links to a searchable catalog, simplifies the purchase of the society's many publications and features the California Names Index, a database of over 350,000 names. Full text copies of indexed items from this database and a number of other sources are available for a small fee. The society provides expert research assistance for a reasonable hourly fee, offers frequent instructional sessions and publishes a blog, a monthly electronic newsletter and a biannual journal, *The California Nugget*. Membership brings a discount on research services and publications. Recent publications, which can be ordered from the society, include:

- *San Francisco Deaths, 1865-1905: Abstracts from Surviving Civil Records.* Published in four volumes in 2010, this series indexes over 96,000 civil death records that survived the 1906 earthquake and fire. Compiled by Barbara Close and Vernon A. Deubler, it is available softbound. Vol. 1 covers surnames A-D; vol. 2: E-K; vol. 3: L-P; vol. 4: Q-Z.

- *San Francisco Probate, 1906-1942: Register of Actions.* Compiled by Vernon A. Deubler and published in two volumes in 2010, this indexes 179 Registers of Actions to proceedings that took place following the 1906 earthquake and fire through March 27, 1942. Over 85,000 probates and guardianships are represented, some of which were continuations and reconstructions of ongoing cases. Softbound.

- *A Most Dreadful Earthquake: A First-Hand Account of the 1906 San Francisco Earthquake and Fire with Glimpses into the Lives of the Phillips-Jones Letter Writers*. Dorothy Fowler. Published 2006, softbound, 190 pages.

- *San Francisco, California: I.O.O.F. Crematory Records*. Barbara Ross Close, compiler. Published in 2001, this indexes approximately 10,000 cremations that occurred over the years 1895-1911 in the crematory on the grounds of the old Odd Fellows Cemetery. It includes a provision for ordering digitizations of the full ledger entries, which include birthplace, date of death and age, place and cause of death and frequently an inserted newspaper obituary. Softbound, 413 pages.

- *San Francisco, California: Columbarium Records, 1847-1980*, Vernon A. Deubler, compiler. Published in 2003, this softbound publication of 130 pages provides the location and date of inurnment of over 4,300 remains. Many represent cremations of remains disinterred from the original cemetery during the period of removals. Years of birth are included when known.

- *San Francisco Probate Index, 1880-1906: A Partial Reconstruction*. Compiled by Kathleen C. Beals and published in 1996, this 239-page index was constructed from surviving probate receipt books, from names found in reconstructed probates following the 1906 earthquake, from the *San Francisco Municipal Reports* and from previously published newspaper abstracts. Softbound.

- *Index to San Francisco Marriage Returns, 1850-1858*. Although the marriage records themselves were lost in 1906, San Francisco marriage returns were indexed in the early general indexes to deeds over the first eight years following statehood. These were extracted from the filmed records by Kathleen C. Beals, who supplemented the list with names garnered from previously published extractions from four San Francisco newspapers, yielding a total of over 4,000 names. Published in 1992, softbound, 109 pages.

- *The Ancestry of Theodore Timothy Judge and Ellen Sheehy Judge, Including the Families of Boland, Roussel, Harman, McMurphy, Kelley, Bohane, Chapin, Freiermuth, Taylor, Moore and Farneman*. Compiled by society members, this 240-page family history, published in 2010, is softbound. It received a Certificate of Appreciation from the Federation of Genealogical Societies for "duty performend in an exemplary and outstanding manner."

Details and ordering instructions for this and the above publications are available at the CGS website, CaliforniaAncestors.org.

About the Author

A fifth–generation Californian, Nancy Simons Peterson is a certified genealogist whose work has appeared in prominent genealogical periodicals, including the *National Genealogical Society Quarterly*. She received undergraduate and graduate degrees from Stanford University, where she worked part-time for many years until moving to the Pacific Northwest in 1986. Nancy has taught beginning and intermediate genealogy and for six years was editor of the Tacoma-Pierce County quarterly *The Researcher*. In 1998, she won the National Genealogical Society Family History Writing Contest, and in 2003, was awarded the American Society of Genealogists Scholar Award. In 2004 she and her husband returned to the Bay Area. Since then she has sought to uncover details surrounding her mother's pre- and post-Gold Rush San Francisco immigrant German, Irish and Cornish roots and currently serves as director of research services at the California Genealogical Society.

Praise for the First Edition of *Raking the Ashes*

"Every large city deserves a guide to researching its people and families. What Nancy S. Peterson has done for San Francisco provides one of the best of this genre. Ms. Peterson's wonderful treatment of working around the lost documents makes pre-1906 San Francisco research more than a hope. Her thorough coverage of a wide variety of records will be helpful for researching in any American city, burned or unburned, especially in the nineteenth century."

— Roger D. Joslyn, CG, FASG
Immediate Past President, American Society of Genealogists

"'I'm sorry. Those records burned.' That reply to a genealogist's question makes my researcher's heart sink. For those, however, working in early Northern California, help has arrived in the form of *Raking the Ashes: Genealogical Strategies for Pre-1906 San Francisco Research* by Nancy S. Peterson, Certified Genealogist. This is a better gold mine for genealogists than the one discovered in 1849 at Sutter's Mill. Well organized, clearly written and filled with little-known sources, the California Genealogical Society has done a great service in publishing this source and methodology book."

— (the late) *Marsha H. Rising, CG, FASG*
Author, **The Family Tree Problem-Solver: Proven Methods for Scaling the Inevitable Brick Wall**

"Nancy S. Peterson's ***Raking the Ashes: Genealogical Strategies for Pre-1906 San Francisco Research*** is an extremely consequential work on a critically important topic for anyone doing genealogical research in the San Francisco area of California. Well-researched and clearly written, this work is literally packed with meaningful data, from the poignant title and rich illustrations to the descriptive contents pages and marginal text boxes . . . The work not only identifies records destroyed and those that survived, it also gives the researcher specific, consequential work-arounds for continuing genealogical research despite record loss. So excellent is the caliber of work presented in ***Raking the Ashes***, it should be used as a recommended primer for anyone doing research in a burned city or county as well as anyone engaging in California research."

— *Curt Witcher*
Historical Genealogy Department Manager
Allen County Public Library

"***Raking the Ashes*** knocks down the brick walls that plague researchers with San Francisco roots. I highly recommend this book for anyone wanting to learn more of their San Francisco family . . . . ***Raking the Ashes*** belongs on every genealogist's desk."

— *James R. Smith*
Author, **San Francisco's Lost Landmarks**

The Call=Chronicle=Examiner

SAN FRANCISCO, THURSDAY, APRIL 19, 1906.

EARTHQUAKE AND FIRE: SAN FRANCISCO IN RUINS

DEATH AND DESTRUCTION HAVE BEEN THE FATE OF SAN FRANCISCO. SHAKEN BY A TEMBLOR AT 5:13 O'CLOCK YESTERDAY MORNING, THE SHOCK LASTING 48 SECONDS, AND SCOURGED BY FLAMES THAT RAGED DIAMETRICALLY IN ALL DIRECTIONS, THE CITY IS A MASS OF SMOULDERING RUINS. AT SIX O'CLOCK LAST EVENING THE FLAMES SEEMINGLY PLAYING WITH INCREASED VIGOR, THREATENED TO DESTROY SUCH SECTIONS AS THEIR FURY HAD SPARED DURING THE EARLIER PORTION OF THE DAY. BUILDING THEIR PATH IN A TRIANGUAR CIRCUIT FROM THE START IN THE EARLY MORNING, THEY JOCKEYED AS THE DAY WANED, LEFT THE BUSINESS SECTION, WHICH THEY HAD ENTIRELY DEVASTATED, AND SKIPPED IN A DOZEN DIRECTIONS TO THE RESIDENCE PORTIONS. AS NIGHT FELL THEY HAD MADE THEIR WAY OVER INTO THE NORTH BEACH SECTION AND SPRINGING ANEW TO THE SOUTH THEY REACHED OUT ALONG THE SHIPPING SECTION DOWN THE BAY SHORE, OVER THE HILLS AND ACROSS TOWARD THIRD AND TOWNSEND STREETS. WAREHOUSES, WHOLESALE HOUSES AND MANUFACTURING CONCERNS FELL IN THEIR PATH. THIS COMPLETED THE DESTRUCTION OF THE ENTIRE DISTRICT KNOWN AS THE "SOUTH OF MARKET STREET." HOW FAR THEY ARE REACHING TO THE SOUTH ACROSS THE CHANNEL CANNOT BE TOLD AS THIS PART OF THE CITY IS SHUT OFF FROM SAN FRANCISCO PAPERS.

AFTER DARKNESS, THOUSANDS OF THE HOMELESS WERE MAKING THEIR WAY WITH THEIR BLANKETS AND SCANT PROVISIONS TO GOLDEN GATE PARK AND THE BEACH TO FIND SHELTER. THOSE IN THE HOMES ON THE HILLS JUST NORTH OF THE HAYES VALLEY WRECKED SECTION PILED THEIR BELONGINGS IN THE STREETS AND EXPRESS WAGONS AND AUTOMOBILES WERE HAULING THE THINGS AWAY TO THE SPARSELY SETTLED REGIONS. EVERYBODY IN SAN FRANCISCO IS PREPARED TO LEAVE THE CITY, FOR THE BELIEF IS FIRM THAT SAN FRANCISCO WILL BE TOTALLY DESTROYED.

DOWNTOWN EVERYTHING IS RUIN. NOT A BUSINESS HOUSE STANDS. THEATRES ARE CRUMBLED INTO HEAPS. FACTORIES AND COMMISSION HOUSES LIE SMOULDERING ON THEIR FORMER SITES. ALL OF THE NEWSPAPER PLANTS HAVE BEEN RENDERED USELESS, THE "CALL" AND THE "EXAMINER" BUILDINGS, EXCLUDING THE "CALL'S" EDITORIAL ROOMS ON STEVENSON STREET BEING ENTIRELY DESTROYED.

IT IS ESTIMATED THAT THE LOSS IN SAN FRANCISCO WILL REACH FROM $150,000,000 TO $200,000,000. THESE FIGURES ARE IN THE ROUGH AND NOTHING CAN BE TOLD UNTIL PARTIAL ACCOUNTING IS TAKEN.

ON EVERY SIDE THERE WAS DEATH AND SUFFERING YESTERDAY. HUNDREDS WERE INJURED, EITHR BURNED, CRUSHED OR STRUCK BY FALLING PIECES FROM THE BUILDINGS AND ONE OF TEN DIED WHILE ON THE OPOPERATING TABLE AT MECHANICS' PAVILION IMPROVISED AS A HOSPITAL FOR THE COMFORT AND CARE OF 200 OR THE INJURED. THE NUMBER OF DEAD IS NOT KNOWN BUT IT IS ESTIMATED THAT AT LEAST 500 MET THEIR DEATH IN THE HORROR.

AT NINE O'CLOCK, UNDER A SPECIAL MESSAGE FROM PRESIDENT ROOSEVELT, THE CITY WAS PLACED UNDER MARTIAL LAW. HUNDREDS OF TROOPS PATROLLED THE STREETS AND DROVE THE CROWDS BACK, WHILE HUNDREDS MORE WERE SET AT WORK ASSISTING THE FIRE AND POLICE DEPARTMENTS. THE STRICTEST ORDERS WERE ISSUED, AND IN TRUE MILITARY SPIRIT THE SOLDIERS OBEYED DURING THE AFTERNOON THREE THIEVES MET THEIR DEATH BY RIFLE BULLETS WHILE AT WORK IN THE RUINS. THE CURIOUS WERE DRIVEN BACK AT THE BREASTS OF THE HORSES THAT THE CAVALRYMEN RODE AND ALL THE CROWDS WERE FORCED FROM THE LEVEL DISTRICT TO THE HILLY SECTION BEYOND TO THE NORTH

THE WATER SUPPLY WAS ENTIRELY CUT OFF, AND MAY BE IT WAS JUST AS WELL, FOR THE LINES OF FIRE DEPARTMENT WOULD HAVE BEEN ABSOLUTELY USELESS AT ANY STAGE. ASSISTANT CHIEF DOUGHERTY SUPERVISED THE WORK OF HIS MEN AND EARLY IN THE MORNING IT WAS SEEN THAT THE ONLY POSSIBLE CHANCE TO SAVE THE CITY LAY IN EFFORT TO CHECK THE FLAMES BY THE USE OF DYNAMITE. DURING THE DAY A BLAST COULD BE HEARD IN ANY SECTION AT INTERVALS OF ONLY A FEW MINUTES, AND BUILDINGS NOT DESTROYED BY FIRE WERE BLOWN TO ATOMS. BUT THROUGH THE GAPS MADE THE FLAMES JUMPED AND ALTHOUGH THE FAILURES OF THE HEROIC EFFORTS OF THE POLICE FIREMEN AND SOLDIERS WERE AT TIMES SICKENING, THE WORK WAS CONTINUED WITH A DESPERATION THAT WILL LIVE AS ONE OF THE FEATURES OF THE TERRIBLE DISASTER. MEN WORKED LIKE FIENDS TO COMBAT THE LAUGHING, ROARING, ONRUSHING FIRE DEMON.

NO HOPE LEFT FOR SAFETY OF ANY BUILDINGS

San Francisco seems doomed to entire destruction. With a lapse in the raging of the flames just before dark, the hope was raised that with the use of the tons of dynamite the course of the fire might be checked and confined to the triangular sections it had cut out for its path. But on the Barbary Coast the fire broke out anew and as night closed in the flames were eating their way into parts untouched in their ravages during the day. To the south and the north they spread; down to the docks and out into the resident sortion, in and to the north of Hayes Valley.. By six o'clock practically all of St. Ignatius' great buildings were no more. They had been leveled to the fiery heap that marked what was once the metropolis of the West.

The first of the big structures to go to ruin was the Call Building, the famous skyscraper. At eleven o'clock the big 18-story building was a furnace.. Flames leaped from every window and shot skyward from the circular windows in the dome. In less than two hours nothing remained but the tall skeleton.

By five o'clock the Palace Hotel was in ruins. The old hostelry, famous the world over, withstood the seige until the last and although dynamite was used in frequent blasts to drive

Continued on Page Two

BLOW BUILDINGS UP TO CHECK FLAMES

The dynamiting of buildings in the track of the fire, to stay the progress of the flames, was in charge of John Bermingham, Jr., superintendent of the California Powder Works. Several experienced men from the powder works, assisted by policemen and members of the fire department, did the hazardous work of blowing up the buildings. They were razed in sets of threes, but the open spaces where the shattered buildings fell were quickly turned into holocausts of flame. The work was most effective in the business blocks east of Kearny street.

WHOLE CITY IS ABLAZE

At 10 o'clock last night the Occidental Hotel was destroyed by the flames which swept unchecked across Montgomery street and attacked the block bounded by Montgomery, Sutter, Bush and Kearny. The new Merchants' Exchange building was a mass of flames from basement to tower.

The Union Trust building and Crocker-Wolworth Bank were both ablaze and the Chronicle building and other buildings in that block were threatened by the flames.

Shortly after 10 o'clock the fire had eaten its way southward from Portsmouth Square to Kearny and California streets.

At the building adjoining the Hall of Justice were ablaze and the firemen were striving to save the structure by using dynamite. It is almost a certainty that every building contained in the section bounded by Clay, Kearny, Market and East streets will be consumed.

The flames had eaten their way westward in the residence section as far as Gough street. There, by dynamiting blocks after blocks, the firemen succeeded in checking the devouring element.

CHURCH OF SAINT IGNATIUS IS DESTROYED

The magnificent church and College of St. Ignatius, on the northwest corner of Van Ness avenue and Hayes street represents in its destruction a material loss of over $1,000,000. The actual cost of the great building was over $900,000, but during the years which have elapsed since its erection the church has been enriched by paintings and frescoes, which were priceless. Some of them were works of art which can never be replaced, however willing those interested in the church might be to meet any expense in the effort.

MAYOR CONFERS WITH MILITARY AND CITIZENS

At 1 o'clock yesterday afternoon 50 representative citizens of San Francisco met the Mayor, the Chief of Police and the United States Military authorities in the police office in the basement of the Hall of Justice. They had been summoned thither by Mayor Schmitz early in the forenoon, the fearful possibilities of the situation having forced themselves upon him immediately after the shock of earthquake in the morning, and the news which at once reached him of the completeness of the disaster. He lost no time in making out a list of citizens from whom to seek advice and assistance, and in summoning them to the conference. It was called at the Hall of Justice, as virtually the first news which reached the Mayor regarding the extent of the disaster was that of the ruin of the City Hall. He did not realize that even while the conference was to be going on cornices would be crashing down and windows falling in fragments in the Hall of Justice also, and that before sunset desperate efforts would be made to blow the structure up in the vain endeavor by this means to check the advance of the flames in the northern section of the downtown district.

All, or nearly all of the citizens summoned to the conference

Continued on Page Two